STRATFORD-UPON-AVON STUDIES 17

General Editors

MALCOLM BRADBURY
& DAVID PALMER

Also available in this series

3 EARLY SHAKESPEARE

5 HAMLET

6 RESTORATION THEATRE

7 AMERICAN POETRY

8 LATER SHAKESPEARE

9 ELIZABETHAN THEATRE

Under the General Editorship of Malcolm Bradbury and David Palmer

11 METAPHYSICAL POETRY

12 CONTEMPORARY CRITICISM

13 THE AMERICAN NOVEL AND THE NINETEEN TWENTIES

14 SHAKESPEAREAN COMEDY

15 VICTORIAN POETRY

16 MEDIEVAL DRAMA

DECADENCE AND THE 1890s

ASSOCIATE EDITOR
IAN FLETCHER

HOLMES & MEIER PUBLISHERS, INC.
New York

© EDWARD ARNOLD (PUBLISHERS) LTD 1979

First published in the
United States of America 1980 by
HOLMES & MEIER PUBLISHERS, INC.
30 Irving Place, New York
N.Y. 10003

Library of Congress Cataloging in Publication Data

Main entry under title:
Decadence and the 1890s.
    (Stratford-upon-Avon studies; 17)
    Includes bibliographical references and index.
    1. English literature—19th century—History and
criticism—Addresses, essays, lectures. 2. Decadence
(Literary movement)—Addresses, essays, lectures.
I. Fletcher, Ian. II. Series.
PR469.D4D4 1980   820'.9'008   79-20174

ISBN 0-8419-0568-1 (Cloth)
ISBN 0-8419-0569-X (Paper)

Printed in Great Britain

Contents

		PAGE
Preface		7
I	'Decadence' in Later Nineteenth–Century England R. K. R. THORNTON	15
II	'Decadent Spaces': Notes for a Phenomenology of the *Fin de Siècle* JAN B. GORDON	31
III	Swinburne's Circle of Desire: A Decadent Theme CHRIS SNODGRASS	61
IV	Fierce Midnights: Algolagniac Fantasy and the Literature of the Decadence JERRY PALMER	89
V	The Decadent Writer as Producer JOHN GOODE	109
VI	From Naturalism to Symbolism JOHN LUCAS	131
VII	The Legend of Duse JOHN STOKES	151
VIII	Decadence and the Little Magazines IAN FLETCHER	173
Bibliographical Note		203
Index		209

Preface

THE EDITOR of an anthology of late nineteenth-century verse once wrote to A. E. Housman, asking permission to include some poems from *A Shropshire Lad* (1896). Housman returned a lapidary refusal: 'To include me in an anthology of the Nineties would be just as technically correct, and just as essentially inappropriate, as to include Lot in a book on Sodomites.' Housman was perhaps being sensitive to the autobiographical background (his interest in Moses Jackson) of some of the poems; he was certainly invoking one of the veteran cliches of literary history—that the writers of the Nineties were the deployers and victims of the myth of *fin de siècle, fin du globe*. For the English, the Decadence was simply shorthand for the 1890s, much as for Sherlock Holmes Irene Adler was *the* woman. Yet there had been decadences before (the English 1590s were just such another *fin de siècle*, presided over by another ageing iconic queen), and some had been prolonged; Callimachus, Petronius, Statius, Bernini and the Italian painters of the *seicento* were, for the writers of the late nineteenth century, recognizable antecedents. But something about round numbers, and the terror of turning centuries, encourages the equation: when better to discern an apocalypse, or begin a secular 'new age'? Hence another type-casting of the period, which has been stabilized as 'an age of transition': the closing phase of the Victorian synthesis, the opening phase in those tendencies we call for convenience 'modernism'.

The 1890s have long been thought a decisive decade, yet they have been obscured by a series of gestures extending over the past sixty years. Yeats and Pound evolved the myth of the 'tragic generation' *à la fin de siècle*: Yeats as part of his self-mythology, Pound (followed later by Eliot and Virginia Woolf) as part of his version of the anxiety of influence. Linda Dowling has taught us to recognize the activity as 'the parthenogenesis of the *avant garde* disavowing its past in order to regenerate itself and gain creative space. By treating aestheticism and decadence as the last exotic pendants of a hopelessly frumpish Victorianism modernists made modernism newer, fathering themselves.' Since then the students of modernism have reversed the process, searching for the tendency's origins in the devotion of certain aesthetes and decadents to colloquial speech, urban themes, and, most importantly, 'the image'. The years between 1870 and 1914 became the age of transition into modernism—a view that, as Linda Dowling says in the prefatory essay to her bibliography of Aestheticism and Decadence, superficially offers an attractive version of the period, allowing us to view it both as 'a genuine divergence from Victorian literary culture and an authentic participation in the modern movement'. Certainly it permitted literary historians to search for unifying themes through a multiplicity of 'movements'—Parnassianism, Realism, Impressionism, Symbolism, and so on, down to Imagism and Vorticism—without imposing a single reductive scheme on them all, and had value at a time when detailed discussion of decadence might have met the stern rebukes of moral critics. Yet ideas on modernism have themselves changed greatly, becoming more internationalist and more plural; in the process it has grown vastly harder to say with any great clarity what modernism—a *post facto* definition, laid over many different phenomena in many different countries in different periods—actually is.

Thus, important as are many of the essential transactions of the 1890s—those between scientific positivism and the role of subjective consciousness, for example—to what follows, it can be constricting and methodologically naive to insist on the period as ur-modern. In another area, Northrop Frye has attacked the dangers of the concept of 'Pre-Romanticism'; the same risks apply to the 1890s. For who—besides Dryden, who had his own reasons for suggesting that men of letters were a dynastic breed—ever saw his own poetry as being fulfilled by his successors? Did Dowson bite a desperate nail as he waited for a messianic Eliot to appear? Certainly veils trembled, and apocalyptics had a vogue. Yet for those who went on elsewhere decadence was merely a phase, though in Yeats's case the decadent characterization, the aesthetics of failure, persisted for a considerable time after the turn of the century, until he established a 'system' to usurp the failed systems contemporary culture had to offer. Transitions, then, mattered profoundly to the 1890s: evanescence, instability, failure, the enterprise of internalizing history and manifesting it as style, an historical and personal sense of decline and fall, are, of course, primary motifs. Yet the notion of 'an age of transition' can become a false application of the motif—one more version of the myth of *fin de siècle* from which it attempted, initially, to deliver us.

We are coming to see that one way beyond the impasse lies in not defining the last two decades of the nineteenth century in terms of a single myth, theme, image or movement; rather in stressing the inter-

connectedness of the period's writers, even those who do not assent to
fin de siècle, fin du globe. It was an era of complex mergers, variant
affiliations; one good recent sign is a movement toward the 'lateral'
study of the period, through the critical examination of diverse figures,
the building of fuller primary and secondary bibliographies, the new
accessibility of important texts from an era of limited editions and even
suppressed ones. The problem of analysis is complicated by the emphasis on movements, which now looks like a nominalist imposition on
the period's variousness. It was an age of terms and 'isms', as Holbrook
Jackson said; yet the terms were themselves features of evanescence, and
not applied with exactitude. Following the examples of earlier seces-
sionists, the 'Decadents' gracefully accepted the pejorative label thrust
on them by the higher journalism and the progressive critique. Yet
terms like 'Pre-Raphaelite', 'Aesthetic 'and 'Decadent' intersect with
each other, and even tendencies like 'Naturalism' are not discrete and
distinct: Zola, founding this last, recognized that people like movement
names so that they can identify an art as 'new'. Because of this self-consciousness about group roles, 'vertical' studies still retain a validity, but
it is precisely that commitment to fluidity, that aversion to the canon-
ical, dominant in the period, that most invites analysis, through minute
study of style, through a recognition of the role of failed systems,
through an attention to minor figures and the nature of their minority.

Much of this is called up in the concept of 'Decadence' itself, by no
means a new term; literary formulations about it considerably pre-
date the French movement of 1884–5 or the English tone of the years
following 1890. It was Désiré Nisard who first deployed the term 'art
for art's sake' in English, in the *Westminster Review* in 1837, and who
set out, in a critical spirit, the lore that Decadents came to espouse. His
Etudes de mœurs et de critiques sur les poètes latins de la décadence (1834) had
as its subject Persius, Juvenal, Statius and Martial, but its target was
Hugo and the generation of 1830. Nisard's points were that decadent or
devitalizing *mœurs* encourage certain kinds of literary developments—
especially a penchant for individual eccentricity, recondite subject
matter, description for its own sake, and images of 'le règne exclusif
de procédé sur les ruines de l'inspiration'. Behind this is a crude
Viconian model of how literature connects with the growth or
decline of civilization: first there are primitives (Homer, Dante,
Shakespeare); then Golden Ages (Pericles, Augustus, the Medicis,
Louis XIV) producing treasures of common sense and reason; there-
after there is Decadence, when little remains to be discovered, and

enfeebled latecomers must make do with 'what the great authors have
disdained'. The cyclical historiography was not new; what was new,
as A. G. Lehmann emphasizes, was the link between Decadence and
free imagery, following from the collapse of rhetorical rules. Hence
decadence forms *style*, and poets are at the mercy of the time-spirit.
The stylistic characteristics are failure of invention, insistence on
manner without substance, use of description for physical rather than
philosophic functions, addressed not to reason but the eye, conveying
colour and nuance. The application to the French nineteenth century is
clear: poets now seek the ugly rather than the beautiful, the peripheral
rather than the central, an art void of moral clarity. In 1830 Hugo had
fractured the Alexandrine, an event equated with the bringing back of
the tumbrils of 1789, though what 1830 brought was not the tumbrils
but Louis Philippe. Indeed for Nisard it was the new industrial era the
king inaugurated that poems should be hymning, not romantic *mal du
siècle*.

Industrialism was indeed a central issue in the 1830s and 1840s debate
about decadence. Indeed, for romantic primitivists, industrialism *was*
decadence. Up to the 1850s the French considered the British as the
modern decadents, looking at the sinister example of the factory
system, and of London as 'monster city'. Some Frenchmen insisted
that the British were to be admired; others derided progress as regression, and for Gautier and Baudelaire progress was 'a doctrine of
Belgians'; they expatiated on the charm of decadent civilizations. Sade,
with his exaltation of the criminal asserting freedom from a demonic
nature, with his anti-heroine and hero of prostitute, homosexual,
adulterer, was celebrated. Gautier's description of the style of
Baudelaire's poetry is a classic definition of decadence: it is ingenious,
learned, complicated, diseased, 'gamy', nuanced, borrowing from all
the technical vocabularies, expressing the vaguest and most fleeting of
contours, alert to the subtle confidences of the neuropath, the avowals
of ageing or depraved passion, and the singular hallucinations of the
idée fixe. Gautier mimes the style he describes; the language used by
Nisard to *condemn* the generation of the 1830s is now used to *praise*
Baudelaire. Gautier also stresses the city, and the equation of *decadent*
with *modern*: so Baudelaire's poetry embodies the crisis of contemporary civilization. Baudelaire, who had read Nisard, wrote in the preface
to the Poe translations 'the words decadent literature imply something
fatal and providential. . . . All that I can grasp in this academic impression is that it is shameful to take pleasure in obeying such a law, and

that we are guilty when we rejoice in our destiny. . . .' And, in the year of Gautier's and Baudelaire's comments, Mallarmé was shaping a prose poem, in memory of a dead sister, which refers to his taste for Latin decadent poems, praised and imitated by Baudelaire; and affirms that all he loved is summed up in the word *chute*, fall. The barbarians did indeed come: Paris fell to the Prussians, and Verlaine wrote 'Je suis la décadence et la fin de l'Empire'. This was 1883; the sonnet and Verlaine were taken up by the Decadent school of 1884, a movement that embodied the fallen spirit and expressed itself in coteries and little magazines.

Self-conscious Decadence progressed more slowly in England. The Aesthetic movement—an amorphous affair, embodying manuals from 'House Beautiful', ritualism, the Kyrle Society, and rational dress reform—shades rather mysteriously into Decadence in the 1880s. The decline of provincial culture, the continuous economic and agricultural depressions from the 1870s, the rise of German industrial and military hegemony, the persistent Romantic critique of mechanical progress, and the waning of Victorian cultural confidence all furnish a plausible context. The Aesthetic type had appeared earlier in the century—in the Regency Dandy; in the effeminacy that provided Kingsley with a model for distrust of the newly established Roman Catholic hierarchy (1850); in the Spasmodics; and so on. The exposure of the *avant garde* artist was rehearsed in the 1870s: the Fleshly School controversy, Whistler's suit with Ruskin, and the Paterian spirit in Oxford were all part of this. The early letters of Wilde offer glimpses of a homosexual world—though one still Uranian and public schoolish, far from the 'renters' of the London 'gay' underworld of the 1880s and 1890s. The word 'decadence' had been making its way into the language to replace 'decay' and 'decline'; a writer in *The Journal of Philosophy* in 1871 urged resistance to this 'barbarous Gallicism'. In the Imperial era after 1874 the fear of degeneration and fall becomes more present; indeed Imperialism and the cult of adventure was a response to it. This was partly a fear of racial degeneration, following on from Darwin, Malthus and eugenics, with those least fit to breed overbreeding and those who should be renewing the race neglecting the matter. It is thus an apt degenerate or decadent reversal for C. Kains Jackson to advocate 'Uranian' homosexual love not on Sadian but neo-Malthusian grounds.

But acceptance of decadence was a possible response to the way of the times, and it was further stimulated by the impact of French Decadents, known in England by 1886. 'The London correspondents of our dailies have spoken of them as "the school of collapse", a grace-ful translation, certainly, and one worthy of the *largest circulation in the world*,' George Moore wrote, anonymously, in *The Court and Society* of 19 January, 1887, describing the Decadents as the '*contre coup* of Zola and his school', mentioning Huysmans, and translating two examples of Mallarmé's prose poems, including the famous *chute* passage. English decadence evidently owes much to French, though the parallels are not exact: themes rather than language define the English decadence. There are shrugging ironies here and there in Symons's poems, parody and self-mockery in Johnson, Beardsley and Wilde; and, just as the French decadent poets spice their poems with English words, so the English use French, archaism occasionally jostles colloquialism and natural word order. Similar sounds are arbitrarily repeated: assonance is not infrequent in John Gray's poetry, and attempts are made by 'colour' words to fix elusive shades precisely, though these are the colours of artefacts rather than natural objects. Wilde's and Symons's impressionist cityscapes may not escape from verbs, but they are often deliberately weak ones:

> A bright train flashed with all its squares
> Of warm light where the bridge lay mistily . . .

The word 'fall' has peculiar resonances for Lionel Johnson: 'Go from me, I am one of those that fall.' He himself embodied all that was summed up in that word; indeed was always himself falling, morally, physically, downstairs, out of hansom cabs, off bar stools and chairs, until he finally took one fall too many and died. In novels too there is some-times a decadence of style as well as subject matter: in some of George Moore's prose, for example. But, though portraits of the *névrosé*, the artist, beginning with Pre-Raphaelite *romans à clef* like Vernon Lee's *Miss Brown* or Mrs M. Hunt's *Thorneycroft's Model*, present the Deca-dent 'type', it is difficult to isolate any purely decadent novel other than *The Picture of Dorian Gray* or George Moore's *Mike Fletcher*.

The essays in this volume meet around the crossing point of Deca-dence and the 1890s. Some, like Jan Gordon's and Chris Snodgrass's, consider the evolution of that narcissism, that sense of emptiness within, that incapacity to look without, which corresponds to the successive closures of the nineteenth-century poetic tradition, to that loss of metaphor and metonymy which leads to the painful tautology whereby the poet can only affirm that 'immortal diamond' in the wake of col-lapsing inscape is indeed 'immortal diamond' and '(my god)' is 'My

God'. Ian Fletcher's essay on little magazines follows another path of this evolution, from the Pre-Raphaelites through the House Beautiful movement to the tone of the 1890s. Other essays concentrate more 'laterally' on the decade. Kelsey Thornton lays out some of its essential issues; John Stokes looks to one of its central motifs, that of the actress, in a consideration of Duse; Jerry Palmer looks at an essential sexual theme; John Goode examines alienation from commercial and philistine society with a socio-literary exactingness. We hope the volume will encourage the extending recognition that Decadence is not only a central moment in the evolution of the modern arts because of its place in larger transitions, but a moment of a distinctive kind meriting a quite distinctive attention. Finally, the editors would like to express their gratitude to Jan B. Gordon and John Stokes, for their invaluable editorial assistance at two stages of this project.

IAN FLETCHER
MALCOLM BRADBURY

April 1978

Note

The history of Decadence is confused by disagreement among the ranks of the Decadents themselves, a confusion compounded by the vagueness, one-sidedness, inaccuracy, and derivativeness of many subsequent accounts. Holbrook Jackson's *The Eighteen Nineties* (1913) has never been superseded as a general survey, and substantially merits its many reprintings. The most concentrated general survey of critical approaches is Helmut Gerber's essay on 'The Nineties: Beginning, End, or Transition?' in *Edwardians and Late Victorians*, edited by Richard Ellmann (English Institute Essays, 1959), and an informed account of the poetry is in John M. Munro's *The Decadent Poetry of the Eighteen-Nineties* (Beirut, 1970). A. E. Carter's *The Idea of Decadence in French Literature 1830–1900* (Toronto, 1958) covers much of the French background, which is given a broader and more exciting context by Koenraad Swart's *The Sense of Decadence in Nineteenth-Century France* (The Hague, 1964). Frank Kermode's *Romantic Image* (1957), Mario Praz's *Romantic Agony* (1933), and Ian Fletcher's collection of essays by various hands, *Romantic Mythologies* (1967), provide approaches to some of the dominant images and ideas, and John Lester's *Journey Through Despair* (Princeton, 1968) is full of exciting ideas. Two books whose long subtitles indicate their scope are Ruth Z. Temple's *The Critic's Alchemy: a Study of the Introduction of French Symbolism into England* (New Haven, 1953), and Barbara Charlesworth's *Dark Passages: The Decadent Consciousness in Victorian Literature* (Madison, 1965). There are some insights into the connection of Decadence and Imperialism in David Daiches's *Some Late Victorian Attitudes* (1969). Also see, for aestheticism, Albert J. Guerard, *Art for Art's Sake* (New York, 1936; repr. 1963), and Robert V. Johnson, *Aestheticism* (Critical Idiom series, 1969).

Five articles in periodicals might lead to further discussion: Clyde de L. Ryals, 'Towards a Definition of "Decadent" as applied to British Literature of the Nineteenth Century' in the *Journal of Aesthetics and Art Criticism* XVII (September, 1958), pp. 85–92; Robert L. Peters's reply, 'Towards an "Un-Definition" of Decadence ...' in the *Journal of Aesthetics and Art Criticism* XVIII (December, 1959), pp. 258–64; Helmut Gerber, 'The Editor's Fence' in *English Literature in Transition: 1880–1920* VI, 1 (1963), pp. iv–v; Ruth Z. Temple, 'Truth in Labelling: Pre-Raphaelitism, Aestheticism, Decadence, Fin-de-Siècle' in *English Literature in Transition* XVII (1974), pp. 201–222; and Jean Wilson's intriguing challenge, 'The "Nineties" Movement in Poetry: Myth or Reality?' in *The Yearbook of English Studies* I (1971), pp. 160–174.

Aestheticism and Decadence: a Selective Annotated Bibliography by Linda C. Dowling appeared in 1977. See the bibliographical note at the end of this book for fuller listings.

I

'Decadence' in Later Nineteenth-Century England

R. K. R. THORNTON

I

THERE ARE those who question whether there was a Decadent Movement in England at all. Vincent O'Sullivan—to take not merely a critic but a writer who has been said to be part of such a movement—claimed of Arthur Symons that 'though he was perhaps the only decadent in London, he has managed . . . to pass into history as the leader of a definite movement called Decadent'.[1] Many other critics have despaired of using the word Decadent with any precise meaning, apparently forgetting that at least since Gautier's 1868 essay on Baudelaire the very men who used the word and praised the style to which it refers have consistently noted its difficulty and inaccuracy. For them, and for a time, it was an appropriate word; and I suggest that if we steer by the period's landmarks we can find our way into what they understood by it.

If it existed, the Decadent Movement in England was given a fatal blow on 25 May, 1895, when Oscar Wilde was found guilty of acts of gross indecency with other males and sentenced to two years' imprisonment with hard labour. On the streets outside the Old Bailey, we are told, prostitutes danced in professional delight at the decision. But it was not only Wilde's homosexual behaviour which was being tried—and not only Wilde. A whole body of ideas, moral, literary, and aesthetic, and the relationship between them, were on trial—a fact which newspapers were eager to point out both before and after the sentence. When the libel action against Queensberry was withdrawn, the *National Observer* published a leader which attacked Wilde as a figurehead (the irony of W. E. Henley's association with this attack, as editor rather than author, will be apparent later):

> There is not a man or woman in the English-speaking world possessed of the treasure of a wholesome mind who is not under a

[1] *Opinions* (1959), p. 199.

deep debt of gratitude to the Marquess of Queensberry for destroying the High Priest of the Decadents. The obscene imposter, whose prominence has been a social outrage ever since he transferred from Trinity Dublin to Oxford his vices, his follies, and his vanities, has been exposed, and that thoroughly at last. But to the exposure there must be legal and social sequels. There must be another trial at the Old Bailey, or a coroner's inquest—the latter for choice; and of the Decadents, of their hideous conceptions of the meaning of Art, of their worse than Eleusinian mysteries, there must be an absolute end.[2]

After the sentence had been announced, the *Daily Telegraph* continued this note of criticism, writing that 'No sterner rebuke could well have been inflicted on some of the artistic tendencies of the time than the condemnation of Oscar Wilde at the Central Criminal Court,' and insisting on

the terrible warning of his fate. Young men at the universities, silly women who lend an ear to any chatter which is petulant and vivacious, novelists who have sought to imitate the style of paradox and unreality, poets who have lisped the language of nerveless and effeminate libertinage—these are the persons who should ponder with themselves the doctrines and career of the man who now has to undergo the righteous sentence of the law.[3]

The *Evening News*, in like vein, called Wilde 'one of the high priests of a school which attacks all the wholesome, manly, simple ideals of English life, and sets up false gods of decadent culture and intellectual debauchery'.[4] Writers in the last years of the century undoubtedly felt the cold wind of conventional morality blowing into their hothouse pages; the increasing freedom which they had been winning seemed to be in danger, and Decadence as a term to focus their ideas became so loaded as to be worse than useless.

Arthur Symons, who must always be at the centre of a discussion of Decadence, stood valiantly by its theoretical positions in his Prefaces to the second editions of *Silhouettes* (1896) and *London Nights* (1897); but he abandoned any hopes of continuing under the old name. When Aubrey Beardsley and much of the quality had been driven away from

[2] *National Observer*, 6 April, 1895, as quoted in H. Mongomery Hyde, *Famous Trials: Seventh Series: Oscar Wilde* (1962), p. 156.

[3] Quoted in H. Montgomery Hyde, *The Trials of Oscar Wilde* (1948), pp. 11–12.

[4] *Ibid.*, p. 12.

the *Yellow Book* because of unfounded suspicions of association with Wilde, they found a place in Symons's new *Savoy*. But in the journal's prospectus of November 1895, Symons denied links with any one movement:

> We have no formulas and we desire no false unity of form or matter. We have not invented a new point of view. We are not Realists or Romanticists or Decadents. For us, all art is good which is good art.[5]

If one does link the *Savoy* with any movement, it is more likely to be Symbolism than Decadence; indeed this was the direction in which Symons was moving. In December of 1896 he was still planning and advertising a book to be called *The Decadent Movement in Literature*, an altered and expanded version of his earlier article; but in 1899 his book, concerned with many of the same authors, appeared with the title *The Symbolist Movement in Literature*. In a passage the end of which recalls Yeats's Preface to *Poems* (1895), Symons explains the change in what is the last word in the history of the Decadent Movement:

> Meanwhile, something which is vaguely called Decadence had come into being. That name, rarely used with any precise meaning, was usually either hurled as a reproach or hurled back as a defiance. I pleased some young men in various countries to call themselves Decadents, with all the thrill of unsatisfied virtue masquerading as uncomprehended vice. As a matter of fact, the term is in its place only when applied to style; to that ingenious deformation of the language, in Mallarmé, for instance, which can be compared with what we are accustomed to call the Greek and Latin of the Decadence. No doubt perversity of form and perversity of matter are often found together, and, among the lesser men especially, experiment was carried far, not only in the direction of style. But a movement which in this sense might be called Decadent could but have been a straying aside from the main road of literature. Nothing, not even conventional virtue, is so provincial as conventional vice; and the desire to 'bewilder the middle-classes' is in itself middle-class. The interlude, half a mock-interlude, of Decadence, diverted the attention of the critics while something more serious was in preparation. That something more serious has crystallized for the time, under the form of Symbolism, in which art returns to the one pathway, leading through beautiful things to the eternal beauty.[6]

[5] Quoted in R. Lhombreaud, *Arthur Symons* (1963), p. 126.
[6] *The Symbolist Movement in Literature* (1899), pp. 6–7.

The Decadent Movement was over by the end of the century. Many of those who had been associated with it had died or were soon to die; its chief champion had repudiated it, its main force had been diverted into another channel, and the word itself was no longer the emotive and vogue word which for a few years it had been.

II

Even allowing that it lasted until the turn of the century, the movement, particularly in England, had been short-lived. The French movement had a longer history, beginning in 1834 when Désiré Nisard (who was also responsible for the introduction of the term 'art for art's sake' into England in 1837)[7] mounted an attack on contemporary poets in his *Etudes de mœurs et de critique sur les poètes latins de la décadence*. Nisard set the character and perhaps the tone of subsequent criticism by noting that both contemporary and Roman Decadents showed the same 'recherche des nuances, même esprit de mots, mêmes subtilités, mêmes exagérations, et parmi les exagérations même préférence pour le laid'.[8] The subsequent history of Decadence in France has been well explored by A. E. Carter in his *The Idea of Decadence in French Literature 1830–1900* (Toronto, 1958), and I need here only mention the main landmarks. Nisard's term was picked up and the subject elaborated by Gautier, most significantly in his 'Notice' to Baudelaire's *Les fleurs du mal*, in 1868, while Baudelaire himself added the authority and subtlety of his greater talents. The eighties in France saw a burst of interest in the subject, with Anatole Baju's *Le décadent* (1886–8), its successor *Le décadisme*, and later the *Scapin*, while the popularity of the subject was sufficient to prompt a parody in the shape of *Les déliquescences. Poèmes décadents d'Adoré Floupette* (Byzance [Paris], 1885). The greatest stimulus for this activity was no doubt Huysmans's complete picture of the Decadent in *A Rebours*, which Symons considered the 'breviary of the Decadence', and which contained that mixture of literary leg-pull (as its author insisted to Zola) and serious study which became characteristic of portraits of Decadents. The name was attached at various times to both Verlaine and Mallarmé; but the former moved easily in and out of any association which suited him and the latter was more aptly associated with Symbolism, a term which was increasingly taking over from Decadence in the late eighties in France.

[7] L. M. Findlay, *Notes and Queries*, n.s. XX, 7, pp. 246–8.
[8] *Op. cit.* 2nd ed., Paris (1849), II, p. 216.

It is at this same period, specifically 1889, that Decadence with particular reference to a literary movement can be said to have come to England, although one should not forget that Walter Pater could write in the *Renaissance* in 1873 that in the poems of du Bellay the Renaissance was 'putting forth in France an aftermath, a wonderful later growth, the products of which have to the full that subtle and delicate sweetness which belongs to a fine and comely decadence'. In October of 1889 Havelock Ellis wrote 'A Note on Paul Bourget' for the *Pioneer*, discussing Bourget's *Essais de psychologie contemporaine* (1881) and *Nouveaux essais de psychologie contemporaine* (1885), two books on contemporary authors whose approach would particularly attract Ellis. Among the writers whose work is seen as profoundly pessimistic, a later expression of *le mal du siècle*—Leconte de Lisle, Turgenev, Amiel, Renan, Flaubert, Taine, Stendhal, Dumas *fils*, and the Goncourts—Bourget discusses Baudelaire, and it is in this essay that he writes of the *Théorie de la Décadence* which forms the point of departure for Ellis's comments. The whole tone and italicizing of the word add weight to the suggestions that this is an introduction of the term to his English readers:

> Bourget uses this word as it is generally used (but, as Gautier pointed out, rather unfortunately) to express the literary methods of a society which has reached the limits of expansion and maturity— 'the state of society,' in his own words, 'which produces too large a number of individuals who are unsuited to the labours of common life. A society should be like an organism. Like an organism, in fact, it may be resolved into a federation of smaller organisms, which may themselves be resolved into a federation of cells. The individual is the social cell. In order that the organism should perform its functions with energy it is necessary that the organisms composing it should perform their functions with energy, but with a subordinated energy, and in order that these lesser organisms should perform their functions with energy, it is necessary that the cells comprising them should perform their functions with energy, but with a subordinated energy. If the energy of the cells becomes independent, the lesser organisms will likewise cease to subordinate their energy to the total energy and the anarchy which is established constitutes the *decadence* of the whole. The social organism does not escape this law and enters into decadence as soon as the individual life becomes exaggerated beneath the influence of acquired well-being, and of heredity. A similar law governs the development and decadence of that other organism which we call language. A style of

decadence is one in which the unity of the book is decomposed to give place to the independence of the page, in which the page is decomposed to give place to the independence of the phrase, and the phrase to give place to the independence of the word.'[9]

Ellis emphasizes style above content in his summary of Bourget, but notes the tendency to 'represent what Baudelaire called "la phosphorescence de la pourriture" '.

English writers were still obviously learning from their French masters when, in April 1891, Lionel Johnson wrote for the *Century Guild Hobby Horse* 'A Note upon the Practice and Theory of Verse at the Present Time Obtaining in France', an article subtly illuminated by the appearance opposite its final page of Ernest Dowson's 'Non sum qualis eram bonae sub regno Cynarae'. Retaining the French accent for the word, and quoting liberally from Anton Lange, Johnson writes a rather academic definition:

> In English, *décadence* and the literature thereof, mean this: the period, at which passion, or romance, or tragedy, or sorrow, or any other form of activity or of emotion, must be refined upon, and curiously considered, for literary treatment: an age of afterthought, of reflection. Hence come one great virtue, and one great vice: the virtue of much and careful meditation upon life, its emotions and its incidents: the vice of over-subtilty and of affectation, when thought thinks upon itself, and when emotions become entangled with the consciousness of them.[10]

After a similar precise definition of *symbolisme*, Johnson concludes:

> Now, in either of these schools, poetry becomes a matter of infinite pains, and of a singular attention: to catch the precise aspect of a thing, as you see or feel it; to express, not the obvious and barren fact, but the inner and fruitful force of it; this is far from easy, far from trivial.[11]

This is as Paterian as it is French, and looks forward to Symons and Eliot. Pater in the Preface to the *Renaissance* takes, as the aim of the true student of aesthetics, 'To define beauty, not in the most abstract, but in the most concrete terms possible, to find, not a universal formula for it, but the formula which expresses most adequately this or that special manifestation of it.' Symons, relying on Johnson and Pater

9 *Views and Reviews*, First Series (1932), pp. 51–2.
10 *The Century Guild Hobby Horse* VI, p. 65.   11 *Ibid.*

for his definition in 'The Decadent Movement in Literature', says that the ideal of Decadence is 'To fix the last fine shade, the quintessence of things; to fix it fleetingly; to be a disembodied voice, and yet the voice of a human soul.' Eliot's 'objective correlative', the 'set of objects, a situation, a chain of events which shall be the formula of that *particular* emotion', is not far away.

III

While a serious discussion of the stylistic aspects of Decadence was going on, however, the public had caught hold of the more sensational and moral aspect of the word and the movement. 'For oneself the prayer. From decadence, Good Lord deliver us!' wrote 'Michael Field' in a diary for 5 April, 1891. And indeed it is in the parodic and satirical writings about Decadence that the ideas and characteristics become clarified into caricature. As was said in '1894', a *Punch* parody of Max Beerbohm's essay '1880', which had appeared in the fourth volume of the *Yellow Book*, 'we may learn from the Caricatures of the day what the Decadents were in outward semblance; from the Lampoons what was their mode of life'.[12] *Punch* indeed drew a good deal of copy from the Decadents from 1892 to 1895—satirizing effeminate long hair, the world-weary attitude of the Decadent, the infantile nature of impressionist pictures (Flipbutt—Wilde's cigarette was never wholly forgiven—mistakes a child's drawing for an impressionist work), the lack of enthusiasm for exercise, and the expected love of the ugly. It is not difficult to see the target of 'Disenchantment' and 'Abasement', two items from 'Select Passages from a Coming Poet':

> My love has sicklied unto Loath
> And foul seems all that fair I fancied—
> The lily's sheen a leprous growth,
> The very buttercups are rancid!

or:

> With matted head a-dabble in the dust,
> And eyes tear-sealèd in a saline crust,
> I lie all loathly in my rags and rust—
> Yet learn that strange delight may lurk in self-disgust.[13]

[12] *Punch*, 2 February, 1895, p. 58.   [13] *Ibid.*, 14 July, 1894, p. 16.

To this last a character remarks, 'I rather like that—it's so very decadent!'

But it was not only the moralists who caricatured or the comic papers who poked fun. All who wrote of it were conscious of the unsatisfactoriness of the term, and also conscious that complete espousal of the anti-natural tendencies was impossible; hence the criticism and parody manifested even in those most centrally involved in it. The hero of Huysmans's *A Rebours* finds that his body will not survive the unnatural things he asks of it and finds that 'only the impossible belief in a future life could bring him peace of mind'. Max Beerbohm's 'A Defence of Cosmetics', in the first volume of the *Yellow Book*, is at once a penetrating insight into typically Decadent themes in a style of mannered particularity *and* a criticism of it—as he pointed out in a letter to the editor in Volume II. Purporting to find it incredible that critics should 'fail to see that my essay, so grotesque in subject, in opinion so flippant, in style so wildly affected, was meant for a burlesque upon the "precious" school of writers', he turned the satire back to his critics, in a passage that recalls those descriptions of books in *A Picture of Dorian Gray*, *A Rebours*, and *Marius the Epicurean*:

> There are signs that our English literature has reached that point, when, like the literature of all the nations that have been, it must fall at length into the hands of the decadents. The qualities that I tried in my essay to travesty—paradox and marivaudage, lassitude, a love of horror and unusual things, a love of argot and archaism and the mysteries of style—are not all these displayed, some by one, some by another of les jeunes écrivains? Who knows but that Artifice is in truth at our gates and that soon she may pass through our streets? Already the windows of Grub Street are crowded with watchful, evil faces.[14]

Lionel Johnson's 'Cultured Faun', with his universal boredom, his precise appearance, his 'exquisite appreciation of pain, exquisite thrills of anguish, exquisite adoration of suffering', and love of beauty, is similarly convincing both as parody and portrait.[15]

Parody and mockery were, as they had been for Oscar Wilde earlier, a major force in putting Decadence before the public, an important element in disseminating its ideas, and one reason for some coherence in our ideas about it. But there was earnest debate too. Richard Le

[14] *The Yellow Book* II, July, 1894, p. 284.
[15] *The Anti-Jacobin*, 14 March, 1891.

Gallienne was earnest enough, though his apparent desire to be on both sides at once adds an element of self-parody to his comments. In the *Century Guild Hobby Horse*, in some 'Considerations suggested by Mr Churton Collins's "Illustrations of Tennyson" ', Le Gallienne took up Johnson's arguments in the same magazine, along with some of his Arnoldian tendencies, in his wish that writers should 'see life steadily and see it whole':

> But decadence in literature is more than a question of style, nor is it, as some suppose, a question of theme. It is in the character of the treatment that we must seek it. In all great vital literature, the theme, great or small, is always considered in all its relations near and far and above all in relation to the sum total of things, to the infinite, as we phrase it; in decadent literature the relations, the due proportions, are ignored. One might say that decadence consists in the euphuistic expression of isolated observations.[16]

Le Gallienne expanded on these ideas both in prose and verse. In his *The Religion of a Literary Man* he elaborated the theme of his contributions to the debate on Christianity and Decadence which had been conducted in the pages of the *Daily Chronicle*. In his reassuringly entitled *English Poems* (1892) he opened with an address 'To the Reader' which complains that Art, which was once a palace, is now a 'lazar-house of leprous men'; but it is in 'The Décadent to his Soul' that we find the clearest picture of his idea of the contemporary writer. The Décadent of the poem had thought that 'the body were enough' but, seeing the attractive soul, he 'dreamed of a new sin: / An incest 'twixt the body and the soul'.

> Then from that day, he used his soul
> As bitters to the over dulcet sins. . . .

> Sin is no sin when virtue is forgot.
> It is so good in sin to keep in sight
> The white hills whence we fell, to measure by—
> To say I was so high, so white, so pure,
> And am so low, so blood-stained and so base;
> I revel here amid the sweet sweet mire
> And yonder are the hills of morning flowers;
> So high, so low; so lost and with me yet;
> To stretch the octave 'twixt the dream and deed,

16 *The Century Guild Hobby Horse* VII (1892), pp. 80–1.

Ah, that's the thrill!
To dream so well, to do so ill,—
There comes the bitter-sweet that makes the sin.[17]

As E. K. Chambers pointed out, in a review of Le Gallienne's book in the *Academy*,[18] 'Beauty Accurst' in the same volume seems to display all those characteristics against which Le Gallienne inveighs. It was as a reply to Le Gallienne's attack that Symons wrote his article on 'The Decadent Movement in Literature', and one wonders with what maliciousness Symons chose—after a discussion of the Goncourts, Verlaine, Mallarmé, Maeterlinck, Villiers de l'Isle Adam, and Huysmans—to represent Decadence in England by the work of Pater and W. E. Henley. When the essay was reprinted in *Dramatis Personae* (1925), and the contentiousness had gone from the subject, Symons left out the section on Pater and Henley. The central statements and definitions of Symons's article, however, are clear and, though he too begins by saying that the names are 'none of them quite exact or comprehensive', his views at the time are not obscure:

> Taken frankly as epithets which express their own meaning, both Impressionism and Symbolism convey some notion of that new kind of literature which is perhaps more broadly characterized by the word Decadence. The most representative literature of the day— the writing which appeals to, which has done so much to form, the younger generation—is certainly not classic, nor has it any relation with that old antithesis of the Classic, the Romantic. After a fashion it is no doubt a decadence; it has all the qualities that mark the end of great periods, the qualities that we find in the Greek, the Latin, decadence: an intense self-consciousness, a restless curiosity in research, an over-subtilizing refinement upon refinement, a spiritual and moral perversity. If what we call the classic is indeed the supreme art—those qualities of perfect simplicity, perfect sanity, perfect proportion, the supreme qualities—then this representative literature of to-day, interesting, beautiful, novel as it is, is really a new and beautiful and interesting disease.[19]

The examination of the movement, largely with reference to French authors (and in the reprinted version of *Dramatis Personae* even more exclusively so), suggests that the diseased nerves of modern man have driven him to emphasize the two central characterizations of the

---

[17] *English Poems* (1892), pp. 106–9.   [18] 19 November, 1892, p. 451.
[19] *Dramatis Personae* (1925), pp. 96–7.

movement, subtlety of analysis and curiosity of form. The subtlety of analysis involves the catching of the unique way of seeing things and the precise way of expressing them, and the curiosity of form the self-consciously artificial in life and art.

So closely was Symons involved in the question of decadence in the minds of the critics of the nineties that, even when Symons had abandoned the term, W. B. Yeats had to defend him against it, in a review of 'Mr Arthur Symons's New Book', *Amoris Victima*, in the *Bookman* for April, 1897. Yeats's analysis of the trend of modern poetry—one that he still held by in his introduction to the *Oxford Book of Modern Verse* in 1936—stressed its contraction to the more purely personal and lyrical. He quotes with approval Symons's description of 'the typical modern man, to whom emotions and sensations represent the whole of life', and lists poets (Lang, Dobson, Gosse, Bridges, Francis Thompson, Henley, Lionel Johnson, Davidson, Le Gallienne, Watson, and Symons) who have been gradually 'carrying this change to its momentous fulfilment: the calling of what is personal and solitary to the supreme seat of song'.[20] By this time in the decade, the inaccuracies of the term were outweighing its usefulness; and Yeats ends his review by turning the charge against the critics:

> One may say of Mr Symons that he is in no accurate sense of the word a 'decadent', but a writer who has carried further than most of his contemporaries that revolt against the manifold, the impersonal, the luxuriant, and the external, which is perhaps the great movement of our time, and of more even than literary importance. Popular criticism, which prolongs the ideals and standards of a school of literature, which has finished its great work for this epoch of the world, is on the other hand, in the most accurate sense of the word, 'decadent'.[21]

In the following year, Yeats was abandoning the term decadence and taking the more interesting notion of 'the autumn of the body' in an essay with that name,[22] which uses the same basic arguments and examples.

But the last word from the 'participants and even partisans' to whom Ruth Z. Temple suggests we should return for information to help us

---

[20] *Uncollected Prose by W. B. Yeats*, II, ed. John P. Frayne and Colton Johnson (1975), p. 40.
[21] *Ibid.*, pp. 41–2.   [22] Reprinted in *Essays and Introductions* (1961).

understand the term[23] belongs to Havelock Ellis, who also in England
began it. His essay on Huysmans in *Affirmations* (1898) has as its second
part a discussion of Decadence. He reiterates much of his earlier
material, and two things stand out: that Decadence remains clearer
with reference to French literature than English; and that 'we have to
recognize that decadence is an aesthetic and not a moral conception.
The power of words is great, but they need not befool us. The classic
herring should suggest no moral superiority over the decadent
bloater.'[24] It is evident from Ellis's essay that little has changed, that
the defender still speaks of Decadence as a style, the critic and moralist
of Decadence as a way of life. Even Ellis admits in his Preface that
throughout his book he is 'discussing morality as revealed or disguised by literature'.[25]

IV

What becomes clear from even a brief survey of the decade on its
Decadence is the centrality of the notion of what I would like to call
the Decadent dilemma. The Decadent is a man caught between two
opposite and apparently incompatible pulls: on the one hand he is
drawn by the world, its necessities, and the attractive impressions he
receives from it, while on the other hand he yearns towards the eternal
the ideal, and the unworldly. The play between these two poles forms the
typical Decadent subject matter and is at the root of much of the period's
manner and particularly its mannerisms. Symons saw this polarity
when he wrote that 'Impressionism and Symbolism convey some
notion of that new kind of literature which is perhaps more broadly
characterized by the word Decadence'; and the incompatibility of the
two poles gives rise to the characteristic Decadent notes of disillusion,
frustration and lassitude at the same time as the equally characteristic
self-mockery.

The Decadent who is held by the world is a child of Victorian
materialism, and as precise as a Pre-Raphaelite in his impressions of it.
Pater's grasping at things as they pass is taken without Pater's delicate
but dubious selectivity, for example by Symons who, searching for
the 'quintessence of things', turned his attention to experience, whatever the nature of the experience, merely for its existence; he sought
its *vraie vérité* in the impression. The precise, impressionistic manner

[23] *English Literature in Transition* 17, 4 (1974), p. 216.
[24] *Affirmations* (1898), p. 186.   [25] *Ibid.*, p. iv.

went with an idea that art should represent impartially whatever life
had to offer, and this led inevitably to the late nineteenth-century
debate on the freedom of art, particularly in the field of sexual relationships. The case, which was made by (among many others) Wilde,
Crackanthorpe, Le Gallienne and Symons, is summed up by Yeats in
his *Autobiographies*:

> I think that had we been challenged we might have argued some-
> thing after this fashion: 'Science through much ridicule and some
> persecution has won its right to explore whatever passes before its
> corporeal eye, and merely because it passes, to set as it were upon
> an equality the beetle and the whale, though Ben Jonson could find
> no justification for the entomologist in *The New Inn*, but that he
> had been crossed in love. Literature now demands the same right of
> exploration of all that passes before the mind's eye, and merely
> because it passes.'[26]

Havelock Ellis, who saw Decadence as merely a necessary state,
supported and extended the scientific and unemotional view, which
finds critical expression in the assertion that there is no such thing as a
moral or an immoral work of art.

The fascination of the world and an impressionistic representation of
it are seen in the Decadent writer in conjunction and contrast with a
longing for the unworldly, which moves in natural stages to the anti-
worldly, the anti-natural, the artificial and the unnatural. Many
central poems of the period conform to this simple pattern of contrast
which Le Gallienne caricatured in his 'The Décadent to his Soul'.
Ernest Dowson's 'Non sum qualis eram bonae sub regno Cynarae' is
the most important example, where the real world of the 'bought red
mouth' is made tasteless by the siren call of Cynara:

> Last night, ah, yesternight, betwixt her lips and mine
> There fell thy shadow, Cynara! thy breath was shed
> Upon my soul between the kisses and the wine;
> And I was desolate and sick of an old passion,
>   Yea, I was desolate and bowed my head:
> I have been faithful to thee, Cynara! in my fashion.

This contrast, and his faithfulness to the unattainable in one form or
another, is of course central not only to Dowson's work as a whole but
also, if we take the picture of the man from Symons or Yeats, central to

[26] *Autobiographies* (1955), p. 326.

his whole life. In Lionel Johnson too one finds the same antithesis, if more coldly shown, as in 'By the Statue of King Charles at Charing Cross':

> Yet, when the city sleeps;
> When all the cries are still:
> The stars and heavenly deeps
> Work out a perfect will.

And one could multiply examples, not only from Johnson, but from Yeats's 'Secret Rose' to Symons's poems where imagination transcends the mundane. In some cases the contrast is more evident when one looks at the whole *œuvre*: in John Gray, between his *Silverpoints* (1893) and his *Spiritual Poems* (1896), or in Aubrey Beardsley, between his letters to Smithers and those to Raffalovich. Indeed the very black and white of Beardley's best drawings provides a tempting symbol.

But the crucial distinguishing feature of the Decadent is the nature of his retreat from reality. There is a superficial retreat from reality in the lack of intensity in his grasp on life, the effete casualness, the languid withdrawal—'as for living, our servants will do that for us'—and there is the subtler retreat which accepts only those realities which can be heightened and transformed into spiritualities, particularly those which art creates. Art and artifice become the one way of going beyond the world while remaining in some way of it. The extreme of this is of course impossible; the Decadent who wishes to become artificial must either fail to survive or fail to be totally Decadent, as des Esseintes had shown. It is no accident that Yeats views his contemporaries as 'The Tragic Generation'; nor is it odd to associate the Celtic Revival with Decadence, since the Celtic element in literature was still characterized by the quotation from Ossian which Arnold used as epigraph to his essay, 'They went forth to the war, but they always fell'. And, not surprisingly, self-parody was self-preservation.

In style the Decadent aimed at the consciously artificial, disciplined, formal. Yeats dated the Decadence back to Gosse, Dobson, Lang, and their espousal of forms like the villanelle which Dowson also affected. For Lionel Johnson, 'life is ritual', and he wrote always in a language conscious of its roots, prickly with tradition and quotation. Even Henley experimented in forms. Writers derived word, name, situation, theme from some earlier age; and even Decadence itself gained character from palely imitating Roman decadence. Arthur Symons, whose ornate, narcissistic and circling forms owe more to Verlaine than

Rome, was the most insistent on art and artifice as his subject matter. In his poems, 'Powder and wig, and pink and lace, / And those pathetic eyes of hers' lead towards unfolding wings in 'this miraculous rose of gold' ('Impression: to M.C.'), while the dancing of 'Nora on the Pavement' frees her from her surroundings of nineties grey 'In that blithe madness of the soul of Nora'. Love, especially with an actress or a dancer or a highly made-up woman, or a woman untouchable because of her youth or self-involvement, becomes a favourite symbol of the attempt to escape the bonds of the real world, especially since it also relates to the striving for freedom of subject matter. Symons in 'Idealism' loves a woman as if she were artificial:

> Her body now a silent instrument,
> That 'neath my touch shall wake and make for me
> The strains I have but dreamed of, never known.

Olive Custance in 'The White Statue' begins 'I love you, silent statue!' and yearns 'To press warm lips against your cold white mouth!' in anticipation of the lines in Yeats's 'The Statues'; the Pygmalion story becomes vital again. In *Amoris Victima* (1897) Symons, with a fine Yeatsian burst, reflects the Decadent dilemma and the escape through love or self-denial:

> The world is made for dutiful restraint.
> Its martyrs are the lover and the saint,
> All whom a fine and solitary rage
> Urges on some ecstatic pilgrimage
> In search of any Holy Sepulchre.

But even here he is moving away from Decadence to Symbolism, from the impressionistic world of the theatre to the symbolist landscape of the mind.

Decadence may have been 'half a mock-interlude', but it had *been*. It was a transitional, necessarily brief since self-destructive movement, inhabited by these hollow men for whom between the real world and the ideal fell the shadow. For a time they not only self-consciously but also self-mockingly sang sadly of the shadow and decked it with artificial and theatrical lights and loves. Decadent literature is a literature of failure, but its exploration of that failure helped to create the new modes of dealing with experience. Yeats's 'artifice of eternity' is built on Decadent foundations.

Note

The evolution of a *fin-de-siècle* 'aesthetic' has been the subject of relatively little work, apart from the criticism of individual authors. In addition to references in the footnotes, the reader might be referred to Mario Praz's *Romantic Agony* (1933) and Renato Poggioli's *The Theory of the Avant-Garde* (Cambridge, Mass., 1968). Two less well known books are John Lester's *Journey Through Despair* (Princeton, 1968) and Tom Gibbons's *Rooms at the Darwin Hotel* (Perth, Australia, 1974), containing an account of the various uses of the occult. Barbara Charlesworth's *Dark Passages* (Madison, 1965) contains succinct and occasionally astute observations on individual authors. For a more metaphysical discussion of the yoking of pleasure and pain see G. Bataille, *Literature and Evil* translated by A. Hamilton (1973). One of the more intriguing treatments of a recurrent motif in the literature and art of the nineties is the marvellous essay by A. J. L. Busst, 'The Image of the Androgyne in the Nineteenth Century' in Ian Fletcher, *Romantic Mythologies* (1967). *Edwardians and Late Victorians*, edited by Richard Ellman (the English Institute Essays of 1959), contains a reflection by Helmut E. Gerber entitled 'The Nineties: Beginning, End, or Transition?' that is a tentative approach to an aesthetic. For the legacy of the 'decadents' in contemporary literature and life style Hugh Kenner's *The Pound Era* (Berkeley, 1970) and Susan Sontag's 'Notes on Camp' in *Against Interpretation* (New York, 1967) hold enduring interest. A recent essay on patterns of narcissism in contemporary life is the piece by Christopher Lasch, 'The Narcissistic Personality of Our Times', *Partisan Review* XLIV, 1 (1977), pp. 9–19.

II

'Decadent Spaces': Notes for a Phenomenology of the Fin de Siècle

JAN B. GORDON

What is abnormal in Life stands in normal relations to Art. It is the only thing in Life that stands in normal relations to Art.

Oscar Wilde, 'A Few Maxims for the Instruction of the Over-Educated'

I

IN SO many ways, Tennyson's 'The Lady of Shalott' (1832) serves to summarize the key aesthetic issues at stake in the waning of Romanticism. The lady, perhaps the last of the romantic artists, alone on one of those artistic islands so typical of the poetic landscape of Keats and Shelley, weaves a tapestry through a mirror—doubly removed from the distant, mutable world of the mainland. But, tiring of an aesthetic feast of reflected shadows, she elects to become an artist *engagée*; having worked out her patterned mythology, she attempts to make it part of her own self-development. She hopes to transcend the mirror, escape the imaginative solitude of insular consciousness, authenticate her being-in-the-world. But evidently this is not possible; her inability to achieve outward communion turns what should be a linear pilgrimage into a self-reflective, circuitous journey of the imagination. She finds, in short, the romantic double-bind: the artist-figure can either remain isolated from earthly rhythms in the autotelic world of shadows, or attempt to project his or her biography onto the mainland, synchronizing personal with natural or historical development.[1] To remain on the magic island is to live in an inauthentic fairy realm, where

---

[1] Harold Bloom, *The Ringers in the Tower* (Chicago, 1971), pp. 13–37. Bloom's theory of the 'internalization of quest romance' envisions a dialectic in romanticism between the 'organic', a sort of anxiety principle masquerading as a reality principle and identical to the ego's supportive self-love, and another creative rather than defensive impulse which resists enchantment in favour of some higher empathetic union with the object of affection-attention.

mirrors prompt a masturbatory aesthetic; to move beyond this palace of art into a social involvement that gives the artist relevance is also, eventually, to risk narcissistic destruction. Thus, if the Lady of Shalott were to succeed in making her transition from the island of art to the mainland city, she would, it seems, simply encounter another sequence of mirrors, rather than genuine self-development, or a solution to her problems of identity. Escape from the images of these romantic islands—the 'casement', the tiny 'shallop', the 'reapers'— brings her only to the realm of pseudo-romance; the 'tirra lirra' sung by Sir Lancelot. A descendant of the passengers on Northrop Frye's famous 'drunken boat',[2] she abandons web and loom to enter a world no different from that she left. Now bearing a 'glassy countenance', the Lady of Shalott no longer looks through the mirror of imagination but *is* a mirror:

> In the stormy east-wind straining
> The pale yellow woods were waning,
> The broad stream in his banks complaining,
> Heavily the low sky raining
> Over towered Camelot. . . .
>
> (118–22)

Here is the poetic of autumn, with all the overripeness of decadence. But if romantic poetry was a craft of unfinished connections (as those numerous poems broken off prior to their conclusion suggest),[3] then the art of the *fin de siècle*, which Tennyson prefigures, is the art of half-tones, flickering shadows, rippling pools, feminine endings, and the misty aesthetics of self-reflection. Its existential spaces are overly filled; rather than the ellipses that conclude 'The Fall of Hyperion', 'The Triumph of Life', or 'The Excursion', *fin-de-siècle* art is highly repetitive to the extent that it offers us all surface. This is an art that has self-consciously turned back upon itself, confronted the aesthetics of fatigue and the ontology of boredom. Language, like the Lady of Shalott's tapestry, can no longer appropriate the world. It refers merely to other metaphoric representations; the departure from the archetypal romantic journey is identical to a crisis of language. Structurally the result

[2] Northrop Frye, 'The Drunken Boat: The Revolutionary Element in Romanticism' in *Romanticism Reconsidered*, edited by Northrop Frye (New York, 1963), pp. 62–8.

[3] For a further elaboration of this notion of the 'unfinished' romantic poem, see Edward Bostetter, *The Romantic Ventriloquists* (Seattle, 1966).

is a sort of Chinese-box diagram: words and spaces lead us into a confrontation with other words and spaces, never with an identifiable 'world'. The dialogue of life and art has gone beyond the harvest moment of fruition detailed in Keats's 'To Autumn' and into the stylized oozings of decadence, the other face of romanticism.

II

This shift in sensibility is important in so far as it affects both the life histories and the art of Decadence. If every aesthetic pilgrimage is doomed to failure either because of the isolating nature of the quest, or because every search for cohabitation with Ideal Beauty turns out to be only a sophisticated self-projection, then self-integration is an ephemeral goal. In either case the artist is a victim of mirrors of the self; a conventional notion of self-development is forever denied. The aesthetic voyager becomes a voyeur; unable to encounter the real world, he endures or lives an echo or a reflection or its visual counterpart—hermaphroditism. It is from a recognition of the failed nature of the romantic quest for authentication that the unique stylistic configuration of *fin-de-siècle* art and life springs. The artist, instead of being at the centre of some structural island of art, metaphorically moves to the periphery; this enables him to be everywhere at once, to be both detached and involved, to combine autobiography and art within the frames of a divided existence.

In short, the artist who had gone through romanticism, aesthetically or chronologically, was forced to recognize two competing schemes of personal development—schemes which profoundly alter the structure of nineteenth-century autobiography. At one pole, there was the organic ideal which insists that the self must be allowed to grow with as little interference as possible, assumes an analogy between human development and plant development, and requires that institutions recognize the naturalness of the subject. The other scheme envisions growth as a dialectical process, involving mediation with institutions and individuals who provide the subject with imaginative models; education thus involves a departure from the unique or natural self so that human nature might realize its potential *in experience*. Typical Victorian autobiography usually embodies one or the other of these theories. In one, the child within a *hortus conclusus* is guided into receiving reflected images from the real world (Newman's university); in the other, the child grows through socialization and engagement, and this often involves the mediation of a competing value system (Mill's exposure to Wordsworth in the *Autobiography*). It would seem, though, as if the later nineteenth-century artist wanted an aesthetic and educational system that would involve the best of both worlds: the eternal flower of perpetual childhood, and the gregarious socialization of the dandy. In terms of literary genre, these conflicting theories of development are manifested, on the one hand, in the tremendous growth of children's literature (Kenneth Grahame, James Barrie, George Macdonald); on the other, in the overly stylized aesthetic reponses of the effete and the experienced (Marius, Dorian Gray). The autobiographical mode, which reflects ego development, is altered because the primitive *and* the overly cultivated have equal claims upon the educational process: one through 'minimalization', a narrowing of life's experience against the 'outside' world, the other through the accretion of experiential 'moments', as in Pater's child-artists like Sebastian van Storck.

As one reads one's way through the visual and verbal art of the late nineteenth century, there would appear to have been—certainly in the minds of Morris, Yeats, Wilde, and Pater—some metaphoric era when art and life once were virtually indistinguishable. At these unique periods of history, the argument goes, the individual is virtually indistinguishable from the products of his artistic imagination. For Yeats, those periods of history when man most clearly 'lived' his art were the time of Sato's sword and the golden bird of Byzantium—when primary and antithetical phases became superimposed, one atop the other. This aesthetic configuration took place only when the system of pernes and gyres reached their maximum point of mutual interpenetration, when male and female parts reached a climax, so as to produce a bisexual art that had the perfection of each partner without voiding the identity of the other: 'measureless consummation'. Yeats usually associated these rare periods of Unity of Being with perpetual child-hood—with the polymorphous perversity bespeaking a certain doomed perfection. In the personal cycle, which reduplicates the larger, cosmic one, the poet closest to those states of golden perfection in the history of history was Keats—whose very life had the patterned perfection of artistry that placed him near phase fifteen, the metaphoric juncture of a twenty-eight phase cycle at whose termini were hunchback and fool, decadence and primitive innocence, adjacent on the *Primum Mobile*.

Yeats began his career with the autumnal, misty, wavering journey of Oisin in search of Ideal Beauty through the islands of his youth; he concluded it by trying to reverse the flow that destroyed the Lady of Shalott, ferrying souls back from the mainland to the kingdom of those Byzantine smithies, and redeeming life-as-art by a symbolist spatial and temporal regression which completes the journey by making all history circular. As we shall see, this aesthetic logic impacts in the nature of autobiography in the last years of the nineteenth century; the mode ceases to be merely a way of relating a soul's fruitless search for eternal beauty; it aestheticizes the self by transforming concrete being into artifice. Autobiography becomes the most effective way of living one's art and dying one's life; it corresponds, on the personal, physical level, to the metaphoric eras of Unity of Being on the level of historical consciousness. At the heart of Yeats's *A Vision* is a conception of history as metaphor which implies a certain infinite substitutability—a reincarnation for the individual *and* an internal mirroring of eras (metempsychosis). If the rape of Leda by Zeus disguised as a swan began the classical cycle with its devotion to beauty (Helen of Troy as paradigm), then the rape of Mary by God disguised as a dove commenced the Christian cycle, with its devotion to abnegation, its allegiance to the head. But now, approaching the year two thousand, birds are again gathering; in the coming Magian cycle, some whore slouching toward Bethlehem will again direct our attention to the body. The importance of Yeats's 'system' lies less in glossing his poetry, more in its evidence of crisis in history. History does not proceed linearly; it is rather a 'fiction' that explains one's subjective visions of experience. Rather than the orderly flow of events, to be related incrementally in order that we might adduce causality, history becomes, increasingly, private.

III

The 'orphan' of the typical early or mid-Victorian novel—Lionel Trilling's 'young man from the provinces'—who strives to put his world together episodically thus comes to be replaced after 1860 by an individual who departs from that notion of personal development.[4]

[4] Jerome Buckley, 'Autobiography in the English Bildungsroman' in *The Interpretation of Narrative Theory and Practice*, edited by Morton Bloomfield. Harvard Studies in Literature, Vol. I (Cambridge, Mass., 1970), pp. 93–104.

Instead of looking for origins, or putting himself 'in line' to inherit one of those large Victorian manor houses that lend their names to so many novels, these men seemed doomed to the circular, reflective life of the drifting dandy. Eugene Wrayburn, Will Ladislaw and Clym Yeobright are all predecessors of those cultural eunuchs of the nineties who convert their lives to art; unlike their fellow characters in *Our Mutual Friend*, *Middlemarch*, or *The Return of the Native*, who search for a cosmic or universal history or some similar 'key' to origins, they *internalize* their search for history—meanwhile developing an exterior existence with which to feign compliance. In them, the child (orphan) as a pilgrim-historian questing for occupation is replaced by an aesthete, who renounces occupation in favour of existence. In place of the binary set typical of romanticism—some 'self' seeking out the 'other' in the exterior world—they radically divide their very being, creating an existential hermaphroditism or better—to borrow from Yeats—a distinction between a man and his masks. By definition, the orphan, since he lacks parents, is a child without a history—a step away from that perpetual childhood which so many Nineties dandies like Dowson and Wilde just skirt in their lives and in their art. Disconnected from beginnings, and denying the ending implicit in inheritance, these circuitous wanderers are all 'middle'. Ironic detachment becomes the pyschological corollary to the more real detachment of the orphan earlier in the century.

The 'mirror-effect', so common in the life and art of the late nineteenth century, is thus a visual representation which unifies a number of divergent strains in the phenomenology of the nineties: the *Doppelganger* and the divided self; the voyeurism implicit in romantic self-consciousness; the highly polished surfaces of much Art Nouveau; the labyrinthine structure shared both by geographic quests and a language which seeks an ever more refined nuance. Yeats's statement—'no mind can engender till divided into two'—suggests that Narcissus must engage in perpetual warfare with some anti-self in order to prevent immersion in the pool of abstraction. For Yeats—as for Wilde, Pater and Moore—the possibilities of a divided existence hold out the only hope against the powers of generalization:

> Is not all life the struggle of experience naked, unarmed, timid, but immortal against generalized thought, only that personal history in this is the reverse of the world's history. We see all arts and societies passing from experience, that is to say, not what we call its 'results', which are generalizations, but with its presence,

its energy. All good art is experience, all popular bad art generalization.[5]

The threat, as these lines from Yeats's diary suggest, is generalized abstraction. In the desire to purge his early style of the local and the topical, Yeats encountered a different kind of history, which seemed less personal, devoid of a necessary subjectivity. So, like Ruskin and Morris before him, he became acutely aware that the various notions of nineteenth-century 'progress' and 'development' do not necessarily apply to the individual personality. As civilization advances, technologically and scientifically, the individual is afflicted by the symptoms of alienation: he feels himself as an 'other'. Ruskin and Morris imagine a sociological solution for that crisis: apocalyptically re-starting civilization in its medieval garden (the arts and crafts movement) with the hope of once again synchronizing personal, technological, and historical development. Man must be one with the product of his labours. Besides democratizing the notion of art to include manufacture, such thinking strives to overcome the schism that kills the Lady of Shalott.

But neither a weaver on an island nor the sacrifice of a humanized artist are solutions. If a neo-feudalism is one nineteenth-century solution to the crisis of history, surely there is another way of 'living' time, to borrow from Bergson: the autobiography, which tends to be a convenient mode for linking two types of existence. The flood of autobiographies in the last quarter of the nineteenth century testifies to the attempts made by numerous authors to come to terms with one's own fictional world while, at the same time, maintaining the distance necessary to prevent the infinite regress of meta-art.[6] Autobiography is private or subjective history made public. Whereas the romantic artist typically conceived of the imagination as working analogously to some pre-tuned Aeolian harp situated in an imaginative window to the world, the *fin-de-siècle* artist was more interested in transforming himself into a work of art or some aesthetic intrument, as a way of overcoming the gap between the history of art and the history of one's life. When Lord Henry Wotton suggests to Dorian Gray that he should 'set his days to sonnets', he is in effect suggesting the same thing as the

---

[5] Diary entry made 8 August, 1909, *The Letters of W. B. Yeats*, edited by Alan Wade (London, 1954), p. 535.

[6] Keith Rinehart, 'The Victorian Approach to Autobiography', *Modern Philology* LI (February, 1954), pp. 177–87.

Oscar Wilde who desired to place statues of Apollo in London's maternity wards: life should commence by imitating and thereby embodying the patterned structure of a work of art, rather than the reverse. Of course, the proliferation (and elevation) of the autobiographical mode throughout the nineteenth century might also suggest a crisis of the 'self', doubtless part of the continuing legacy of post-romanticism. But the aesthete prefers, to the Arnoldian goal of the shaped life, which demands the assumption of some limiting *telos*, a life where all options are kept open. Eschewing external formulae, he contrives a history-less existence.

The late Romantic impulse toward wholeness, even at the expense of some internalization of being, is the aesthetic variant of the artisan who was to be integrated with the products of his labour in the Edenic gardens established respectively by Ruskin, Morris and the Fabians. And autobiography is a way of incorporating one's own life within something like the Victorian *deus ex machina*, the General Will. Oscar Wilde noted that Christ, the artist who combined imagination and prophecy, 'pointed out that there was no difference at all between the lives of others and one's own life', giving to man 'an extended personality':

> Since his coming the history of each separate individual is, or can be made, the history of the world ... culture has intensified the personality of man. Art has made us myriad-minded.[7]

Yeats, it is to be remembered, believed that upon death only man lived his life *backwards*, reliving not only his own life, but also the lives of all those whose traits he had assimilated, 'treading the paths we have trodden, growing young again, even childish again'[8] until he had regained the higher innocence of a ritualized origin. In altering the title of the history of his poetic accomplishment from *Autobiographies* to *Autobiography*, Yeats was claiming that to live your own life is to live everyone else's (and *vice-versa*). What both Wilde and Yeats seem to point to is an intensification of one's own history until it reaches the point of becoming a microcosmic history of the world. This assimilative urge to live the most perfect life by exhausting time mixes the intensification inherent in decadent hedonism with the

[7] Oscar Wilde, 'De Profundis', *Complete Works of Oscar Wilde*, introduced by Vyvyan Holland (London, 1948), p. 926. All Wilde citations are from this edition.

[8] W. B. Yeats, *Autobiography* (New York, 1955), p. 251.

attempt to overcome discontinuity between a man and his masks through an aesthetic 'reduction':

> The difference between objective and subjective work is one of external form merely. It is accidental, not essential. All artistic creation is absolutely subjective. . . . For out of ourselves we can never pass, nor can there be in creation what in the creator was not. Nay, I would say that the more objective a creation appears to be, the more subjective it really is. . . . Man is least himself when he talks in his own person.[9]

In design at least, there is a hint that the integration implicit in the auto-biographical mode could be an aesthetic re-working of the earlier socio-economic solutions of Ruskin and Morris.

IV

So if that art is most perfect 'which mirrors man in all his infinite variety', as Wilde alleges in 'The Critic as Artist', then a sort of reversal takes place. The 'natural' or objective world is the most subjective; it is the personal or subjective autobiography that becomes an objective nature. This permutation of the mirror-effect is at the heart of *The Picture of Dorian Gray*: as the effete Dorian comes to live in the static, immutable kingdom of art, the picture becomes ever more life-like. If our very existence has a certain reversible quality, then every subject/object relationship is potentially interchangeable. The aestheticization of the human and the coming to life of a work of art—standard nineties' pygmalionism—also means that history, the lives and deeds of men, is aestheticized. As Dorian Gray initially confronts Basil's finished portrait in the attic that had been his childhood play-room, so art is a

---

[9] Oscar Wilde, 'The Critic as Artist', p. 1045. This transformation or exchange between subjective and objective means that art, that which would normally be part of the 'static' universe, is part of one's development and hence interchangeable with the 'personal history' that we call auto-biography:

> For the artistic life is simple self-development. Humility in the artist is his frank acceptance of all experiences, just as Love in the artist is simply that sense of beauty that reveals to the world its body and soul.
>
> (Wilde, 'De Profundis', p. 922)

Notice that the novelty of Wilde's definition implies that love 'reveals' but does not necessarily *connect*; its narcissism yokes it to Christ's *agape* rather than to human love.

collective past. When Walter Pater changed the title of his history from *Studies in the History of the Renaissance* (1873) to *The Renaissance: Studies in Art and Poetry* (1877), he recognized that history is redeemed by its transposition to art. It is surely evidence of the extent to which nineteenth-century historicism is challenged.

But the price for this 'solution' to the relationship between post-romantic aesthetics and the mythology of ego development is high indeed. Two key metaphors are the Chinese-box diagram and the analogue of the labyrinth: both present the reader with the structural pattern of concentricity or successive layering and both present us with spaces where the initiate encounters his own echo, or its ocular correlate, the reflection. Such a topology is doubtlessly related to those curious return-journeys whereby the aesthetic pilgrim undoes life's experience in some penitential reversal that turns hedonist into saint. The pattern involves, as we shall see, an individual who reverses the linear episodic quest that typified the nineteenth-century *Bildungsroman*, and involves an aesthete who becomes a martyr to his own objectivity. Whereas the romantic quest figure sacrifices himself for his ideals, the voice who speaks from the inner chamber sacrifices himself to live without ideals. In other words, he internalizes the objectivity of the outside world and becomes what the world at large took Alastor to be: an exterior without an interior, whose outer 'style' constitutes the content. If indeed 'style' is part of the man, as Pater charged in 'Style', then autobiography is not merely a literary genre but an existential condition, a way in which people live their mythologies. Parodying Arnold's dictum that the function of criticism is 'to see the object as in itself it really is', Wilde, after Pater, believed that the critic's first responsibility was that of knowing (and indulging) his own impressions. He was thereby claiming that one's own impressions could be simultaneously subject and object; that, more importantly, every act of criticism was but another variant of autobiography: 'The highest, as the lowest, form of criticism is autobiography,' says the Preface to *The Picture of Dorian Gray*.

But this extension of autobiography to include virtually the entire universe stems from one of the necessary conditions of the aesthetic life, one that is a recurrent motif in the *fin de siècle*. Walter Pater in the Preface to *The Renaissance* explicitly sets forth the goal:

> To define beauty not in the most abstract but in the most concrete terms possible, to find not its universal formula, but the formula

which expresses most adequately this or that special manifestation of it, is the aim of the true student of aesthetics.[10]

The various Victorian challenges to faith having made both life's 'beginnings' and its 'endings' uncertain or unknowable, man's goal becomes that of aestheticizing his life by extracting from the train of experience those 'moments' (middles) where perception and existence coalesce. Two alternatives seem to be offered in the choices of two characters in Pater's *Marius the Epicurean*: Marcus Aurelius finds nothing significant because everything passes away; the young Marius finds that at any particular moment everything is significant because it cannot be experienced again in precisely the same way. Pater's emphasis upon beauty as a 'fineness of truth',[11] and his particular attention to the 'concrete' which moves somehow beneath the universal, implies a critical premise that underlies the conduct of his fictional pilgrims. This critical activity has at its base a need for some reduction in surplusage; a narrowing concentration that separates wheat from chaff. And existence—for Pater and Wilde a kind of critical act—clearly requires a similar purging, a transcendental intensity, implicit in the well-known equation of 'success in life' with the flammable corollary to Yeats's unwinding bobbins of history: 'to burn always with this hard, gemlike flame. . . .'[12] To exist at this level of intensity, however, requires a scientific mind; Pater continually notes that true artistic expression is a 'science', idealizing the aesthete-scientist Leonardo da Vinci, who was 'so desirous of beauty . . . in such precise and definite forms.'[13] Another of the heroes of *The Renaissance* combines the aesthetic impulse with the scientific imagination: the classical archaeologist Winckelmann, who always sees 'in the concrete'. For Pater, these men always stand in marked contrast to the fuzzy metaphysics of Coleridge, who denied scientific truth in favour of 'absolute formulas'.[14]

Pater's demand to put the 'finer edge' on life and language is, however, supplemented by a need for that 'wholeness' or 'integration' that was a condition of the *fin-de-siècle* sensibility. His test of an excellent work of art is its 'completeness, the perfectly rounded wholeness and

[10] Walter Pater, *The Renaissance: Studies in Art and Poetry* (London, 1901), p. 235. All citations from Pater's work are taken from this edition, *The Works of Walter Pater*, Library Edition in eight volumes (London, 1901).

[11] 'Style', *Appreciations*, p. 10.

[12] 'Conclusion', *The Renaissance*, p. 235.

[13] *The Renaissance*, p. 154.

[14] 'Coleridge', *Appreciations*, pp. 68–9.

unity of impression'.[15] Life, like art, strives for an existence in which 'form and matter, in their union or identity, present one single effect'.[16] A life or a work of art that reaches such a condition takes upon itself an atmosphere whereby 'a cloudy mysticism is refined to a subdued and graceful mystery. . . .'[17] The language of such wholeness is invariably characterized by the imagery of religious faith. As with so many heirs of the Victorian *Zeitgeist*, the men whose life stories comprise *The Renaissance* seek some permanence in a sea of epistemological fluidity, some centre of stability with which that delicate equilibrium between centrifugal matter and centripetal form might be reconciled in the absence of a knowable God. Pater's 'soul' is no less than man's self-consciousness; reversing Arnold's belief that the strongest part of religion is its unconscious poetry, he sees the devotion to art as an unconscious religion by which incremental time is redeemed:

> The basis of the reconciliation of the religions of the world would thus be the inexplicable activity and creativity of the human mind itself, in which all religions alike have their root, and in which all alike are reconciled.[18]

The stasis which denotes a ritual reconciliation means that *being* is absorbed within *doing*. History and the history of art being virtually identified, conventional linear time sequence is subsumed beneath a notion of time (the notorious Paterian 'moment') that is re-lived in the creative act. *Bildungsroman* is converted into *Künstlerroman*. This involves a thinly disguised notion of aesthetic 'election': the qualification is a key Paterian exercise:

> . . . the end of life is not action but contemplation—being as distinct from doing—a certain disposition of mind is, in some shape or other, the principle of all the higher morality. . . . To treat life in the spirit of art, is to make life a thing in which means and ends are identified: to encourage such treatment, the true moral significance of art and poetry.[19]

Just as the Century Guild's efforts tended toward the creation of a 'total book', where covers, text, spine, and margins would lose a sense of private space, so Pater's wayfarers in *The Renaissance* and the *Imaginary Portraits* dissolve the sense of difference between stasis and

[15] 'Coleridge', *Appreciations*, p. 99.
[16] *The Renaissance*, p. 49.
[17] *Ibid.*, pp. 113–14.
[18] *Ibid.*, p. 179.
[19] 'Wordsworth', *Appreciations*, pp. 62–3.

flux within the posture of self-absorption. Contrary to any advocacy of indiscriminate accumulation of sensations, his aesthetes strive toward a virginal confrontation which always involves a 'casting off [of] all debris, and leaving us only what the imagination has fused and transformed'.[20] They are metaphoric alchemists who, in the process of encountering the phenomenal world, burn off the impurities of vulgar sensation, allowing the subjective touchstone of taste to break to the surface. But since the fall into a tyranny of sensation is absolutely necessary to that higher innocence which occurs when consciousness dwells upon the objects of sensation (a condition that Pater always denotes by metaphors of transparency), there is a certain reciprocal pattern. His aesthetes—Emerald Uthwart, Florian Deleal, and Sebastian van Storck—go out into the world only to return to the confined chamber of the mind. We grow aesthetically, paradoxically, by an act of de-construction:

> At first sight experience seems to bury us under a flood of external objects, pressing upon us with a sharp and importunate reality, calling us out of ourselves in a thousand forms of action. But when reflexion begins to play upon those objects they are dissipated under its influence; the cohesive force seems suspended like some trick of magic; each object is loosed into a group of impressions—colour, odour, texture—in the mind of the observer . . . those impressions of the individual mind to which, for each one of us, experience dwindles down, are in perpetual flight. . . . to reforming itself on the stream, to a single sharp impression, with a sense of it, a relic more or less fleeting, of such moments gone by, what is real in

---

[20] 'Preface', *The Renaissance*, pp. x–xi. See also the idea of Marius, notably that the true aesthete must strive 'to be absolutely virgin towards . . . experience . . . to be rid of the notions we have made for ourselves, and that so often only mis-represent the experience of which they prefer to be the representation' (*Marius the Epicurean*, II, p. 220). The denial of all categories but the *a priori* sensibilities means that the aesthete is a close ally of the perpetual child in theory long before Wilde made the equation practical, in his appearance. The significance of this alliance between the infinite potential of the child and that of the aesthete's confrontation with the phenomenal world may help to account for the fascination of the *fin de siècle* with vicarious participation in childhood via the genre of the children's story or fairytale: William Morris, George Macdonald, Andrew Lang, Oscar Wilde, and others. The demand to reclaim '*temps perdu*' of the Imaginary Portrait's pilgrim is very close to the 'once upon a time' with which so much late Victorian children's literature began.

our life fines itself down . . .—that continual vanishing away, that strange, perpetual weaving and unweaving of ourselves.[21]

This reversion to origins that gives the *Imaginary Portraits* a self-reflexive structure is a return to the condition of pure potential, the virginal, yet all-consuming whiteness that is almost a trademark: the White-Nights of *Marius the Epicurean*; the white heat of the 'hard, gem-like flame'; even the white robes that fascinate Florian Deleal. Such is the world of the 'Diaphaneité', one who participates in the repose of grace rather than the multitudinousness of nature. The 'diaphanous' personality, as imagined by Pater, exudes the austere simplicity of 'the Imitatio Christi', in his expression of 'the repose of perfect intellectual culture'.[22] As this type comes ever nearer the perfect identification of life and art, the 'veil of an outer life not simply expressive of the inward becomes thinner and thinner',[23] in preparation for the awaited regeneration. The condition resembles that phase in Yeats's aesthetic when the gong of the thirteenth hour signals the participation of man in the life of his collective mask; a condition of de-individuation characterized in *A Vision* as 'complete passivity, complete plasticity . . . liquefaction'.[24] The unique particularity of each soul is blurred, as

[21] 'Conclusion', *The Renaissance*, pp. 234–7.
[22] 'Diaphaneité', *Miscellaneous Studies*, p. 249.   [23] *Ibid.*, p. 249.
[24] W. B. Yeats, *A Vision* (New York, 1961), p. 183. After an early poetry filled with wandering questors to romantic islands in the nineties, questors who never could obtain the peace at the centre of the rose or the quietude of the Lake Isle of Innisfree for long, Yeats arrives at a conviction that only by moving in the opposite direction might we obtain some temporary reconciliation between the 'fated' and the 'willed'. Only when the soul has immersed itself in the diversity of experience, the foul rag-and-bone shop of the world, will it be an image of the plenitude of God, and thence capable of being gathered into the artifice of eternity. The development of the theory of Masks, which receives its articulation in the diary of 1909 and its development in *Per Amica Silentia Lunae*, posits creativity from the wearing of the anti-self. The fact that the self needs the anti-self as much as the anti-self needs the self drives each individual to play the role of that which he least resembles. In the process the soul transforms that which stands opposite it into its own nature and comes to draw 'backward into itself, into its own changeless purity, all it has felt or known' (*A Vision*, p. 220). This embrace of the 'contraries' is, in effect, an attempt at liberation by the addition of diverse experiences. Man must be both himself and not himself at the same time in order to achieve spherical wholeness. Yeats no longer wishes to flee the world of his early poetry, the evanescence of 'Ephemera', but rather desires to steep himself in those 'mere complexities'. Instead of moving to the centre of the circle (like the man who

it flows into the 'other', producing the patterned rhythms of the dance where author, participant, and audience form a unity. In Pater's aesthetic, this condition by which Dionysus is transformed into Apollo is described as a suspension of development: 'a moral sexlessness, a kind of impotence, an ineffectual wholeness of nature, yet with a divine beauty and significance of its own'.[25]

If not an absolute counterpart to the Lady of Shalott's 'glassy countenance', the aesthetic orphan undergoes something akin to the torments of a sacrificial victim as part of the aesthetic consummation that is the concluding phase of romantic self-consciousness. Surrendering his individuality by dying into an 'atmosphere' that the reflections of self-consciousness have created, he reverses Darwinian development, where any species was imagined as progressing through ever more sophisticated levels of individuation, by an aesthetic refinement: that 'perpetual weaving and unweaving' of the self by which the fibres of existence and the tapestry of art are made interchangeable.

V

It is, to be sure, a process not without its hazards. A life or work of art that is a 'condition' has, in effect, a symptomatology. That is, it remains vulnerable to physical deterioration or to neurosis. The struggle to formalize random sensation seems to have a cosmic counterpart in the obscure 'inner' deterioration that often afflicts Pater's characters. Watteau is the victim of an 'incurable restlessness' which is a 'symptom of this terrible disease'.[26] La Gioconda's smile mixes a saintly demeanour with a mysterious reflection of all the world's maladies. Some self-consuming illness makes *degeneration*, so crucial to any phenomenology of decadence (as Max Nordau polemically insisted), part of the legacy of lost subjectivity. Behind this inner decay lies a curious process. As similarity between subject and object increases, metaphor becomes unveiled. The ultimate extension is 'perfect similarity' or tautology. If artist and art are identities, we have the beginnings of a world without

---

shoots the arrow that goes to the centre of the sun), he moves along the periphery, first emptying, and then being emptied by experience, with the winding and unwinding of the cones.

[25] 'Diaphaneité', *Miscellaneous Studies*, p. 253.
[26] 'A Prince of Court Painters', *Imaginary Portraits*, p. 40.

metaphor. So some dissimilarity is absolutely necessary in order to prevent language from dissolving into either a uniformity of texture and tone or the visual silence of Mallarmé's blank page—opposite sides of the same *fin-de-siècle* coin. The diaphanous transparency of Pater's culture hero is surely an aesthetic variant of the 'perfect similarity' that has its corollary emblem in symbolic androgyny—an 'ineffectual wholeness of nature'.

There is surely a logical inconsistency in Pater's construction of a religion of art through which the aesthete might hope to escape the randomness of a world without a centre. Perhaps the paradox is inherent in the aesthete's posture before the world at large. After all, the desire to experience random sensations while secretly wishing for an island or similar aesthetic envelope seems as contradictory as wishing for a 'wholeness of nature' while simultaneously worshipping those moments of suspended development among the temporal virgins whom Pater called 'the children of the world'. It is the pantomime of the stereotypical decadent Dandy, convinced that he is unmasking even as he dons the mask. Inverting all values and creating disproportion among those delicate proportions upon which civilization is built, he is unaware of difference. For him all thoughts resemble impressions, and all impressions have the value of thoughts:

> ... if we begin with the inward world of thought and feeling, the whirlpool is still more rapid, the flame more eager and devouring. ... It contracts still further: the whole scope of observation is dwarfed into the narrow chamber of the individual mind. Experience, already reduced to a group of impressions, is ringed around for each one of us by that thick wall of personality. ... Every one of these impressions is the impression of the individual in his isolation, each mind keeping as a solitary prisoner its dream of a world.[27]

The de-generation of the self into art is paradoxically part of generation in the realm of aestheticizing the natural world. The danger, as Sebastian van Storck discovers, is that one's entire impression of the world is 'but a thought'.[28] For, if the self-refining process of Pater's aesthetics results in a condition wherein there is no longer any distinction between 'outward' and 'inward', then the narcissistic projection of the self into the 'outer' world, and the reduction of the self to the status

---

27 'Conclusion', *The Renaissance*, pp. 234, 235.
28 'Sebastian van Storck', *Imaginary Portraits*, p. 83.

of a passive receptor, are not opposites but identities. He who had engaged in a self-refining process, in order to purge experience of its vulgar sensations, finds himself trapped in a maelstrom of subjectivity. If we 'begin with the inward world of thought and feeling', there is implicit the suggestion that, sadly, the journey also ends there. Negation of self and the multiplication of self inherent in narcissism are the twin cones upon which 'the perpetual weaving and unweaving of ourselves' takes place—providing an aesthetic basis for the imagery of Yeats, Vorticism, and post-modernist de-construction.

There is of course a double bind to such an aesthetic; when art's structure is converted to life's conduct by the diaphanous man, aesthetic prescriptions have a way of becoming ethical principles. If the self is projected throughout the universe, then the loss of moral differentiation is a feature concomitant to a life transformed to art. The loss of the human implied in Paterian de-individuation, when carried over into ethics, implies a loss of human values which is often translated by his *fin-de-siècle* successors as either amorality or immorality. Florian Deleal, for example, sees himself increasingly drawn 'to play pain-fugues on the delicate nerve work of living creatures'. Marcus Aurelius seems incredibly detached from the gratuitous slaughter at a Roman amphitheatre and, for Fronto, the other tutor in *Marius the Epicurean*, the disinvolvement from evil is revealed as an aesthetic response: 'there were the evils, the vices, which he avoided as . . . a failure in good taste.' It is a detachment like that of an art object—a thing apart from the world of men which carries with it a smell of interior deterioration, vague illness, or criminality. It is as if the glorious imperfection of the statue were translated into moral weakness or its symptomatic accompaniment, sickly indifference. The detachment of the 'scientific' aesthete who has longed to pare down experience into its ever purer 'moments' turns back upon himself, so that he becomes a voyeur for whom every activity in the 'outer' world testifies to the failure of the romantic quest. And the voyeur, for whom Pater provides an aesthetic justification, is an eye disguising itself as a mirror. Such detachment would find its visual counterpart in Redon's 'Cyclops' series where disembodied and indifferent eyes stare at physically luscious landscapes. Their fictional equivalent would lie in the best-known 'Imaginary Portrait', *The Picture of Dorian Gray*.

VI

Although Pater's aesthetics may at first glance seem isolated from the mainstream of the history of ideas, he was, in fact, formalizing a lore of self-reflexiveness. It was in the 1890s, after all, that the young Freud altered the direction of his investigations from the *Studies of Hysteria* (co-authored with Breuer) to the interests that culminated in the *Project for a Scientific Psychology* (1895) and *The Interpretation of Dreams* (1899). And crucial to that shift is an emphasis upon the relationship between ego-formation and narcissism. The *stade du miroir* or mirror phase of development in childhood comes to be seen as part of a necessary narcissism; development (*bildung*) is a function of replacing the real world with a figure or image (*bild*). This process is essential to development, but it simultaneously contains within itself the seed of that self-destruction much examined by the later Freud of *Mourning and Melancholia*. The beginnings of the psychoanalytical movement show an imagery pattern that seems inherited from the *fin de siècle*: regression to the occasion of childhood trauma brought about by an analyst (one of Pater's alchemists transposed) holding up a figurative mirror to the patient's autobiographical confession. One of Freud's more questionable contributions was that of democratizing guilt, making us all among the *condamnés* (to borrow from Pater). Complete confession and a pseudo-scientist who somewhat voyeuristically (hence transference) holds the mirror up to 'being' is as much a part of the phenomenology of the 1890s as the mirror held to Bram Stoker's *Dracula* so that the beast might undo himself!

This pattern of the emptying of subjectivity, even as one projects it upon the 'others', is surely part of the mythology of naturalism that was to become so fashionable in certain works of Gissing, George Moore, H. G. Wells, and Conrad. Naturalism is not often regarded as part of the 'aesthetic' nineties, except when seen as a reaction against the artificial sensibility of the *fin de siècle*. Yet the scientific detachment that produced an allegedly 'objective' vision can be seen as an authorial ruse enabling the naturalist to project himself onto nature while feigning the passivity of a naive observer. If so, it is a sophisticated legitimization of a 'divided self'. The detached, 'objective' narrator is but another version of the voyeur, vicariously involved while maintaining the illusion of distance behind the paradigm of an experiment. An art which hopes to make an audience 'feel' reality risks being part of a mythology which confuses stylization and bare existence, involving what Lukacs calls the simultaneous manifestation of 'false objectivism' and 'false subjectivism':

> The method of observation and description came into existence with the pretence of rendering literature scientific, of transforming literature into applied natural science and sociology. But the social *moments* grasped by observation and fixed by description are so poor, so schematic, that they easily change into their polar antipode, into complete subjectivism.[29]

Generically speaking, we are in the kingdom of a story such as *Dr Jekyll and Mr Hyde*, where a presumably objective scientist vicariously participates in the life of his 'double'. In the last chapter of Stevenson's novella, the reader learns that Dr Jekyll's will is in Utterson's safe; but, since Hyde can forge Jekyll's signature, the entire story as it is filtered through the human 'frame' is either an autobiography of a divided soul or a confession without an author. We are no longer reading the 'history' of an event, but rather *The Strange Case of Dr Jekyll and Mr Hyde*: a 'case history' wherein the genre of the Imaginary Portrait intersects a medical, criminal, and literary investigation into the nature of 'origins'. In a sense, Dr Jekyll is the ultimate naturalist; he projects a false self as he struggles to experiment with increasingly exquisite sensations. But the fragmentation of the self, the creation of a 'double', is necessary both to create and to redeem an 'underworld'. This kingdom that combines science and a plurality of selves resembles the pairing in the Sherlock Holmes stories: Holmes and his double, Watson, must combine their wits in order to trace the 'clue' back through the labyrinth to some reconstruction of an origin: the crime. The doubling in Stevenson and Doyle comes close to the real-life 'case' of William Sharp, who, in an era of pseudonyms, wrote half of his collected works in a feminine handwriting under the name of Fiona Macleod. The fragmentation of self in the art and lives of *fin-de-siècle* personalities is perhaps the most painful of all the attempts to come to terms with the failures of connection implicit in romantic self-consciousness. Yet the aesthetic foundation for these aberrations is surely to be found in the 'double bind' felt by Pater's aesthete/scientists attempting to order and thereby escape the maelstrom of, first, sensation and, secondly, subjectivity—even as they are accused of indulging both.

Often the careers of *fin-de-siècle* artists exhibit the same compulsion

[29] Georg Lukacs, 'Idea and Form in Literature', in *Marxism and Human Liberation*, edited by E. San Juan Jr (New York, 1973), p. 124.

to seek security in a plurality of selves as do the protagonists of their stories. In George Moore's *Evelyn Innes*, a singer in Tristan comes to live her tragedy. She sees herself projected in every man, and this is indistinguishable from self-love: 'it was like living in a room where there was nothing but mirrors.' Unable to enjoy a mature sexual relationship, and tiring of the sensual intensity of Paris life, the girl enters a convent—and becomes enthralled with the confession, which enables the release of subjectivity to a lecherous Monsignor, as an art form. She elects, not suicide, but a literary analogue: the martyrdom of an autobiographical confession that undoes her previous sensual absorption. Moore's own career is not dissimilar. Unable to approach romantic 'sincerity' in a single utterance, he writes three autobiographies; each treats a different self on a pilgrimage which concludes with the attempt to negate the self. Each volume is a commentary on the preceding one, as if the narrator were in some prison of the autobiographical. In a world where the self is fragmented, and where growth and development are replaced by introjection and/or multiplication, there can only be incomplete attempts at autobiography that eddy and overlap, but seldom communicate. Such is the kingdom of the 'perpetual sequel', an art that, like its creators, wishes to remain perpetually young even at the expense of a loss of 'endings'. The romantic artist dealing with the world at a fragmenting distance—our Lady of Shalott figure—has been replaced in the nineties by its aesthetic antipode: an art about the self writing about the attempt to create another work of art. Meta-art and meta-life become synchronized only with an agonized suspension of ordinary development (hence the perpetually youthful posture of the stereotypical dandy) of a Paterian suppression of self; both involve the reversal that is the objective correlative of self-reflexiveness. Hence the popularity of the confession—in one sense an interiorization of the romantic voyage—in both the *lives* (marked by a penchant for deathbed conversions to Catholicism) and the *literature* of the *fin de siècle*. Stories which commenced as accounts of one's life's development can conclude only in an act of renunciation which converts the chamber of mirrors to the monk's cell, creating an uneasy alliance between criminal, artist, and saint. All three possess an alias; all deny the world; perhaps most importantly, all three imagine themselves martyrs. It is an alliance that Father Rolfe (Baron Corvo) comically, and perhaps Stephen Daedalus (whose very name yokes the saint and the labyrinth), would certainly have understood.

VII

Such sophisticated attempts to escape the labyrinth of subjectivity in order to confront the world virginally shapes the essential art forms of the nineties. The choice would seem to be between a meta-art like Nineties 'purple prose' (which never gets at anything substantive, only at refinements) and the enraptured silence of the martyred saint in some empty cell: both, really, are a species of prison. In an environment where there is little prospect for original utterance, where the structural configuration of an infinitely receding meta-art holds out the only hope for even a temporary escape, the art of parody is, however, a logical consequence. If art and life are subject to a more or less free and random conversion, then it is to be expected that an art about art would come to be a convenient substitute, if not an absolute necessity. The structure of parodic art has a number of familiar features: it spatially echoes an *objet d'art* that is prior in time; it enables the artist to be both outside an object parodied and responsible for its infinite expansion: it can be joined and exited at will by audience participation; it hence has no discernible beginning or ending; finally, it has the sort of mnemonic hallucination of children's verse. An art that parodies inevitably exaggerates individuating characteristics and hence releases a specific genre from its metaphoric space through a process of inversion. The frequency of parodic art in the nineties—Beardsley, W. S. Gilbert, Owen Seaman, Mostyn Piggot, Max Beerbohm—should tell the literary historian something about the conditions under which aesthetic subjects and objects become mutually substitutable, one for the other. In short, parody works by a process of inducing aesthetic neutrality through exaggeration. The structure would be concentric, the geometry of a derivative art form that bombards the original with a thematic mirror.

A corollary to the uses of parody is the functional use of the epigram, especially in Morris and Wilde. Those aphorisims which precede *The Picture of Dorian Gray*, or become part of the wit of *fin-de-siècle* social occasions, function by making words themselves expendable; they participate in philosophical reversals by doing the same thing to standard sentence structure that parody does to its original genre: they enact their own truth in circular form so that the consequence is the revelation of content by form rather than the other way round. The oracular nature of the epigram gives it the character of *received* truth, and hence substantially reduces authorial responsibility not only at the audience level of participation, but at the mode's very commencement It is perhaps the closest one can come to automatic writing, the disappearance of a humanized subject. It is the beginnings of the neutralized, if not neutered, narrator.

Perhaps, with the disappearance of the traditional *bildungsroman*, the closest that the nineties could come to a communal epic is that language which, Heidegger suggests, tends to float baselessly around the culture: gossip and its enactment, scandal. The lives of so many decadents, Ernest Dowson, Lionel Johnson, John Gray, and Oscar Wilde, reach self-definition in some scandalous episode that shocked their friends. Gossip is a mode by which an 'outsider' can vicariously participate in the secret, inner life of someone else, usually of a more elite social position. Hence, it tends to redeem socially sacred space by allowing a passive participant access; the voyeur conspires to invade privacy. Like the epigram, where subjects and verbs are often interchangeable, he who gossips becomes part of the received form merely by repeating the story, participates without risking the discharge of psychic or physical energy. The first gossipers were literally 'god-sibs', siblings of God, who functioned as witnesses at infant baptism in the Middle Ages. They were, even from the outset, voyeurs. And, the more the gossip, the more the truth recedes into the distance. It is an authorless language, totally spontaneous, that creates as much as reflects an 'event'.

A world composed of mirrors, epigrams, and gossip is a world that is decadent in the more traditional sense in which we use that word: it exists under conditions of flagging energy and failed connections where there is no longer any hope of a Unity of Being. It has also a number of the characteristics of pornographic literature. *Lesbia Brandon, Memoirs of a Maid*, and *The Pearl* all testify to the virulence of a counter-culture where mask and mirror are a part of the necessary equipment. That which is private parts or private property ('elite space') must be made communal if the phenomenology of the fictional form is to approximate to the spatial physics of the sex act. Perhaps this accounts for the widespread use of letters, notebooks, and private memoirs by the authors of erotica. But total access de-individuates, so that not only the characters but the authors also have a tendency to remain anonymous. Such a disappearance of self is the enactment of that familiar pseudo-naturalism that we have witnessed in the literature of the nineties; in so many pornographic novels of the period the narrator poses as a scientist or doctor who simply records from a distance. If all have lost their identities in a *mélange* of failed development, then there is no way of distinguishing homosexual from heterosexual activity, since each exists in a realm of polymorphous perversity. And indeed there is a considerable amount of homosexual activity in most late nineteenth-century pornography. When love becomes narcissistic, the self is indistinguishable from the 'other', and any account of development must conclude in a regression where psychic androgynes engage in a full gamut of AC/DC connection. The 'environment' is both public and highly introverted, a paradoxical combination, which makes the prison a marvellous metaphor: the characters are always in the range of someone's guardian eye; there are no events but only the repeated permutation of the same event, now 'done by the number'; and its space is incredibly boring. Like the highly polished surfaces of Art Nouveau or Beardsley's illustration of 'The Rape of the Lock', every object from every angle casts back a transposition of the self. Perhaps it was the nineties' way of calling our attention to the fact that we are all voyeurs, sharing in the criminality around us. In so many Art Nouveau pubs, what appear to be windows are, on second glance, seen to be mirrors which, contrary to providing an opening to nature, reflect the space where we viewers are at the locus of an Imaginary Portrait. It de-natures the world while simultaneously multiplying the self—an allegory of post-romanticism. And of course it prevents the drinker from drinking alone.

The homosexual in jail, whose division of being tempts the world's gossip, is the ultimate reduction of the self-contained, reflex image. And *De Profundis* is the confession of an individual no longer capable of distinguishing self from false-self, where all subjects have become objects. Oscar Wilde's condition, in brief, is the one art form where parody, gossip, the epigram, failed development manifested in the denial of growth, and the dehumanization that is part of the pornographic experience all conspire in an utterance that is the pretence of a failed autobiography. The jailed aesthetic criminal is the final step in spatial interiorization, and the fact that Wilde, emblematically at least on the *via dolorosa* (Clapham Junction), was on public display, with a steady stream of curious onlookers, only heightens the poignancy of his metaphyscial condition. At least a part of the irony is inherent in the parody of a genre. Not unlike Newman, who used his retreat to Littlemore as a metaphoric mental and emotional prison from which to write a pastoral letter both to the faithful and to his accusers, Oscar Wilde uses the confessional overtones and the postponed access inherent in the epistolary form as a precondition for his 'conversion' to the new faith of hedonism and his rebirth as a public work of art—the fruits of martyrdom and its companion, invaded privacy. Behind both confessions lurk the metaphor and the physical presence, respectively, of the prison that has characterized the mode from the time of Augustine. Just as John Henry Newman used his childhood fascination with ghosts as a verifying of the hold of mystery as opposed to ratiocination, so Oscar Wilde denies 'intellectually unworthy motives' by claiming that a 'motive is an aim'. His conversion will be one of the heart rather than the head. As Newman attempted to universalize his confession (to help us all to share in the 'crime'), so Wilde omitted the date and added the Pauline epigraph, '*Epistola: In Carcere et Vinculis*'.

Following an account of the illness of the prodigal, which is often a feature of confessions, Wilde justifies the equivocal nature of his existence by borrowing a theological argument. Man is subject both to free will and to logical necessity, a mixture that feeds the miraculous in religion, and paradox in art. There is no temporal progression in *De Profundis*, only an eddying rhythm—the time dimension of repetition that corresponds to the spatial enclosure: 'With us time itself does not progress. It revolves. It seems to circle round one centre of pain.'[30] As he converts his life to the archetypal pattern of the saint's life, in this most exquisite of labyrinths, Wilde comes to participate in incarnational time: 'What lies before me is my past.'[31] Like Pater's 'moments', and

[30] 'De Profundis', in *The Complete Works of Oscar Wilde*, introduced by V. Holland (London, 1948), p. 904.

[31] *Ibid.*, p. 957. For a rich discussion of the relationship between saint and criminal, see J. P. Sartre, *Saint Genet*, translated from the French by Bernard Frechtman (New York, 1963), pp. 73–138. Although space does not allow a full discussion of Sartre's elaboration of the metaphors of martyrdom, the notion of a 'false detachment' is key. For Sartre, the criminal intelligence desires to 'live the present in the past, to perceive as one remembers'. He relates to himself the events of his life, as they are unfolding, as if they were episodes of a tragic story. The result, for Sartre, is that failure and betrayal are one and the same:

> Genet wants to do Evil, fails, decides to will his failure; whereupon he changes into a traitor, his acts change into gestures and being changes into appearance. Now the law of appearances and gestures is Beauty. We have got to the heart of this strange endeavour, in that secret place where Evil, engendering its own betrayal, is metamorphosed into Beauty.... To carry failure to the point of the destruction of everything, including Evil

Joyce's 'epiphany', this is an experience that cuts across traditional chronology.

Since for Wilde, 'humility in the artist is the frank acceptance of all experiences',[32] the suffering of Christ on the cross became a paradigm for the agony of the aesthete. In a decadent world—where all is mirrored, reflected, capable of infinite expansion or contraction through parody, nuance, and gossip—only suffering provides for the collapse of all masks:

> Pain, unlike Pleasure, wears no mask. Truth in Art is not any correspondence between the actual idea and the accidental existence; it is not the resemblance of shape to shadow, or of the form mirrored in the crystal to the form itself: it is no Echo coming from a hollow hill, anymore than it is the well of silver water in the valley that shows the Moon to the Moon and Narcissus to Narcissus. Truth in Art is the unity of a thing with itself: the outward rendered expressive of the inward: the soul made incarnate: the body instinct with spirit. For this reason there is no truth comparable to Sorrow.[33]

This transcendence through denial may well acount for those numerous death-bed conversions with which so many decadents concluded their pilgrimages, and which Pater was to parody in the death of his Marius. Throughout *De Profundis*, Wilde argues that Alfred Douglas stood between his very self and a devotion to art. Only an objectification-as-art in a single ecstatic act which combines recovery and pleasure can end the Fall. Such martyrdom is one way of making the self into a passive device which merely serves as the focus of attention for a presumed audience: 'the extinction in one's self of all that is but correlative

---

itself, is to betray. But from the point of view of the Other, of the absent and later witness, to betray to the point of despair, to the point of the self-denial that might be called abnegation, is to be a saint. When Evil was possible in his eyes, Genet did Evil in order to be wicked. Now that Evil proves impossible, Genet will do Evil in order to be a saint.

(Sartre, *Saint Genet*, pp. 192–3)

To perceive as one remembers is to will one's own autobiography as a mode of existence. That is to be both inside and outside experience simultaneously. Such a false detachment is perilously close to the *fin-de-siècle* voyeur whose split is the interiorization of the orphan's more real detachment from a sense of history or origins. This stylization is very close to Heidegger's notion of *Dasein* in Being: the outside 'standing in', and hence could represent a philosophical legacy, as well.

[32] *Ibid.*, p. 922.   [33] *Ibid.*, p. 920.

to the finite illusion—by the suppression of ourselves', to borrow from Pater's Sebastian van Storck.[34]

The fact that Wilde had begun to sign his letters with the pseudonymous 'Sebastian Melmoth' only heightens the self-consciousness. Maturin had been a distant relative of Wilde, the part-Jew whose account of the Wandering Jew in *Melmoth the Wanderer* always attracted his attention. By using 'Sebastian' as a prefix, Wilde was perhaps attempting to combine the Hebraic questor without a home with the Hellenic saint, in an equipoise not unlike that sought by Arnold and Pater. It was, perhaps, a way of bringing the androgyne's divided existence into a single, cold focus: the finished product of the process that began with the refined burning of Pater's 'hard, gem-like flame'. There is little distance separating the St Stephen whose diary concludes Joyce's *Portrait*, the Frederick Rolfe who dressed as *Hadrian VII*, Dowson's 'Nuns of the Perpetual Adoration', Hardy's St Jude who dies en route to Christminster, and this St Sebastian of the last, most notably failed autobiography.

Long seeking the regeneration of the world through a new Hellenism in the manner of his splendid Dorian, Wilde lives his mask, at last aestheticizing a split, mirrored self within the confines of a compact, overly filled space occupied by the overly educated fat man. As R. D. Laing, that charter of divided selves, has made abundantly clear, the short-circuiting mirrors of our complex false-self systems leave us with the choice between the diaphanous emptiness of someone who is all surface *sans* interior (the mirror) and what he calls 'petrifaction', the transformation of the self into a stone fortress so as to revel in our martyrdom.[35] The schizoids whose case histories provide the body of Laing's *The Divided Self* all participate in what he calls some variant of the Medusa-myth. They imagine themselves as saints or sinners, saviours

[34] 'Sebastian van Storck', *Imaginary Portraits*, p. 113.
[35] R. D. Laing, *The Divided Self* (1965). Laing tends to blur the boundaries that separate ordinary displacement (schizoid) from illness (schizophrenic). But his analysis of the causes and consequences of the displacement of self are most interesting when read in the light of late Victorian literary history. Laing's patients usually engage in some 'passive' defence in order to avoid dehumanization at the hands of the world at large. Such a fortress for the 'false-self' is very functional in so far as its adaptation enables the victim to avoid the aggression of the 'other'. He becomes an 'other' in order to avoid 'the other', hence the confusion between mask, 'authentic' self, and world symbolized in 'De Profundis' by various confusions of boundaries in the use of pronouns (for example).

or criminals, who alternate in their existence between the mirror and the stone. That imagery is characteristic of *De Profundis*:

> To you the Unseen Powers have been very good. They have permitted you to see the strange and tragic shapes of Life as one sees shadows in a crystal. The head of Medusa that turns living men to stone, you have been allowed to look at in a mirror merely.[36]

Perhaps the extremes are nowhere better illustrated than in Beardsley's 'candelabra signature' which is mirrored virtually everywhere in his art. When directed downward it constitutes a three-fingered papal blessing, but is an obscene gesture when held upright. Wilde's account of his development is arrested when it becomes a willed suicide note. He who had hoped to regenerate the world by aestheticizing it has become the object of a necessary salvation. He was his art, a condition where the metaphor, the genre that we call autobiography, is refined out of existence.

The Lady of Shalott recognized too late that the urge to self-development was inextricably bound up with the urge to self-destruction. In the attempt to exteriorize her fictions of the world, she remained a romantic quest figure, unable to test the fictions of presumed connections on the pulses. Every song became a funeral dirge for both her 'self' and her 'art'; every work of art a sacrificial hymn to an artist whose spaces are the gulfs of romantic alienation. Wilde's *De Profundis*, on the other hand, envisions a man living in his extensions of self, and making a connection which turns out only to be an example of narcissistic feed-back. Or he makes no connections at all and lives in the labyrinthine prison, cut off from normal development. Wilde and late nineteenth-century autobiography are either mirrored into multiple autobiographies (as in Yeats or Moore) or conclude where so many earlier nineteenth-century novels had begun: with a perpetual child in some prison—literal or figurative. But if the fate of autobiography and the mirrors of selfhood look back to the century's beginnings, Wilde's example also looks ahead to another famous poem, twenty or so years later, narrated by another divided saint—that Tiresias who constructs an entire history as the prisoner of history—from failed connections, from voyeurism, and the windy corridors of gossip, all united in a conversion experience called *The Waste Land*. As in the late Victorian furnishings that imprison and eventually suffocate

[36] 'De Profundis', p. 874.

the inhabitants with the down of excess, or the Edwardian feasts that do as much to the body, there are simply no longer any empty or private spaces when everyone is a criminal-voyeur-artist. Des Esseintes, Huysmans's anti-hero of *A Rebours*, is perhaps the ultimate expression of this 'reversal of the flow'. The victim of ever more refined tastes, he resorts during an ultimate 'Last Supper' to seating himself before a plate upon which there is nothing but an enema bag, in order, clearly, to prevent the romantic ego from engaging food. The self-reflexive quest always ends when our endings are our beginnings.

At one stage in his incarceration, some friends conceived of a bold plan to sail up the Thames in a tiny shallop and to rescue Wilde from his stone cell under the veil of darkness. On the eve of the rescue attempt, however, Wilde had second thoughts, and elected to remain on his island, rather than embark upon a journey that would take him to the French mainland, elected instead therefore, a slow death in a museum where the 'other' could watch, gossip, and create the fiction that democratizes the aesthetic experience within the fiction of an Imaginary Portrait. To escape would have been to open up impacted space again, and to deny the viewer his own chance for participation in guilt. In shutting off that last escape route, Wilde was perhaps creating a final mirror image, a public redemption of the Lady of Shalott's private journey to an autumnal death, the gradual 'yellowing' of that 'Autumn of the Body' that was the nineties.

Note

The most nearly complete edition of the works, though very sloppily edited, is still *The Complete Works of Algernon Charles Swinburne*, ed. Edmund Gosse and T. J. Wise, 20 volumes (The Bonchurch Edition, 1925–7). The best collection of the letters is, of course, Cecil Y. Lang's excellent edition, *The Swinburne Letters*, 6 volumes (New Haven, 1959–62). Georges Lafourcade's *La Jeunesse de Swinburne* (*1837–1867*), 2 volumes (Strasbourg, 1928), is still probably the best biography; his *Swinburne: A Literary Biography* (1932), though not as extensive, is also important, and Jean Overton Fuller's *Swinburne: A Biography* (London, 1968; rpt. New York, 1971) is the most valuable recent addition.

A number of older book-length studies have valuable insights, particularly T. Earle Welby's *A Study of Swinburne* (New York, 1926) and Samuel C. Chew's *Swinburne* (Boston, 1929), which is especially sound on the prose criticism. The most important books on Swinburne's critical and poetic theory, however, are Thomas E. Connolly's *Swinburne's Theory of Poetry* (Buffalo, 1964); Robert L. Peters's *The Crowns of Apollo: Swinburne's Principles of Literature and Art* (Detroit, 1965); and Jerome J. McGann's *Swinburne: An Experiment in Criticism* (Chicago, 1972).

The best short general studies of Swinburne are T. S. Eliot's classic 'Swinburne as Poet', in *Selected Essays* (New York, 1950); John D. Rosenberg's 'Swinburne', *Victorian Studies* 11 (December 1967), pp. 131–52; and Morse Peckham's excellent introduction to his collection *Swinburne: Poems and Ballads and Atalanta in Calydon* (New York, 1970), pp. xi–xxxv.

Finally, the most useful articles on Swinburne, dealing with some of the same general issues I have tried to address in my essay, are as follows: Julian Baird's outstanding article, 'Swinburne, Sade, and Blake: The Pleasure-Pain Paradox', *Victorian Poetry* 9 (Spring–Summer 1971), pp. 49–75; David A. Cook, 'The Content and Meaning of Swinburne's "Anactoria"', *Victorian Poetry* 9 (Spring–Summer 1971), pp. 77–93; John O. Jordan, 'The Sweet Face of Mothers: Psychic Pattern in *Atalanta in Calydon*', *Victorian Poetry* 11 (Summer 1973), pp. 101–4; and Douglas C. Fricke, 'The Proserpine Figure in Swinburne's *Poems and Ballads I*' in *Aeolian Harps: Essays in Literature in Honor of Maurice Browning Cramer*, ed. Donna G. and Douglas C. Fricke (Bowling Green, 1975), pp. 191–205.

III

Swinburne's Circle of Desire:
A Decadent Theme

CHRIS SNODGRASS

I

SWINBURNE, who prefigured the Nineties in so many things, pre-figured that era of artistic scandals with the outrage his 1866 volume of *Poems and Ballads* caused. It provoked from the reviewers what Clyde K. Hyder has called 'an attack seldom, if ever, equalled for its fierceness in the annals of English literary history!'[1] 'We do not know when we have read a volume so depressing and misbegotten—in many of its constituents so utterly revolting,' said *The London Review*, calling the poems a 'mere deification of incontinence'.[2] In *The Athenaeum*, Robert Buchanan assailed the poems as 'Unclean', 'rank blasphemy', 'writing of which no true poet, fairly cultured, could have been guilty'[3]—an attack to which he would return later, in 'The Fleshly School in Poetry'. In *The Saturday Review*, John Morley added that instead of a Wordsworthian 'wise passiveness'—'enlarged medi-tation, the note of the highest poetry'—Swinburne displayed a 'reckless contempt for anything like a balance': 'The bottomless pit encompasses us on one side, and stews and bagnios on the other. He is either the vindictive and scornful apostle of a crushing iron-shod despair, or else he is the libidinous laureate of a pack of satyrs.' He loathes 'to throw any veil over pictures which kindle, as these do, all the fires of his imagination in their intensest heat and glow', and these flames melt all moral distinctions into a state of paradox:

His warmest prayer to the gods is that they should
    Come down and redeem us from virtue.
His warmest hope for men is that they should change

[1] Clyde Kenneth Hyder, *Swinburne's Literary Career and Fame* (Durham, N.C., 1933), p. 37.
[2] *The London Review* 13 (4 August 1866), pp. 130–1.
[3] *The Athenaeum* 2023 (4 August 1866), pp. 137–8.

C

The lilies and languors of virtue
For the raptures and roses of vice.[4]

But as amusingly faulty and misguided as these original evaluations may now seem, they cut, in a strangely accurate way, to the core of Swinburne's poetic vision: depict a kind of split world in which, under the white-hot intensity of some passionate quest, there occur blatant transgressions of fundamental social taboos, violations which threaten to obliterate all moral and natural distinctions. This principle of 'heroic criminality', of the fearless invasion of traditionally forbidden areas, is what drew both attacks from Swinburne's scandalized contemporaries and, later, awed veneration from such admirers as the Nineties' Decadents. The Nineties, though, recognized something Swinburne's enemies did not: far from being 'unclean for the mere sake of uncleanness',[5] his poetry, if anything, is 'unclean' for the sake of cleanness, of restoring purity, of resanctification. The poems of *Poems and Ballads* are largely poems of crisis. His heroes desperately seek liberty, immediacy, communion, and the return to some central and sacred absolute because they feel their present condition to be one of confinement, mediation, severed connections, of *absence* within their own experience of any visible sense of the 'sacred'. All those pleading quests for union with Faustines and Doloreses are Swinburne's attempts to return a vital and intense feeling of sacred 'presence' to a world which increasingly feels the bankruptcy of 'sacred space'. This was a condition the Nineties were to re-experience and re-express. Related to this, however, is another dimension to Swinburne's poetic vision, noticeably ignored by his Nineties' admirers, though it in fact places Swinburne spiritually still closer to them. This is an uneasy recognition within his verse of the tremendous *destructive* power of those 'fires of the imagination'—flames which may be destructive not only of Philistine moral distinctions, but possibly of all life's distinctions, flames which reduce the world to paradox. It is an uneasiness stemming both from a definite and frustrating awareness of 'the characteristic paradox of an antithetical God', a God 'delighting in antithetics',[6] and a vague and guilt-tinged fear of the 'latent mystery of terror which lurks in all the highest poetry

[4] *The Saturday Review* 22 (4 August 1866), pp. 145–7.
[5] *The Athenaeum* 2023 (4 August 1866), p. 137.
[6] See 'Victor Marie Hugo', *The Complete Works of Algernon Charles Swinburne*, Vol. XIII, ed. Edmund Gosse and Thomas James Wise (1925–7), pp. 182–8.

or beauty'.[7] These were anxieties and fears, after all, held by a man who thought his frequent and severe 'bilious attacks' to be 'an act of God'.[8]

Though it has been said of Swinburne's career that 'a single note is struck early and held obsessively long',[9] it is interesting to observe that he rarely again, if ever, dealt so freely or intensely with the erotic situations and problems raised in his first volume. As Georges Lafourcade suggests, of the 1878 series of *Poems and Ballads*, 'the poet has exchanged the lyrical outbursts of *Poems and Ballads* and *Songs Before Sunrise* for the vaguest themes of undefined melancholy and sorrow', and the quest for divine immediacy is mitigated by 'a sort of dramatic detachment of self'.[10] This applies to other later volumes. Such unsettling recognition in Swinburne's early poetry of an ever-present potential might indeed suggest why a poet who once displayed 'a reckless contempt for anything like a balance' would accept so genially and passively the strictly regimented order and discipline of The Pines. It may also provide a partial explanation of why Swinburne (like Arnold before him) turned increasingly in later years from verse to literary criticism—and a criticism, moreover, which manifested an almost Aristotelian passion for categories and concrete distinctions, feared a loss of 'moral certitude', and proclaimed that great art is 'that immortal and immutable instinct . . . which not only serves freedom and seeks harmony' but 'whose instinct is for law'.[11] But the crisis that early Swinburne explores continued, and is, finally, that of the middle and late nineteenth century generally. It is much the same crisis that the Decadents of the nineties were to feel even more intensely —what J. Hillis Miller has called 'the disappearance of God', the inability of Victorian artists to sustain an unequivocal belief in a unifying transcendental authority and any absolute standard of value, the fear that no such absolute standard exists.[12] Like so many artists

[7] 'John Webster', in *The Complete Works*, XI, p. 295.

[8] Humphrey Hare, *Swinburne* (1949), p. 118.

[9] John D. Rosenberg, 'Swinburne', *Victorian Studies* 11 (December 1967), p. 152.

[10] Georges Lafourcade, *Swinburne, A Literary Biography* (New York, 1932), p. 226.

[11] See Robert L. Peters, *The Crowns of Apollo: Swinburne's Principles of Literature and Art* (Detroit, 1965), pp. 109–49.

[12] J. Hillis Miller, *The Disappearance of God* (1963; rpt. New York, 1965). Although, of course, the nineties' attempts at resolutions in this regard were not strictly theological, the effort to claim Art or an aesthetic consciousness as

who were to follow, the Swinburne of *Poems and Ballads* shows himself
to be another of those *fin-de-siècle* 'spiritual orphans'—in the words of
Max Beerbohm, 'a singing bird that could build no nest'.[13]

II

In some sense Swinburne's analysis of the first plate of William Blake's
'Gates of Paradise' encapsulates the central spiritual crisis. Like the
figures in Blake's engraving, the hero-lover in *Poems and Ballads* finds
himself 'orphaned', in a state of separation, divorced from his sacred
origins and the harmonizing divine. He, too, becomes a kind of 'dark
hermaphrodite'—'enlightened by the light within him, which is
darkness'—trapped in and possessed by a world of endless paradox.[14]
For, in Swinburne's reading of Blake, the act of creation is not a
charitable act by a benevolent deity but a malicious power-play by a
God who 'invents' the distinctions of virtue and vice, and divides
perfect, unified man into flesh and spirit, casting out the spiritual, and
sequestering man in a thick wall of materiality. The 'Creator God', in
fact, does not represent what can be called the 'true sacred'. Indeed, he
is an imposter who deceives 'perfect and eternal man' into subservience
and institutes the 'flaming sword of Law' and the 'winds and snows of
prohibition' to condition the man-god into perpetuating his false
power.[15] Man's imprisonment is due not so much to the Usurper's

a sacred 'centre' of meaning and value addresses itself to the same problem,
and indicates that their sense of the 'crisis of meaning' is basically the same as
their more theologically oriented predecessors.

[13] Max Beerbohm, 'No. 2 The Pines', in *The Incomparable Max: A Collection
of Writings of Sir Max Beerbohm* (New York, 1962).

[14] 'William Blake', in *The Complete Works*, Vol. XVI, pp. 71–3. Georges
Lafourcade in *Jeunesse de Swinburne*, Vol. II, p. 358, indicates that Swinburne
superimposes his own ideas on Blake's poems; Julian Baird, in 'Swinburne,
Sade, and Blake: The Pleasure—Pain Paradox', *Victorian Poetry* 9 (Spring–
Summer 1971), pp. 49–75, makes the same point. Although our conclusions
differ somewhat, both Baird and I see in parts of Swinburne's *William Blake* a
crystallization of Swinburne's poetic vision.

[15] Swinburne refers elsewhere to this man-god as the 'Pantheistic', as
opposed to the 'Theistic', god. He writes in a fascinating footnote to his
William Blake, under the guise of an anonymous correspondent:

These poems or essays at prophecy [he says] seem to me to represent in an
obscure and forcible manner the real naked question to which all theologies
and all philosophies must in the end be pared down. . . . On the right hand

might as to man's own abdication of his divine aspect. 'Fallen spiritual man' is referred to as 'deluded': his 'divine humanity' was supreme and free until he allowed the false Creator God to form the conditions of division, Law, and prohibition which constitute the merely 'earthly' state of existence:

> For the divine nature is not greater than the human; they are one from eternity, sundered by the separative creation or fall, severed into type and antitype by bodily generation, but to be made one again when life and death shall both have died; not greater than the human nature, but greater than the qualities which the human nature assumes upon earth.... The other 'God' or 'Angel of the Presence' who created the sexual and separate body of man did but cleave in twain the 'divine humanity', which becoming reunited shall redeem man without price and without covenant and without law; he meantime, the Creator, is a divine demon, liable to error, subduable by and through this very created nature of his invention, which he for the present imprisons and torments.

> *(William Blake*, pp. 199–200)

Indeed, this 'Angel of the Presence' is not all omnipotent; man has the intrinsic power to overthrow him and recover divine harmony. But, meantime, encased by the limits, the fears, and the guilt associated with earthly taboos, man's human nature is no longer identical with un-restrained and undifferentiated divine nature, he can only stare across the abyss in a vague attempt to find his 'other self'. Although man may continually feel within himself an absence, the subverting tactics of the false God make his divine complement increasingly more difficult to locate. Swinburne chooses to emphasize repeatedly in his Blake study that the greatest danger to man's full potentiality of being lies, not in

---

... is the Theist—the 'man of God', if you may take his own word for it; the believer in a separate or divisible deity capable or conceivably capable of existence apart from ours who conceive of it; a conscious and absolute Creator. On the left hand is the Pantheist; to whom such a creed is mainly incredibly and wholly insufficient. His creed is or should be much like that of your prophet here ... and that creed, as I take it, is simply enough expressible in Blake's own words, or deducible from them; that 'all deities reside in the human breast'; that except humanity there is no divine thing or person [p. 269n].

Throughout this essay I try to use the terms 'sacred' or 'true sacred', instead of 'God', 'gods', or other theistic designations, in an attempt to be faithful to Swinburne's distinction.

his initial enslavement, but in his blind and collusive acceptance of it. The danger is that if man does not act forcefully to reassume his divine nature, the Usurper-God will replace the true sacred altogether. Man may 'forget' his divine aspect, his 'natural state', becoming a mere tool of Urizen, and being forced to announce, like the hero of 'Hymn to Proserpine': 'Thou hast conquered, O pale Galilean; / . . . We have drunken of things Lethean, and fed on the fulness of death' (ll. 35–6).

In 'Faustine', the bankruptcy of spirit in the 'divine' Faustina's last incarnation can be attributed directly to this kind of undermining Lethean forgetfulness (ll. 81–9). Instead of striving to develop her own god-like potential, the 'fallen Faustine' submits to the will of a theistic, perverted God 'who metes the gardens with his rod' (l. 147). Faustine's vibrant, Faustian soul is hence subverted, entrapped in a 'love-machine / With clockwork joints' which appears to tick out 'This ghastly thin-faced time of ours' (ll. 142–3, 139). This 'fall' is perhaps most strikingly represented by the change in Faustine's hair: at the start of the poem, she is encouraged to 'Let your head lean / Back to the shoulder with its fleece / Of locks'; by the end, her hair is 'heavily bound back' (ll. 2–4, 153). But 'Hertha', the poem Swinburne once referred to as embodying his most 'intense and clarified thought', is his largest assault on Urizen. His letter to William Michael Rossetti (8 January, 1870) announces that 'At the tottering throne of that dignitary Urizen I have just discharged the most formidable piece of artillary yet cast or launched in his direction—the best stanzas written of "Hertha" strike such a blow at the very root of Theism.'[16] The poem begins with a striking refutation of any theistic (or Blakean) Creator-God as 'first cause' or as the agent of man's salvation (ll. 1–11). Hertha is shown to be the original and continuing life force—the Greater Soul in which man's soul and all living things, including 'God', participate. As she more fully describes herself, true and false Gods are differentiated (ll. 66–85). Unlike the Blakean Creator-God, Hertha is 'Mother, not maker'; man is 'Born, and not made'. And man, her emanated self, gives worship 'Not as servant to Lord, nor as master to slave' but in freedom as an equal, by being 'the ways of thy giving / As mine were to thee'. Worship of the true God becomes worship of the free self, for the true God is 'To be a man with thy might, / To grow straight in the strength of thy spirit.' Man refuses an identity imposed by a God of 'creeds' and 'rods'; instead, he seeks self-definition, 'to live out thy life as the light', in the

16 *The Swinburne Letters*, ed. Cecil Y. Lang (New Haven, 1959), Vol. I, pp. 79–80.

struggle towards reunification. To overcome the false God and re-store his 'divine humanity', he must realize his god-like potentiality, recognizing that 'the one thing unclean is the belief in uncleanness, the one thing forbidden is to believe in the existence of forbidden things' (*William Blake*, p. 167). 'I am in thee to save thee,' Hertha informs man, and man's salvation depends on his willingness to engage in what Swinburne refers to in *William Blake* as 'holy insurrection':

> a divine revolt against divine law; an evidence that man must become as God only by resistance to God—the 'God of this world'; that if Prometheus cannot, Zeus will not deliver us; and that man, if saved at all, must indeed be saved 'so as by fire'—by ardour of rebellion and strenuous battle against the God of nature, the Creator-God of pure materiality. . . .
>
> (*William Blake*, p. 202)

The issue comes down to a battle of wills: between the forces of transgression, liberty, growth, and immediacy on the one hand, and the forces of law, restraint, stasis, and mediation on the other. Man-god must assert his will over the will of the Usurper. And, in fact, man-god's 'holy insurrection' authenticates not only his own being, but also that of the sacred in which he participates. Hertha's fulfilment, her fruition, also depends on man's assuming his true destiny: she needs man free 'That my heart may be greater within me, beholding the fruits of me fair / . . . Man, pulse of my centre, and fruit of my body, and seed of my soul' (ll. 160, 195). Reciprocity becomes total: if man fulfils his divine destiny, the stasis of Urizen is overcome, Hertha is fruitful, sacred 'presence' is made manifest; if he fails, then the world is 'grown grey with thy breath', Hertha is rendered sterile, the sacred impotent. In a sense, the model is the medieval one of the will and the *anima*: the *anima* or the soul (Hertha) endows man with meaning, yet it is characteristically a passive, amorphous, completely plastic force; it depends for its shape, direction, and fulfilment on the will's moulding of it. In Swinburne's poetry as well, the affirmation of the sacred depends on man's uniting his will with it.

III

As passionate love has been traditionally considered a mode of sancti-fication and deification, it is not surprising that in Swinburne's poetry it becomes the primary vehicle for heroic rebellion: the means to divine immediacy is erotic desire. Indeed, the natural dynamics of sanctification and taboo virtually mandate an erotic element. As Georges Bataille notes in *Death and Sensuality* (New York, 1969), the transition from the state of normal human equilibrium to that of erotic desire presupposes a kind of violence—the partial dissolution of the self as it moves from the separateness and discrete distinctions of stable life to the ecstatic unity and loss of distinctions which constitute 'transcendence'. Erotic passion, pressing beyond the boundaries of normal human existence, causes in the process a disruption of order a fundamental loss of 'difference'. Furthermore, by its threat to plunge man into ultimate obliterating 'unity'—death—this intense erotic 'violence' represents what must be forbidden to human beings; that is, it becomes 'sacred' (from *sacré* or *sacer*, to set apart). In the works of a number of commentators (Bataille, Roger Caillois in *L'Homme et le Sacré* [Paris, 1950], and René Girard in a number of essays, including 'Dionysos et la genèse violente du sacré', *Poétique*, III [1970]) the sacred is defined as fundamental violence. The traditional and mythic function of taboo is precisely to expel this violence, to enable man to order his world. Since acts of violence (including such 'disordering' acts as incest) disrupt the human and social order and make impossible the productive work (and stability) necessary for survival, man is forced to prohibit those acts from the realm of everyday life. Yet, while the taboo, in assigning a negative definition to these forbidden objects and experiences, inspires fear, it also inspires religious-erotic fascination, sometimes even adoration and devotion: it evokes desire. The prohibition becomes erotically charged and invites its own transgression; one comes to desire what is most forbidden. Consequently, the violation of taboos is not at all contrary to what is divine; the 'sacred' (forbidden) aspect of the taboo is precisely what draws man towards it and transfigures ('sanctifies') any violation of it. Just as the primitive priest was invested with a sacramental character in the act of killing the sacrificial victim,[17] so we discover in Swinburne's early poems that the hero-lover who 'invades the sacred' through erotic desire becomes himself a sanctified figure. Paradoxically,

---

[17] Bataille, p. 68. Ritual sacrifice, through the death of the victim (or through the destruction of some inanimate object), reveals sacred 'continuity' to the witnesses; likewise, in the process of 'dissolving' the separate beings which participate in it, erotic activity reveals that 'awe-ful' obliteration of differences which the sacred embodies—an effect similar to the ones produced by the annihilating waves of all those Swinburnean seas.

by flagrantly violating the false God's taboos, the hero's erotic passion reconstitutes and once again makes immediately present the sacred 'centre'.[18]

This process of sanctification through violation is clearly demonstrated in 'The Leper', a poem where the hero-lover's flaunted necrophilia establishes the dominance of the truly sacred over the strictures of a Urizen-God:

> They cursed her, seeing how God had wrought
> This curse to plague her, a curse of his.
> Fools were they surely, seeing not
> How sweeter than all sweet she is. . . .
> Falling on her, such joy I had
> To do the service God forbids. . . .
> Yea, though God hateth us, he knows
> That hardly in a little thing
> Love faileth of the work it does
> Till it grow ripe for gathering.
>
> (ll. 53–6, 79–80, 89–92)

The lover's belief that 'new shame could make love new' (l. 119) is an article of faith throughout *Poems and Ballads*. In 'Dolores', the Lady of Pain, whose sins are 'seventy times seven' and for whose disciples 'The desire of thy furious embraces / Is more than the wisdom of years', is an emblem of transgression. Unlike the Creator-God, who severs spirit from flesh, Dolores shall 'quicken the soul through the blood'. The obedience to the false God's decrees of abstinence and non-passion has caused man to lose any sense of the 'presence' of the sacred, but Dolores will 'Come down and redeem us from virtue' (ll. 277–84). It becomes clear that man's apostasy was caused, in fact, by a failure of the will—the will to freedom, the will towards passionate transgression:

> What broke off the garlands that girt you?
> What sundered you spirit and clay?

[18] As Georges Poulet has pointed out in *The Metamorphoses of the Circle* (Baltimore, 1966), throughout Western history God has been conceived as an infinite, absolute 'centre'—*logos*—from which all creation, meaning, and value emanate. As we have seen, Swinburne did not depart from this logocentric tradition. He, too, felt that in order for man to return to harmony he must recover his origins; he must again feel within him the 'presence' of the sacred 'logocentre'.

> Weak sins yet alive are as virtue
> To the strength of the sins of that day.
>
> (ll. 321-4)

As the poet-lover knows, the return to 'grace' demands a disregard of normal limits and recognition of life's true altar, 'the shrine where a sin is a prayer'—even at the risk that 'the service be mortal' (ll. 129-31). Swinburne explained in an enthusiastic passage of *William Blake* that 'The extremest fulness of indulgence in such desire and such delight as the senses can aim at was absolutely good, eternally just, and universally requisite' (*William Blake*, p. 232). Under the guidance of Dolores, the 'chosen people' are redefined:

> Ah thy people, thy children, thy chosen,
> Marked cross from the womb and perverse!
> They have found out the secret to cozen
> Thy gods that constrain us and curse;
> They alone, they are wise, and none other. . . .
>
> (ll. 145-9)

This passage recalls another redefinition of the 'chosen' in 'The Masque of Queen Bersabe'. King David confesses that 'For all my wrong-doing with my queen, / I grew not of our heartés clean, / But it began of her body' and proceeds to describe his queen's 'piety': 'And ever she gave God thank, / Yea, God wot I can well see yet / Both her breast and her sides all wet' (ll. 271-3, 305-7). But upon hearing this the prophet Nathan simply replies:

> Now, sir, be merry anon,
> For ye shall have a full wise son,
> Goodly and great of flesh and bone;
> There shall no king be such an one.
> I swear by Godis rood.
>
> (ll. 325-9)

The sterile rod of the false God is replaced by the 'spirit of the flesh'.

In 'Laus Veneris', it is through Tannhäuser's 'sin' that Venus is revealed as the greater deity; 'her mouth is lovelier' (l. 20), and Christ is urged to 'lift up thine eyes and see' (l. 22). The poem's conclusion reinforces the distinction:

> Ah love, there is no better life than this;
> To have known love, how bitter a thing it is,
> And afterward be cast out of God's sight;

Yea, those that know not, shall they have such bliss
High up in barren heaven before his face
As we twain in the heavy-hearted place . . . ?
For till the thunder in the trumpet be,
Soul may divide from body, but not we
    One from another . . .
I seal myself upon thee with my might. . . .
                                        (ll. 409–14, 418–19, 421)

Venus allows union (however problematic) whereas the Christian God
does not. Tannhäuser, even under the threat of damnation, clings to
Venus. Moreover, like Meleager in *Atalanta in Calydon*, who sacrifices
potential immortality in affirming the true sacred, Tannhäuser's
defection is of particular significance since he has told us, I was of
Christ's choosing, I God's Knight' (l. 209). Venus has not won a
weakling; she has taken the best God has to offer. Heroic criminality
reaches perhaps its extreme extension, however, in 'Anactoria,' where
Sappho's self-deifying passion is intensified to the point where it
becomes demoniacal: in order to assure that 'Of me the high God hath
not all his will', she would seek the ultimate transgression—his murder:

Him would I reach, him smite, him desecrate,
Pierce the cold lips of God with human breath,
And mix his immortality with death. . . .
Yea, thou shalt be forgotten like spilt wine,
Except these kisses of my lips on thine
Brand them with immortality. . . .
                                        (ll. 182–4, 201–3)

The roles are reversed: God is mortal, made immortal (in his destruction) only by Sappho's sanctifying, boundless passion. Even in 'Hymn
to Prosperpine', where passionate intensity has been lost, the poet-
hero still seeks to affirm the true sacred and renounce any allegiance to
'the pale Galilean'. In contrast to the lovers' 'mother' Venus, who was
'Clothed round with the world's desire as a raiment', Christ's mother
is described as 'pale and a maiden', 'sister to sorrow', and 'Weeping, a
slave among slaves' (ll. 79, 85, 81). The poet-hero mocks blatantly all
of the Galilean's theistic brethren and affirms their ultimate impotence
in the face of Prosperpine, the representative of that sacred violence
which in the end will reclaim all things.

Will ye bridle the deep sea with reins, will ye
    chasten the high sea with rods?

Will ye take her to chain her with chains, who is
    older than all ye Gods?
All ye as a wind shall go by, as a fire shall ye
    pass and be past;
Ye are Gods, and behold, ye shall die, and the
    waves be upon you at last.

(ll. 65–8)

In the final analysis, however, the Gordian knot is not so easily severed: while Swinburne's transgressing heroes affirm the liberty and intensity of the true sacred, many of them experience great personal torment and guilt—even to the point of feeling themselves damned. As Julian Baird has noted, these troubled heroes are unable to see their personal destinies as potentially separate from the rod of the Creator-God.[19] Swinburne's remarks about Tannhäuser serve to describe a number of others: '. . . the Knight who has renounced Christ believes in him, the lover who has embraced Venus disbelieves in her.'[20] These heroes never truly manifest the kind of sanctifying freedom which would be their salvation, because their rebellions paradoxically affirm not only the true sacred but the false sacred as well.

Part of the problem lies in the dynamics of transgression itself. As we have seen, taboos plunge man into continual paradox: he is simultaneously driven away by terror and drawn by an awed fascination. And since, in a sense, the sacred world depends for its continuing reinforcement and validity on limited acts of transgression (acts which, like ritual sacrifice, periodically evoke the awe-inspiring 'presence' of the sacred), the man who quests for the sacred is forced to live constantly in that intensified double bind. Swinburne champions transgression over Christian asceticism precisely because transgression reveals what Christianity (and Swinburne's Urizen-God) conceals: that the sacred and the forbidden are one, and that the sacred can be reached—in fact, can only be reached—not through 'mediation' and sublimation, but through the violence of broken taboos, through heroic criminality. But in effect, the dynamics of Swinburne's 'holy insurrection' reduplicate the circular and paradoxical relationship between transgression and taboo: taboos both attract and repel, representing not only means for the recovery of the sacred but also malicious tools available to a false Creator-God who wishes to suppress man's divine destiny, to displace the sacred 'presence' man seeks.

[19] Baird, pp. 63–74.
[20] 'Notes on Poems and Reviews', *Works*, Vol. XVI, p. 365.

The distinctions between the two 'divines' blur the Swinburnean hero's mind, as he is frequently unable to separate the force of the true sacred from its counterfeit double; his rebellion appears to authenticate both at the same time. He attempts to restore the lost logocentre and validate the superiority of his 'divine humanity', yet the very act of transgression presupposes a more powerful 'other'—an Oppressor-God who must be rebelled against. Consequently, the hero-lover, as Swinburne himself noted, 'cries out for freedom and confesses the chain'.[21] Against his every effort the Swinburnean hero still feels himself bound by a *logos* which he knows to be false; his struggle does not reorganize and reunify the world but only further fragments it. Divine rebellion becomes self-subverting collusion. This conflict accounts for much of the torment and guilt Swinburne's heroes experience. But it does not really explain another even more disturbing paradox underlying their quest for a sacred 'centre'—a paradox present in 'Laus Veneris', 'Anactoria', 'Dolores', and most of *Poems and Ballads*: that man's divine destiny and personal salvation often demands his sacrifice, that the Dolores who redeems also devours, that man's 'life' is also his death. These truths, most often embodied in the constant association of love with death, mark the paradox which Swinburne perceives at the heart of man's attempt to reconstitute sacred space.

IV

The Swinburnean hero's attempt to break the chains of the false Urizen-God are manifested in his continual transgression of taboos, perpetual struggle, and unceasing passion—in short, in acts stemming from overwhelming desire. And desire, especially in Swinburne's poetic vision, demands at some point an act of the will. His scattered cases of burnt-out love can all be traced to a failure of the will. As devouring as his *femmes fatales* often seem, they are fundamentally passive. The lover feels the need to gain access; he pleads for his beloved to respond to his passion. Tannhäuser's Venus appears to be in a state of languorous 'deep sleep'; Sappho grows furious over Anactoria's hesitations, over her inability or refusal to match Sappho's passion; the narrators of 'Dolores', 'The Leper', and a number of other poems beseech their beloveds to 'Give me place'. What the hero-lover desires is a penetration of sanctified space, a union which will restore a sense of sacred 'presence' and authenticate his being. And, as we have previously noted, what is really willed, what desires to be authenticated, is the hero's own potentiality, his god-like destiny. He seeks through his will to give shape to his soul, a soul which participates in and is potentially identical with the 'Oversoul' of Hertha.

In *Victor Marie Hugo*, a study of another of his 'poet-prophets', Swinburne selects a remarkable passage from *Les Misérables* to support his definition of 'a *great* act' as the 'lifting of the mind to God':

> At the same time that there is an Infinite outside us, is there not an Infinite within us? Do not these two Infinites (monstrous plural) lie one over the other? The second Infinite, does it not, so to say, underlie the first? Is it not the mirror, the reflection, the echo of that other; the abyss concentric with the other abyss? This second Infinite, is it also intelligent? Does it think? Does it love? Does it will? If the two Infinites are intelligent, each of them has a willing principle, and there is an 'I' in the Infinite above, as there is an 'I' in the Infinite below. The 'I' below is the soul; the 'I' above is God. *To place in thought, the Infinite below in contact with the Infinite above*, that *is called* 'prayer'.
>
> (*Victor Marie Hugo*, pp. 185–6; Swinburne's italics)

Even suspending for a moment the problematic nature of 'two Infinites', the striking image of the abyss of man mirroring the abyss of God betrays a subversive element at the core of this cosmological theory. In a system of continual mirroring there is an imminent danger of a total 'loss of difference'. Not only is there a threat of interpenetration to the point of 'doubling', but there also soon arises in a hall of mirrors the question of origins—which is the echo and which is the source; who is created in whose image?

The problem is central to the crisis manifested in Swinburne's poetry. The problematic nature of the issue can be seen even in 'Hertha' —the poem, we remember, which Swinburne considered to contain his 'most intense and clarified thought'. The *logos* which the mother-spirit represents is not at all a stable one. When she defines man as 'Man, equal and one with me, man that is made of me, man that is I' (l. 200), she calls into question the entire premise of a prior, organizing *logos*. Her instructions that man must authenticate himself in reciprocity, that he should 'Give thou as I gave thee / . . . Do the ways of the giving / As mine were to thee' (ll. 78, 81–2), indicate that Promethean man unites with the sacred through a process of reduplicating the mother-spirit—in short, by participating in a kind of theological and ontological incest.[22] In some sense Hertha's word is not very different from that of the false Gods whose existence she seeks to disprove, the 'Gods of your fashion / That take and that give' (ll. 101-2). If, indeed,

> ... This thing is God,
> To be man with thy might,
> To grow straight in the strength of thy spirit,
> and live out thy life as the light,
>
> (ll. 73-5)

who is to say whether Hertha is generative of man or whether she is only an idealization of man's self-generated 'life-light', another 'God of your fashion'? The mother-spirit of the poem tells man. 'I am thou, whom thou seekest to find him; find thou but thyself, thou art I' (l. 35). The hero's striving for connection with the sacred translates into desire for his own god-like potentiality. In other words, the hero's quest is a quest for his own idealized self-image, the projected image of his own desire.

Psychoanalysis, of course, has much to say about the dynamics of desire; and its insights are particularly helpful with respect to the way the problem manifests itself in Swinburne's poetry. Freud explains[23] that the self's inability to accept its fundamental separation from the 'other' (posited originally in the infant's separation from a nourishing and ego-fulfilling mother) causes it to seek to restore the primal condition in which the 'ego-libido' and the 'object-libido' were indistinguishable. According to Freud, man attempts this reunification by introjecting or incorporating the 'lost' love-object into the self; that is, by either passively making himself like it or actively projecting his own image into it—or a combination of the two. Reunification is thus sought by making the self and the other identical; thus every quest for

---

[22] This motif pervades Swinburne's verse. In 'Dolores', the poet-lover refers to 'our Lady of Pain' as 'my sister, my spouse, and my mother'; the poet-lover of 'Hymn to Proserpine' names himself the brother of the goddess whom he desires. In 'Laus Veneris' Tannhäuser makes an allusion to incest in an attempt to implicate Christ in his affirmation of Venus: 'Had now thy mother such a lip—like this? / Thou knowest how sweet a thing it is to me' (ll. 23-4). And Sappho's narcissistic brutalization and deification of Anactoria manifests itself as incestuous; such self-reflexive homosexuality is perhaps merely the most extreme and inverted form of incest.

[23] Sigmund Freud, *Collected Papers*, ed. J. Riviere and J. Strachey, 5 vols. (New York, 1924-50), pp. 57, 152-70. Norman O. Brown in *Life Against Death* (Middleton, Conn., 1959), especially pp. 40-55, gives his own interpretations and amendments to Freud's reading of this relationship.

a lost love-object becomes a narcissistic desire for one's own mirrored image. And we find that the prophecy in 'A Ballad of Burdens' that 'as the thing thou seest thy face shall be' (l. 27) is fulfilled through Tannhäuser in 'Laus Veneris'. Venus is described throughout the poem as his soul's incarnation:

> Behold, my Venus, my soul's body, lies
> With my love laid upon her garment-wise
> Feeling my love in all her limbs and hair
> And shed between her eyelids through her eyes. . . .
> And lo my love, mine own soul's heart, more dear
> Than mine own soul, more beautiful than God,
> Who hath my being between the hands of her.
>
> (ll. 29-32, 386-8)

Venus is pictured as being both autonomous and yet at the same time defined by the lover's desire; she imprisons the lover's being and yet is also an extension of it. And when the image of the lover's self is not projected onto the beloved, hers is introjected:

> I knew the beauty of her, what she was,
> The beauty of her body and her sin,
> And in my flesh the sin of hers, alas!
>
> (ll. 310-12)

In any case, the lover's penetration of this sacred space manifests a 'loss of difference' between the lover and his deified beloved. Their relationship is described in terms of an interfused mirroring, 'Lips that cling hard till the kissed face has grown / Of one same fire and colour with their own' (ll. 289-90), a motif recalled even more vividly in 'Fragoletta':

> Thy barren bosom takes my kiss
> And turns my soul to thine
> And turns thy lip to mine,
> And mine it is.
>
> (ll. 47-50)

In Swinburne's world, life itself comes to be seen as an unstable mirror, the poet of 'Hymn to Proserpine' noting that 'The glass of the years is brittle wherein we gaze for a span' (l. 107). The distinctions between self and other, 'inside' and 'outside', are wiped away; the outer environment dissolves into a mere reflection of the inner one. In such a setting there can be little rest; the hero-lover's life is transported into a theatre of continual 'violence', of constant temptation and denial, in which his desire becomes both self-perpetuating and self-devouring:

> The scent and shadow shed about me make
> The very soul in all my senses ache;
> The hot hard night is fed upon my breath,
> And sleep beholds me from afar awake. . . .
> There lover-like with lips and limbs that meet
> They lie, they pluck sweet fruit of life and eat;
> But me the hot and hungry days devour,
> And in my mouth no fruit of theirs is sweet.
> No fruit of theirs, but fruit of my desire,
> For her love's sake whose lips through mine respire.
>
> ('Laus Veneris', ll. 89–92, 97–102)

The lover's only food is himself; he can never get outside the limits of his own desire. And a desire which can only struggle after its own idealized image is a desire which can never be consummated. As in 'Dolores', 'The delight that consumes the desire, / The desire that outruns the delight' gives rise to a world in which every quest becomes circular, every gesture self-reflexive. Even Cupid himself, labouring at love's loom, is caught up in the fruitless, self-generated cycle: 'Labouring he dreams, and labours in the dream / . . . His web, reeled off, curls and goes out like steam' (ll. 46, 48).

Meredith's much-abused remark that Swinburne did not have 'any internal centre',[24] though formalistically false, is psychologically acute. Desire itself is the recognition of a need, a lack, and Swinburne's hero-lovers are quite literally defined by their desire (the ontological value of the lovers being measured by the intensity of their passion). But clearly what they actually desire is not some pale earthly refraction of the divine but the totality of the sacred itself. They perceive themselves to be missing their divine 'other self', their essence; they strive constantly for 'completion', fulfilment, validation, 'place'. The Swinburnean hero's beloveds—Venus, Dolores, Faustine—are generally not earthbound beings with individualized human characteristics, but cosmic figures, emblems of pure Desire, incarnations of sacred space.[25]

[24] *Letters of George Meredith*, collected and edited by his son (New York, 1912), Vol. I, p. 55.

[25] Even the more obviously human beloveds are perceived as emblems; the beloved of 'The Leper', for instance, is described as 'The body of love wherein she abode' (l. 48).

The hero-lover's desire becomes, therefore, a quest for a projected dream of purity—and a quest which, like those of Shelley's 'Alastor' and 'Epipsychidion', is destined to be endless and endlessly self-torturing. In his attempt to shatter the bonds of Urizen, the Swinburnean lover only succeeds in becoming trapped in a 'prison of the self', unable to find outside authentication because he has transfigured the whole world into a mere extension of his own desire. T. S. Eliot was more profound than even he suspected when he wrote about *Poems and Ballads*: 'the object has ceased to exist . . . because language, uprooted, has adapted itself to an independent life of atmospheric nourishment.'[26] The hero-lover experiences himself as 'uprooted', cast out of the sacred 'centre' and, consequently, forced to struggle to rediscover or reconstitute it. In some sense, Swinburne's style, which Arnold indicted as 'using one hundred words where one would suffice', is very appropriate for depicting a world of infinite extension and redoubling. The hero's *raison d'être* is to 'make connections' and to fill man again with a sense of sacred 'presence'; but his self-deifying quest only results in increased fragmentation and the sense of the self as an 'absence'.[27]

In such a world, to put a Swinburnean twist on Wallace Stevens's famous formulation, the violence without becomes the violence

[26] T. S. Eliot, *Selected Essays* (New York, 1950), p. 285. We might recall that Swinburne himself wrote that poetry's concern is 'rather to render the effect of the thing than the thing itself' ('Notes on the Text of Shelley', *Works*, Vol. XV, p. 380).

[27] My design has not consciously been to draw parallels with R. D. Laing's 'schizoid condition', first discussed in *The Divided Self* (London, 1959; rpt. Baltimore, 1965), but there are some obvious areas of correspondence. Laing's 'schizoid' also experiences fears of imprisonment and of impinging reality obliterating the 'empty self'; yet he may, paradoxically, also feel himself to be at the same time totally free and omnipotent (in his 'inner, unembodied self'). Laing explains that in this seeking to remain omnipotent—a pure potentiality, 'uncommitted to the objective element'—the self renders itself impotent, attains no freedom *in* 'reality'. Furthermore, Laing indicates that often in a 'schizoid condition', 'one feels one's being to be bound up in the other, or that the other is bound up in oneself' (p. 53), that the other is both 'me' and 'not me' at the same time. Finally, in a passage which is, for my purposes, most revealing, Laing speaks of the schizoid's 'being a mirror to himself' and notes: '*This identification of the self with the phantasy of the person by whom one is seen* may contribute decisively to the characteristics of the observing self . . . this observing self often kills and withers anything that is under scrutiny. The individual has now a persecuting observer in the very core of his being' (Laing's italics, p. 117).

within.[28] As Sappho demonstrates in 'Anactoria', every sadistic act is also simultaneously masochistic. Sappho's inability to find a reciprocating passion which will achieve sexual fulfilment and authenticate her selfhood inevitably leads her to sadism, to a desire to appropriate Anactoria's being by forcibly consuming it into her own:

> I could drink thy veins as wine, and eat
> Thy breasts like honey! that from face to feet
> Thy body were abolished and consumed,
> And in my flesh thy very flesh entombed!
>
> (ll. 111–14)

But, as David A. Cook has indicated, Sappho's desire is fundamentally 'masturbatory', and the annihilation of her double, instead of completing Sappho's self, would only destroy it:

> ... pain made perfect in thy lips
> For my sake when I hurt thee; O that I
> Durst crush thee out of life with love, and die,
> Die of thy pain and my delight, and be
> Mixed with thy blood and molten into thee![29]
>
> (ll. 128–32)

Sappho's intense need for a sanctifying union cannot be authenticated; the violence is trapped inside. Her attempt to overcome the split she feels between flesh and spirit by wringing the 'very spirit through the flesh' ultimately fails. After finding Aphrodite, Anactoria, and even God inadequate, she still 'thirsts'. In fact, we discover that her 'introjection' is total, as the entire world comes to mirror the sterile circularity of her divided self:

> ... and mine eyes
> Burn as that beamless fire which fills the skies
> With troubled stars and travailing things of flame;
> And in my heart the grief consuming them
> Labours, and in my veins the thirst of these,
> ... and the earth,
> Filled full with deadly works of death and birth,

[28] Wallace Stevens, 'The Noble Rider and The Sound of Words', *The Necessary Angel* (New York, 1942). The original remark is 'It is a violence from within that protects us from a violence without'.

[29] David A. Cook, 'The Content and Meaning of Swinburne's "Anactoria"', *Victorian Poetry* 9 (Spring–Summer 1971), pp. 77–93. Norman O. Brown, in *Life Against Death*, p. 115, notes that one of the effects of the inability to accept separation is an attempt to eroticize death—to activate a morbid wish to die.

> Sore spent with hungry lusts of birth and death,
> Has pain like mine in her divided breath;
> Her spring of leaves is barren, and her fruit
> Ashes. . . .
>
> (ll. 227–31, 233–8)

Erotic desire is inseparable from a kind of psychic violence; its function is to break down the divisions between the self and the desired object and make possible their union. But for the Swinburnean lover, whose 'schizoid consciousness' accentuates those divisions even while it incorporates the other, the erotic violence has been inverted, interiorized. He feels, like Althea, that 'all my life turns round on me; / I am severed from myself . . . / My name is a consuming' (*Atalanta in Calydon*, ll. 1942–3, 1945).

v

Just as the Victorians in general saw man's sense of self to be informed by his sense of the divine, so Swinburne also perceives the state of man's internal psychic 'centre' to be inextricably related to his sense of the external and sacred logocentre. The dilemma which becomes so manifest in *Poems and Ballads* is that, in a world so desperately organized around a central Absolute, the 'absence' of the one implies, if not precipitates, the 'absence' of the other.

All men, as Bataille has indicated, accept some limit to define the ordered parameters of their lives, a kind of boundary of selfhood—a limit beyond which exists that undifferentiated fundamental violence of sacred things, that condition of 'nothingness' from which all order arose and which underlies all existence. In his 'heroic criminality' the Swinburnean hero-lover, that breacher of limits, seems to call into question not only the distinctions between 'self' and 'others' but all of life's distinctions—and in the process seems to discover Hegel's maxim that 'pure Being and pure Nothing are the same'. Upon 'invading the sacred', Swinburne's hero, like Kierkegaard's, experiences a fundamental 'dread of being', sensing that, as Swinburne implies in 'Hymn to Proserpine', man's soul is a 'rock' whose 'ground' is not a mainland but a chaotic sea:

> Fate is a sea without shore, and the soul is a rock that abides;
> But her eyes are vexed with the roar and her face with the foam
> of the tides.
>
> (ll. 41–2)

Confronting the sacred in all its overpowering totality, the Swinburnean lover perceives reality begin to dissolve into a condition of
'oxymoronic identity', the paradox preceding what appears to be a
complete 'loss of difference'. Standing before Dolores 'in the twilight
where virtues are vices',

> Pain melted in tears, and was pleasure;
> Death tingled with blood, and was life.
> Like lovers they melted and mingled,
> In the dusk of thine innermost fane. . . .
>
> ('Dolores', ll. 179–82)

The quester in 'Dolores' discovers the same phenomenon as the quester
of 'Laus Veneris': 'hills grow deep' and 'the sea's panting mouth'
emits 'dry desire'. Both confront a world in which 'Day smiteth day
in twain, night sundereth night, / and on mine eyes the dark sits as
the light'. An alchemical breakdown has occurred, one extreme
being transmuted into its opposite. And the further the hero presses
into the 'abyss' of the sacred, the more life's distinctions collapse until
they approximate a state of tautology:

> Ah God, that love were as a flower or flame,
> That life were as the naming of a name,
> That death were not more pitiful than desire,
> That these things were not one thing and the same!
>
> ('Laus Veneris', ll. 65–8)

Hertha, after all, is simultaneously 'the mouth that is kissed / And
the breath in the kiss, / The search, and the sought, and the seeker'
(ll. 23–4). Althea of *Atalanta in Calydon* finds that she has become both
'a spoiler and a spoil'; Proserpine, the goddess of Death, is described as
earth's 'crown and blossom of birth' (l. 93). What the invading hero
finds is that life's pervading 'oxymoronic identity' is merely the last
veil which masks the condition and underlying essence of all reality—
an obliteration of all distinctions, an absence of absolutes. For in a
world in which one's own image has pervaded all existence, not
merely ontological distinctions but all human distinctions are obliter-
ated; and man is plunged, without any clear sense of direction, into a
sea of flux. One road becomes as good as another; each element contains
its opposite. The Swinburnean hero is paralysed by an infinity of
meaningless choices, and every attempt to reach out is turned back
upon the self. We can see, then, why Swinburne—and the nineteenth
century in general—was so desperate to affirm an absolute and sacred

'centre' of life: the absence of an ordering *logos* 'out there' threatened to be translated into violence and loss of distinctions 'in here'.

As A. J. L. Busst has pointed out, the supreme emblem in the nineteenth century for this imprisoning, oxymoronic loss of difference is the figure of the hermaphrodite.[30] It came to represent in the *fin de siècle* not only the incorporation and confusion of male and female, spirit and flesh, good and evil, and other contraries, but also self-reflective, incestuous desire. We have witnessed already the highly incestuous nature of the Swinburnean hero's quest for the sacred; and incest—with its correlate, homosexuality—is, of course, the paramount sexual symbol for 'loss of difference'. The hermaphrodite reflects perfectly the paradoxical nature of Swinburnean sacred space: it represents both completion and sterility, unified totality and imprisoning stasis. Swinburne found the figure especially appealing; he remarked that Simeon Solomon's androgyne figures were representative of the 'intermixture of spiritual forces' characteristic of truly beautiful art, 'the same profound suggestion of unity between opposites, the same recognition of the identity of contraries'.[31] Yet later in the same essay Swinburne applies to this 'identity of contraries' a more disconcerting hue; it becomes a 'mystery of beauty' that is both 'great' and 'terrible':

> In the features of these groups and figures ... we see the latent relations of pain and pleasure, the subtle conspiracies of good with evil, the deep alliances of death and life, of love and hate, of attraction and abhorrence. Whether suffering or enjoyment be the master expression of a face, and whether that enjoyment or that suffering be merely or mainly spiritual or sensual, it is often hard to say— hard often to make sure whether the look of loveliest features be the look of a cruel or a pitiful soul.[32]

This paradoxical 'centre' also reveals itself in Swinburne's 'Hermaphroditus'. The hermaphrodite is depicted not as an emblem of peaceful union, but as a figure embracing the endless struggle of

[30] A. J. L. Busst, 'The Androgyne', *Romantic Mythologies*, ed. Ian Fletcher (1967), pp. 1–95. Busst's superb essay emphasized the ambiguity of the figure, explaining that at different times in the course of the nineteenth century the androgyne was considered to be a 'sanctifying' symbol (representative of reunion, perfection), a 'destructive' symbol (representative of self-enclosed sterility, evil), and even both simultaneously.

[31] Swinburne, 'Simeon Solomon: Notes on His "Vision of Love" and Other Studies', *Works*, Vol. XV, pp. 443, 454–5. Also see Peters, *The Crowns of Apollo*, pp. 94–108.

[32] 'Simeon Solomon', in *The Complete Works*, Vol. XV, pp. 454–6.

'Blind love that comes by night and casts out rest' (ll. 1–10). The androgynous figure involves everyone in the circular double bind it exemplifies: the poet explains that

> ... whosoever hath seen thee, being so fair,
> Two things turn all his life and blood to fire;
> A strong desire begot on great despair,
> A great despair cast out by strong desire.
>
> (ll. 11–14)

It exists in that no-man's-land 'between sleep and life', fusing 'Sex to sweet sex' and thereby 'Turning the fruitful feud of hers and his / To the waste wedlock of a sterile kiss' (ll. 18–19). Although this fusion of contraries emits 'something like as fire ... / That shall not be assuaged till death be dead' (ll. 20–1), its passion is non-productive, barren. Love himself, having produced this monstrous union, finds it uninhabitable:

> Love made himself of flesh that perisheth
> A pleasure house for all the loves his kin;
> But on the one side sat a man like death,
> And on the other a woman sat like sin.
> So with veiled eyes and sobs between his breath
> Love turned himself and would not enter in.
>
> (ll. 23–8)

Like Milton's Sin and Death which flank the gates of Hell, this union, too, can only constitute an inverted sterility The androgyne is emblematic of the paralysis of overfilled space; it is representative of that 'sacred totality' whose centre is an *absence*. Even though 'Love stands upon thy left hand and thy right' and hides 'love in all the folds of thy hair',

> Yet by no sunset and by no moonrise
> Shall make thee man and ease a woman's sighs,
> Or make thee woman for a man's delight.
>
> (ll. 34–6)

Like the hermaphrodite, the Swinburnean hero-lover experiences the fruitless passion and loss of distinctions which accompany having an internalized other. And he, too, feels himself imprisoned in impacted space-time; Tannhäuser begs for 'A little space of time ere time expire, / A little day, a little way of breath' (ll. 71–2). But his fear of suffocation only takes on more menacing proportions:

> Ah, with blind lips I felt for you, and found
> About my neck your hands and hair enwound,
>   The hands that stifle and the hair that stings,
> I felt them fasten sharply without sound.
>
> (ll. 317–20)

The hero seeks to escape, pleading for more 'spaces of time', but Time itself is an enemy; it only serves to perpetuate man's self-destructive, labyrinthine struggle. Either it drains desire until the lover must live a life-in-death where love is impossible, or it extends and intensifies the flames of desire until they gradually consume the self:

> There is a feverish famine in my veins;
> Below her bosom, where a crushed grape stains
>   The white and blue; there my lips caught and clove
> An hour since, and what mark of me remains?
> I dare not always touch her, lest the kiss
> Leave my lips charred.
>
> ('Laus Veneris', ll. 165–70)

So, like Hermaphroditus, the self-reflexive hero-lover is trapped: any attempt to break through his prison of fruitless desire, and create a space where Love can dwell, must necessarily draw upon elements of the same 'sin' and 'death' which originally gave rise to that desire. That maze of mirrors leads only to the funeral pyre. The shrine in 'Dolores' where 'a sin is a prayer' is, after all, 'mortal' to the worshipper. The lover-priest who sanctifies the sacred at that altar finds, like Meleager, that he must himself become the sacrifice: 'This death was mixed with all my life, / Mine end with my beginning . . . overloving men / Slay and are slain for love's sake' (*Atalanta in Calydon*, ll. 2238, 2244–5). Swinburne's hero-lovers reveal a world in which everything rushes toward a 'centre' that is really nothingness. Man's desire for sanctified reunification is a desire inextricably linked with his own sacrifice. His invasion of sacred space exposes the horrifying paradox which underlies all existence:

>   . . . Life and lust
> Forsake thee, and the face of thy delight;
> And underfoot the heavy hour strews dust,
>   And overhead strange weathers burn and bite . . .
> And where day was, the likeness of the night;
> This is the end of every man's desire.
>
> ('A Ballad of Burdens', ll. 65–72)

Thus the Swinburnean hero is very much Lucien Goldmann's 'tragic man', who—like the divine 'presence' he so desperately seeks—is 'absent and present in the world at one and the same time':

> ... there stretches before tragic man only 'the eternal silence of infinite space'; not even of the narrowest and most insignificant sector of human life can a completely clear and unequivocal statement be made without the opposite and contradictory statement being immediately added; ... paradox is the only valid expression of reality. And, for tragic man, paradox is a constant source of scandal and concern: to accept paradox, to accept human weakness, the ambiguity and confusion of the world, its 'sense and non-sense' as Merleau-Ponty puts it, means giving up any attempt to endow life with meaning.[33]

VI

Meaning has indeed gone from life; Swinburne's hero is suddenly faced with the terrifying possibility that *logos* is non-existent. He has sought a total reunification of his fragmented world; but he becomes increasingly aware that life holds no such reunion. Even death, towards which all things flow, is not reconciliation but merely a cessation of the struggle—those figures in 'The Garden of Proserpine' do not find fruition, but 'Only the sleep eternal / In an eternal night' (ll. 95–6). He yearns to stand in the unifying light of the sacred; yet he discovers that the sacred is not a 'presence' in which things are logo-centrically resolved, but a pervasive paradox in which everything is plunged into a state of oxymoronic identity. The sacred 'centre' is found to be an absence: the only reconciliation is obliteration, the only *logos* death.

The hero's failure is inevitable, for 'to live out thy life as the light' is to interiorize *logos* and define it in process—an act which negates the very concept of a prior absolute. The sacred is no longer separate from its manifestation, and consequently, as sacred essence increasingly becomes human fact, it loses its 'sacred' character. The hero's desire for authentication becomes more unfulfillable even as it becomes more passionately insatiable; when the mirrors of the heros' desire proliferate, sacred space vanishes—all 'sanctifying' violations become acts

---

[33] Lucien Goldmann, 'The Tragic Vision: The World', *Moderns on Tragedy*, ed. Lionel Abel (New York, 1967), pp. 293–4; reprinted from *The Hidden God*, trans. by Philip Thody (New York, 1964). Goldmann's concept of 'tragic man' is, of course, historical.

of masochism. In a fascinating footnote to *William Blake*, Swinburne —or rather, an anonymous source which Swinburne refers to as 'a modern pagan philosopher'—discusses a crisis in may ways analogous to that of his hero-lover:

> But what evil is here for us to do, where the whole body of things is evil? The day's spider kills the day's fly, and calls it a crime? Nay, could we thwart nature, then might crime become possible and sin an actual thing. . . . Nay, and not then: for nature would fain have it so, that she might create a world of new things; . . . she would fain create afresh, and cannot, except it be by destroying: in all her energies she is athirst for mortal food, and with all her forces she labours in desire of death.
>
> (*William Blake*, p. 203)

Under such circumstances, either erotic love itself becomes impossible, as the 'sacred' core of eroticism lies bankrupt, or the perpetuated violence of the hero-lover's desire is trapped 'inside' and can only slowly devour itself and its possessor. In either case, the hero is plunged into the shadow of Nietzsche's dead God. Unlike Nietzsche, however, he cannot engage in the 'joyful wisdom' of complete freedom, of what Jacques Derrida has termed 'free play',[34] because his sense of freedom is inseparably tied to a search for origins, to a quest for the 'logocentre'. Attempting to free himself from the Creator-God's taboos the Swinburnean hero struggles to resanctify the true sacred. Yet, ironically his quest reveals that complete human freedom and divine 'presence' are diametric opposites, that human boundaries define the sacred, that human existence demands a Urizen. His only means of authenticating his 'divine humanity' necessitates his destruction, for if Urizen is overthrown, 'chaos is come again'; in his sacred beloveds he confronts not a redeeming and unifying *logos* but an inscrutable and

---

[34] Jacques Derrida, 'Structure, Sign, and Play in the Discourse of the Human Sciences', *The Languages of Criticism and the Sciences of Man: The Structuralist Controversy*, ed. R. Macksey and E. Donato (Baltimore, 1970), pp. 247–72. Derrida indicates that Nietzsche's critique of metaphysics, which freed philosophical thought from absolute truth, gave rise to a concept of a world structured *without* a 'centre'. In such a world man was no longer bound to any one transcendental 'centre' or origin. Instead of being bound to an organizing force or standard of value 'outside' himself, man can order his world in any way he sees fit; in a sense, everything becomes discourse, interpretation. The one origin or centre gives way to an infinite number of substitutable 'centres'. There is complete 'free play', as the domain and the interplay of signification—'the game'—is extended *ad infinitum*.

terrifying paradox, the last veil masking a complete annihilation of difference.

J. Hillis Miller's statement about the nihilism of the Nietzschean world is an apt description of the Swinburnean hero's plight: 'Nihilism is the nothingness of consciousness when consciousness becomes the foundation for everything. Man the murderer of God and drinker of the sea of creation wanders through the infinite nothingness of his own ego. Nothing now has any worth except the arbitrary value he sets on things as he assimilates them into his consciousness.'[35] But of course, the Swinburnean hero can never accept this verdict. Committed with his late-Victorian contemporaries to the need for absolute truth, for a sacred 'logo-centre', he can only continue the quest, even at the risk of his own destruction. He remains throughout *Poems and Ballads* a disembodied wanderer seeking a ground for his being: another of those Victorian orphans, searching for a home.

[35] J. Hillis Miller, *Poets of Reality: Six Twentieth Century Writers* (1965; rpt. New York, 1969), pp. 3–4.

Note

H. S. Ashbee's *Index Librorum Prohibitorum, Centuria Librorum Absconditum* and *Catena Librorum Tacendorum* (privately printed 1877, 1879 and 1885) remain the best bibliographies of English erotica despite lacunae and idiosyncrasies. D. Foxon, 'Libertine Literature in England 1600–1745', *The Book Collector* XII, nos. 1, 2 and 3, is standard for an earlier period which establishes traditions for the nineteenth century. The difficulties in the way of serious research into pornography are summarized in P. Fryer, *Private Case, Public Scandal* (London, 1966). The French scene is covered in L. Perceau, *Bibliographie du Roman Erotique au 19e Siècle* (Paris, 1930). Special aspects of algolagniac sensibility in nineteenth century authors are discussed in M. Blanchot, *Lautréamont et Sade* (Paris, 1963), and G. Blin, *Le Sadisme de Baudelaire* (Paris, 1948). Mario Praz's *Romantic Agony* (Oxford, 1933) remains useful for its wide-ranging *exempla*; S. Marcus, *The Other Victorians* (1968) is more critical and less of a pathography of nineteenth-century literature and art. G. Deleuze, *Présentation de Sacher-Masoch* (Paris, 1967; trans. as *Introduction to Sacher-Masoch*, 1972), is both an extended assessment of Sade and Sacher-Masoch, and a major reworking of Freudian and neo-Freudian conceptions of sado-masochism. J. H. Gagnon and W. Simon, 'On Psychosexual Development' (in D. Goslin, ed., *Handbook of Socialization: Theory and Research*, New York, 1969), is the classic exposition of gender-role theory. The relation between pornography and gender-role is the subject of continuing study by J. N. J. Palmer.

IV

Fierce Midnights: Algolagniac Fantasy and the Literature of the Decadence

JERRY PALMER

PORNOGRAPHY AND GENDER-ROLES

THE TASTE for pornography must be interpreted as a social fact, and I have argued elsewhere that there is a case for an interpretation that takes as its basis the social-psychological concept of gender-role.[1] In summary, that analysis starts from the interactionist argument that 'gender' is not primarily a physiological matter, but a social matter: in other words, from the perception that what affects our sexual behaviour is not chemistry but the way in which we learn to use our chemistry. This learnt use is our 'gender-role'. Pornography is used in two social settings: at 'stag parties', and as an aid to solitary masturbation; its audience is—or was until very recently—exclusively male, and in so far as women use pornography it is in the company of men. The distinctive feature of pornography is that it portrays (explicitly) the pursuit of sexual pleasure for its own sake, and in isolation from any other moral context. Hedonism considered as an autonomous value in sexual behaviour is an integral component of male gender-role training, but not of the female equivalent; boys learn that the end of sex is pleasure, whereas girls learn that what counts is reciprocated emotion. The use of pornography at stag parties clearly reinforces this aspect of male gender-role training in an unproblematic way. Used as an aid to masturbation, pornography is a fantasy solution to a real problem: the problem is that although hedonism is perceived as an autonomous value in male gender-role training, it is placed in a

[1] Cf. 'Solitary, Poore, Nasty, Brutish and Short: Pornography, Gender-Role and Political Cosmologies', co-written with Iain Manson, in Brake and Pearce (eds.), *Circles and Arrows: Critical Perspectives on Sexuality*. The locus classicus for an exposition of the notion of gender-role is Gagnon and Simon, 'On Psycho-Sexual Development', in D. Goslin (ed.), *Handbook of Socialization: Theory and Research* (New York: Rand-Macnally, 1969).

contradictory relationship with other equally important and equally autonomous values: deferment and respect. Boys learn that sex is first and foremost about pleasure, but that it is illicit before marriage—which is always, effectively, a long time thence. They learn that women are the source of pleasure, but that in order to find that pleasure—defined egoistically—you have to love—defined altruistically. Normal maturity consists in learning to negotiate these contradictions. Many fail, perhaps temporarily, and one of the many attempted solutions to failure is the recourse to masturbatory fantasy, in which women play out in an unproblematic, non-contradictory way the hedonistic role assigned to them in the male gender-role. Pornography is the publically available representation of these fantasies, intended to provoke their re-enactment.

The preceding analysis is ahistorical, but what is known about sexual mores in the past suggests that it applies at least from the Industrial Revolution to the present day, perhaps with its gestation in the respectable middle classes in the previous century.[2] The present paper will concentrate on the ways in which a particular fantasy, algolagnia, is to be found not only in pornography but more generally, albeit in disguised forms, in the literature of the nineteenth century. Specifically, it will examine Mario Praz's thesis in *The Romantic Agony* that 'the shadow of the Divine Marquis' falls across the whole of that century, and it will trace the presence of algolagniac fantasy in certain well-known themes of 'the literature of Decadence': the Persecuted Virgin, the Femme Fatale and aestheticism. Nevertheless it will be helpful first of all to make some observations about the presence or otherwise of algolagnia in the specific genre of pornography. Readers of Praz will recognize algolagnia as the synoptic term for the sexual attraction of pain, whether inflicted or suffered.

FLAGELLANT PORNOGRAPHY

The famous and voluminous bibliography of pornographic literature that was assembled by 'Pisanus Fraxi', H. S. Ashbee, in the late nineteenth century is more remarkable for its thoroughness than its acumen.[3] Nonetheless, buried in this congeries of exotica is at least one historical

[2] See for example Alex Comfort's remarks on eighteenth-century ideas on sexuality in *The Anxiety Makers*, esp. chs. 2 and 3 (1968).

[3] Pisanus Fraxi (pseud., H. S. Ashbee), *Index Librorum Prohibitorum, Centuria Librorum Absconditorum* and *Catena Librorum Tacendorum* (1877, 1879 and 1885). See S. Marcus, *The Other Victorians* (1969), ch. 2, for details and analysis.

observation that is original, important and true: of the first volume of a series entitled *The Curiosities of Flagellation* Ashbee observes: 'flagellation is here looked upon as an aphrodisiac, as a means to an end, not as the end in itself, *as is not infrequently the case in flagellation books published early in the century*'. And in the 'Preliminary Remarks' to the third part of his collection, the *Catena*, he makes a related point with the charge that 'the writers of the present day have allowed themselves to be influenced by the pernicious, bloodthirsty, anti-natural doctrines of the Marquis de Sade ... Thus the nature of English erotic fiction has been changed, and its wholesome tone ... entirely lost ...'[4]

Ashbee may have misunderstood the phenomenon he observed, for elsewhere he asserts: 'Flagellation, if it has any value, is a preparation for, an incentive to, a higher pleasure (for it can scarcely be called a pleasure itself), a means towards an end, not the end itself' (*Index*, p. 242). Some theoreticians, basing their argument upon the experience of psychoanalysis, would assert the autonomy of algolagnia, and would want to contradict Ashbee's attempt to save sexual normality. But Ashbee's possible misunderstanding does not detract from the validity and importance of his observation: an emergence during the nineteenth century of a body of literature where flagellation is no longer the occasional accompaniment of genital eroticism, but has largely replaced it.

Flagellation as an aphrodisiac forms part of pornography from its earliest days as a genre. According to David Foxon,[5] Nicholas Chorier's mid-seventeenth-century *Satyra Sotadica* contains flogging episodes, and Ashbee comments *à propos The Adventures of Sir Henry Loveall*, published 'early in the (nineteenth) century', that 'one or two flagellation scenes occur, as in every English erotic work ...' while *The Favourite of Venus* evokes the terse 'one or two flogging scenes are of course introduced'.[6] Foxon cites another early text, Meibomius's *De la Flagellation Venerienne*, one of the two works for which the bookseller / publisher Curll was prosecuted in 1725 in what was effectively the first English obscene-publications trial.[7] Perceau's bibliography of erotic literature in French gives support to Ashbee's thesis that the

[4] *Index Librorum Prohibitorum* (1969), p. 72; *Catena Librorum Tacendorum*, pp. xlii f. My italics.
[5] 'Libertine Literature in England, 1600–1745', *The Book Collector*, Vol. XII, nos. 1, 2 and 3, pp. 21–36, 159–77, 294–307; p. 304.
[6] *Index Librorum Prohibitorum*, *art. cit.*; *Catena Librorum Tacendorum*, p. 145.
[7] Foxon, *op. cit.*, p. 32.

quantity of flagellation literature increased in the late nineteenth century:[8] after the mid-1860s he indicates a few exclusively flagellation texts, and in the last two decades of the century a considerable number; before the the mid-century none appear. The invasion of pornography by algolagnia in the late century is such that one of his titles reassures the potential reader 'no flagellation, no dildos ... nothing but human flesh' (no. 140, publ. 1894).

But we should beware of inferring too much about the early nineteenth century from Perceau's bibliography because it is purely concerned with books published for the first time in the nineteenth century, and therefore makes no mention of Sade. In any case Sade's influence was certainly disproportionate to the number of titles that he published: he was sufficiently widely read, in France at least, to prompt Sainte-Beuve's remark that—along with Byron—he was perhaps the greatest inspiration of *'nos modernes'*.[9] Sade's rapid impact must be compared with Ashbee's point that it was rare for early nineteeth-century works not to treat flagellation as a means to an end since Sade certainly promoted the autonomy of algolagnia even if he was alone in doing so. But more typical than Sade of the late eighteenth century is the flagellation episode in *Fanny Hill*. Towards the end of her narrative the heroine is involved in a scene in which she both beats and is beaten. The man is unable to achieve an erection without being beaten, but requires no further stimulus to orgasm—which is probably a correct representation of masochism.[10] He is presented as an object of pity:

> she rather compassionated, than blamed those unhappy persons, who are under subjection they cannot shake off, to those arbitrary tastes that rule their appetites of pleasure with an unaccountable control: ...[11]

The heroine, on the other hand, has no taste for flagellation, but nonetheless finds, as the pain wears off, that she is very excited:

> But scarce was supper well over, before a change so incredible was wrought in me, such violent, yet pleasingly irksome sensations

[8] L. Perceau, *Bibliographie du Roman Erotique au 19e Siècle* (Paris, 1930).

[9] Quoted in Mario Praz, *The Romantic Agony* (1933), pp. 80–1.

[10] Though the severity of the beating he requests is likely to be exaggerated; cf. the far more plausible account of a masochistic incident in Walter's *My Secret Life* recounted and analysed in Marcus, *op. cit.*, pp. 126–7.

[11] 1970, p. 174.

took possession of me that I scarce knew how to contain myself; . . .
No wonder then, that in such a taking, and devoured by flames
that licked up all modesty and reserve, my eyes, now charged
brimful of the most intense desire, fired on my companion very
intelligible signals of distress. . . .

(p. 181)

Whatever the degree of clinical accuracy of this observation, the
incident shows very clearly that for Cleland algolagnia is not a valid
autonomous sexual taste, and in this he is typical of his period.

It is often argued that the emphasis on painful defloration common in
early pornography is itself sadistic. Both David Foxon and Peter Fryer
refer to a 'sadistic vein' in the emphasis on defloration in Chorier's
Satyra Sotadica,[12] and Steven Marcus comments *à propos The Lustful
Turk:* 'The deflowering is conventionally represented as rape-murder-
sacrifice' (*op. cit.*, p. 201). However, in texts such as these girls come to
delight in what was originally forced upon them, and this marks the
distance that separates them from Sade: Justine and the other victims
never accept the roles into which they are thrust, and if they did
their tormentors would cease to value them. We must recall Freud's
distinction between 'aggressive sadism' and 'hedonistic sadism';
aggressive sadism consists essentially in not taking 'no' for an answer,
perhaps in finding resistance provoking; hedonistic sadism dis-
places pleasure entirely, completely abandoning heterosexual intercourse.[13]

If Ashbee was right then, as it seems he was, what inferences may we
make about nineteenth-century sensibility? In the first place we may
certainly not infer that algolagnia was a new taste in real life: the
existence of flogging parlours in eighteenth-century London is well
attested; there are earlier literary references to algolagnia—Pisanus
Fraxi cites a Marlowe epigram, Shadwell's *Virtuoso* and Otway's
Venice Preserved; and the existence of 'amateurs of suffering' in the
eighteenth century is well known—George Augustus Selwyn, for
instance, created a minor legend by travelling to Paris especially to see
Damien's death by torture for the attempted murder of Louis XV. In
the second place, any inference must carefully distinguish between the

---

[12] Foxon, *loc. cit.*; P. Fryer, *Private Case, Public Scandal* (1966), p. 88.
[13] Cf. G. Deleuze, *Présentation de Sacher-Masoch* (Paris, 1967), p. 39.

D

content of the text, and the construction placed upon it by the audience in their response. Conventionally, both literary criticism and the hermeneutic tradition of sociology either ignore or reject this distinction: the reader's experience of the text is taken to be an immanent function of the text itself, and the text is therefore thought to be an unequivocal guide to sensibility. Nowhere is the questionable nature of this assumption more obvious than in flagellation literature.

In real life the infliction of pain (whether enjoyed passively or actively) provokes—or is intended to provoke—orgasm. In specialized algolagniac literature it is commonly the case that no mention is made of genital activity, and if one failed to distinguish between the text and its reception, one might take literally Sacher-Masoch's portrait of the algolagniac as the 'new man without sexuality':[14] but it is in the reader that the orgasm is intended to be provoked, and this 'non-textual' function is in fact as important as anything actually 'in' the text. This means—inter alia—that the flogging sequence in Fanny Hill, although carefully structured to avoid a direct and explicit appeal to algolagnia as an autonomous taste, could well be construed in these terms by an algolagniac reader. This is of course in large part due to the ambivalent presentation of pleasure in the text, but also to a principle which is fundamental to the reading of pornography, and which Sade recognized:

> Many of the extravagances you are about to see illustrated will doubtless displease you, yes, I am well aware of it, but there are amongst them a few that will warm you to the point of costing you some fuck, and that, reader, is all we ask of you; if we have not said everything, analysed everything, tax us not with partiality, for you cannot expect us to have guessed what suits you best. Rather, it is up to you to take what you please and leave the rest alone, another reader will do the same, and little by little everyone will find himself satisfied.[15]

The principle of self-selection by the reader—so that all pornographic texts become, formally, like encyclopaedias—is what is largely responsible for the monotony with which they are charged by literary

---

[14] Cf. idem, pp. 27 ff.
[15] The Hundred and Twenty Days of Sodom (New York, 1966), p. 254.

critics.[16] But these restrictions do not prevent valid inferences about nineteenth-century sensibility from the emergence of specialized algolagniac literature. In the first place that emergence implies a recognition (of a proto-clinical nature) of the autonomy of algolagnia. In the second place it implies an increase in the number of people amenable to algolagniac fantasy, since not only is there an absolute increase in the number of algolagniac texts, but also a relative increase in the sense that the expansion of algolagniac pornography is out of proportion to the general increase in pornographic publishing that marked the second half of the century.[17] The first implication (recognition) is perhaps to be seen as a function of the second.

MORAL AMBIVALENCE AS A FUNCTION OF GENDER-ROLE: THE PERSECUTED VIRGIN AND THE FEMME FATALE

The success of the persecuted beauty as a subject in the novel of the nineteenth century owes more to the motives which dictated the work of the Divine Marquis than to those which caused Richardson to write *Clarissa*.

(*The Romantic Agony*, p. 107)

Praz is arguing here that in the eighteenth century the portrait of vice was dictated by moral concerns: it had to be horrifying in order to render convincing the triumph (moral, if not actual) of virtue, whereas in the nineteenth century this concern gives way to a certain ambivalence in the presentation of suffering, a 'complaisance' in persecution that leaves the reader on the side of the dark angels. Praz advances this argument on the basis of an analysis of Shelley's *Cenci*, where he finds an ambivalence that is the legacy of Sade's *Justine*. But Praz's

[16] In the case of Sade, all philosophical commentators agree that monotonous repetition has an added function, intrinsic to his philosophy. There is little agreement over what the function is, but—minimally—the consensus over its importance and the possibility of finding functions for it should warn us that dismissal on the grounds of paucity of imagination is jejune.

[17] Examples are: *The Pearl*, 1879–83; *The Whippingham Papers*, 1888; *My Secret Life*, Volume 10, c. 1890; *The Yellow Room*, 1893; *The Petticoat Dominant*, 1898; *Frank and I*, 1902; and the Mr Sackville series, c. 1905. Pornography was—and is thought still to be—a largely middle-class market (prices alone ensured that in the nineteenth century, for most of the figures Ashbee quotes are in guineas) and this would reduce the effect of the increased literacy of the late nineteenth century.

concern is with the Gothic tradition, and because he enlists everything from Maturin's *Melmoth the Wanderer* to Le Fanu's *Uncle Silas* in order to reinforce his thesis, it may be that his judgment is at times uncertain. Melmoth certainly looks like a *prima facie* candidate: his thirst for experience, his destructiveness and his energy, all would seem to align him with Sade's heroes. For Sade, as Maurice Blanchot suggests,[18] 'Everything is good when it is excessive'. However, the eponymous villain of *Uncle Silas* merely seeks an inheritance by peculiarly unpleasant means; and such everyday cupidity, the incarnation of no special energy, is a far cry from the unprincipled, breathless pursuit of evil that animates Sade's heroes. Perhaps the portrait of his accomplice, the governess, is more genuinely horrifying, since in her we sense a gratuitous perversity. And there is a more fundamental reason for removing *Uncle Silas* from the shadow of the Divine Marquis. In Sade's novels the pursuit of evil is to be experienced as its opposite, as something unequivocally good, a positive 'delirium of reason':[19] *Uncle Silas* is melodrama: we are entirely on the side of Maud Ruthyn and we experience Silas and Mademoiselle as negative forces, incompatible with the outright exhilaration that Sade intended. The contemporary German term for the Gothic novel was 'Schauerroman', 'shudder-novel', and the term provides the key to the reader's anticipated reaction which is to be a negative one: horror, even though that horror is unquestionably tempered by a pleasurable frisson.

These reservations do not however amount to a complete dismissal of Praz's case: the ambivalence toward suffering in the Gothic tradition remains, and *prima facie* there is a case to be made for seeing it as algolagniac in structure. This becomes clearer when the Persecuted Virgin is seen in the context of the Femme Fatale, a type that Praz finds originally in Lewis's Matilda and Sainte-Beuve's Mme R. Although she is far from unknown in the early century, it is in the late century, and especially in the Decadent Movement, that the Femme Fatale acquires her real clarity of outline. Praz quotes Des Esseintes, hero of Huysmans's *A Rebours*, on Moreau's Salomé:

the symbolic goddess of indestructible Lewdness, goddess of immortal Hysteria, Beauty damned, chosen among all others for the catalepsy that makes her flesh firm and hardens her muscles; a monstrous

[18] *Lautréamont et Sade* (Paris, 1963), pp. 42–3.
[19] The phrase is taken from Deleuze, *op. cit.*, p. 26.

Beast, indifferent, irresponsible, insensitive, poisoning everyone who approaches her, like Helen of old, everyone who sees her, everyone she touches. . . .

And Moreau himself refers to the women in his paintings as woman 'in the form of perverse and diabolical seduction'.[20] The Femme Fatale, who ensnares, uses and discards her lovers, has clearly acquired the characteristics of the demonic hero of the early Romantic period as Praz claims.

At first sight, it is tempting to posit an equivalence between the themes of 'Fatal Beauty' and 'Persecuted Innocence', to interpret them as Juliette and Justine, to equate the destructiveness of the Femme Fatale with the destructiveness of Sade's heroine and with the destructiveness of Melmoth and Cenci: all persecute. But in reality there is no such equivalence. The man who is destroyed by the Fatal Beauty is destroyed, so to speak, from within (and it is not necessary to accept Freud's interpretation of the Medusa to make this point): it is his own appetite, from Prévost's des Grieux onwards, that is as much responsible for his fate as the woman herself. But none of Juliette's victims fall through love of her. Or—to look at it from the opposite point of view— the Femme Fatale is far from necessarily destructive on purpose: Manon Lescaut genuinely regrets what she does to des Grieux, Keats's Belle Dame sans Merci has no attitude at all. Juliette, on the other hand, makes destructiveness the meaning of her life: men are her victims because of her qualities, whereas the conventional Femme Fatale finds victims through their qualities.

On second thoughts, then, we may want to suggest that the theme of the Fatal Beauty should be equated with masochism, and the Persecuted Beauty with sadism, rather than both with sadism. And perhaps even this statement is too schematic: sadism and masochism refer to behaviour patterns and associated fantasies that have been clinically defined with considerable rigour, and the patterns of behaviour that are described in the literary works Praz cites are by no means those of clinical descriptions. Is the conflation of the two literary themes and two clinical concepts justified, or is it an unwarranted extension of Freud into territory he is not entitled to? We can begin to answer that question by noting how striking it is that both the Persecuted Virgin and the Fatal Beauty are explored from a male point of view: the

[20] All in *op. cit.* For Lewis and Sainte-Beuve, cf. p. 191. For Huysmans, pp. 292–3. For Moreau, p. 295.

Fatal Beauty is that which saps the male ego, with scant attention paid to the effects the situation has on the lady; and the Justine-figure is similarly restricted by her function as reinforcement of the male ego. Both figures are male gender-role fantasies; this is clear if we examine them in the light of the distinction between sadism and masochism. Deleuze has pointed out an immediate discontinuity between sadism and masochism: no sadist seeks a masochistic victim, no masochist seeks a sadistic tormentor. It is resistance to humiliation that the sadist seeks, to be certain that the humiliation really is such. The masochist, on the other hand, seeks to educate his tormentor into his new role because a 'contractual' relationship between victim and tormentor is essential to create the masochistic ritual and to reinforce the notion— central to the masochistic phantasm—that the masochist is breaking a rule and being punished for it. A sadist would be no use in this role, since the infliction of pain would then be the result of a personal desire, not of the impersonal process of a law; and for the obverse reason, no sadist would accept such a contract.[21] In other words, the masochist's tormentor is posited by his masochism: the torturer is a function of the victim's phantasm. Correlatively, the sadist's victim is a function of the torturer's phantasm, posited by his sadism. Thus algolagnia posits four distinct roles: sadist, victim, masochist, tormentor.

In a sadistic fantasy we may expect a greater degree of verisimilitude in the portrayal of the sadist than in the portrayal of his victim, since although the sadistic behaviour may be a fantasy, rather than an observation of real life, it is a fantasy which is really lived as a fantastic self-image; whereas the role of victim is a fantasy within a fantasy. If Deleuze is right there is never, in real life, a fantastic self-image 'victim' which produces a correlative fantasy 'sadist'. These non-existent fantasy roles are displaced by the roles 'masochist' and tormentor' in masochistic fantasies. Therefore, in a masochistic fantasy one could expect a greater degree of verisimilitude in the portrayal of the masochist than in the portrayal of the tormentor. This difference in verisimilitude is observable even in de Sade, where one would expect that everything is too steeped in fantasy for any differences to be observable. In practice, if one compares the rhythms and the tone of Justine's laments and attempts at philosophical counter-argument, it is clear that they have less of reality in them than those of her tormentors. And in the *120 Days of Sodom* the victims never actually say anything; they are the

---

[21] Deleuze, *op. cit.*, pp. 20, 36–7, 68–74.

perfect sadistic phantasm: just active enough to suffer, otherwise passive participants. Now, *a priori*, there is no reason why any of the roles should be the apanage of either sex. Even if we were to predict that in a literature predominantly concerned with heterosexual relationships each pair would contain one member of each sex, there would be no grounds on which to anticipate which role within each pair would be filled by which sex.[22] In other words, a female masochist with a male tormentor is as conceivable as the opposite, equally so a female sadist and a male victim, although in practice both of these combinations are rare: *The Story of O* and Sade's *Juliette* exhaust the field, and there is considerable ambivalence involved in the roles in both cases.[23] The norms in algolagniac fantasies are male sadist/female victim and male masochist/female tormentor. At once it is clear that these fantasies are dictated by the male gender-role, since if they were dictated by anything else, there would be no reasons for the (virtual) absence of female sadists and male victims.

It is equally clear that these norms, found quasi-universally in explicitly pornographic algolagniac fantasies, are precisely the norms that it was possible to draw out of Praz's analyses of the Persecuted Virgin and the Fatal Beauty.[24] The problem lies in the fact that the

[22] I am omitting, for convenience's sake, homosexual algolagniac pornography and associated non-pornographic echoes. In its lesbian version there is clearly a direct relationship with heterosexual sadistic fantasies; in its male homosexual version, the attribution of roles is less clear. It must be stressed that this description of the function of lesbian pornography is only possible because it is empirically certain that the consumers of such texts are male.

[23] *The Story of O* concerns the relationship between a male sadist and a female masochist, thus apparently contradicting Deleuze's theory. To save Deleuze, one could argue that the heroine is educated into her masochism in the course of the story and quasi-abandoned when the process is complete—in other words she is a victim who becomes a masochist, and thereby ceases to be what the sadist wants. Sade's *Juliette* maintains the sadist-victim roles while reversing the genders. One might suppose, following Blanchot's interpretation of Sade, that the search for uniqueness, the renunciation of pleasure and the principle of energy which characterize the Sade hero/heroine involve, *inter alia*, the abrogation of gender-roles. It is worth underlining, in this context, that all of Sade's heroes and heroines abhor heterosexual vaginal intercourse, except for the purposes of painful and humiliating defloration.

[24] Praz specifies (p. 206) that the Persecuted Virgin dominates the first half of the century, and the Fatal Beauty the second half—especially, of course, the Decadent Movement—but without offering an explanation. Is the answer, at least in part, political? In England, from 1847 onwards, there is a sustained, and eventually successful attack on the 'penny dreadfuls', and the

literary texts of the nineteenth century are not in fact algolagniac fantasies: they lack the explicitness and repetitiveness that characterize pornography, and they have a framework that posits values other than simple hedonism. In what sense therefore is it possible to assert an isomorphism between the texts Praz cites and pornography? My resolution of the difficulty is both tentative and speculative. Algolagnia is a specifically sexual organization of the psyche, but it involves seeing relationships with other people in a light that affects the perception of what would otherwise be thought non-sexual behaviour: algolagnia, like fetishism, sexualizes the non-sexual. Specifically, it reinterprets relationships of dominance, subordination and brutality as sexual. Correlatively, therefore, the fact that the relationships of dominance and brutality in Praz's texts are clearly related to a male perspective on relationships with the opposite sex, in other words to male gender-role, makes it plausible to see them as algolagniac, since there is no other reason to present such relationships within a specifically sexual framework. If we accept this hypothesis, then the moral framework surrounding and informing what is now recognized as based in (or somorphic to) algolagniac fantasy emerges as an attempt to understand and evaluate that fantasy.

AESTHETICISM: PAIN AND BEAUTY AS EQUIVALENT EK-STASES

Swinburne's algolagnia is well known; the famous statement in *The Whippingham Papers* is an explicit representation of a masochistic phantasm: 'One of the great charms of birching lies in the sentiment that the floggee is the powerless victim of the furious rage of a beautiful woman.'[25] With this statement in mind, the algolagnia implied in the title of 'Dolores, Notre Dame des Sept Douleurs' can scarcely escape notice:

> Love listens, and paler than ashes,
> Through his curls as the crown on them slips,

Persecuted Virgin was a staple of such literature. The attack on popular literature was caused in part by its specifically class nature: the Persecuted Virgin, especially in Reynold's novels, was proletarian, her Lovelace aristocratic or *nouveau riche*. Cf. M. Dalziel, *Popular Fiction 100 Years Ago* (London, 1957), pp. 48–56. The date is striking: 1847 was the height of Chartist activity and 1848 the year of revolutions all over Europe.

[25] Quoted by Praz, *op. cit.*, p. 278n.

Lifts languid wet eyelids and lashes,
And laughs with insatiable lips.
Thou shalt hush him with heavy caresses,
With music that scares the profane;
Thou shalt darken his eyes with thy tresses,
Our Lady of Pain.

Thou shalt blind his bright eyes though he wrestle
Thou shalt chain his light limbs though he strive;
In his lips all thy serpents shall nestle,
In his hands all thy cruelties thrive.
In the daytime thy voice shall go through him,
In his dreams he shall feel thee and ache;
Thou shalt kindle by night and subdue him
Asleep and awake.

Thou shalt touch and make redder his roses
With juice not of fruit or of bud;
When the sense in the spirit reposes,
Thou shalt quicken the soul through the blood.
Thine, thine the one grace we implore is,
Who would live and not languish or feign,
O sleepless and deadly Dolores,
Our Lady of Pain.

(Stanzas 25–7)

'Dolores' is not explicitly about the cult of beauty, since Dolores is less a person than an idea—precisely, the algolagniac phantasm. But although there is no obvious general connection between aestheticism and algolagnia,[26] a connection may be indicated by an unconscious redundancy—or what is apparently a redundancy—in Swinburne's statement in *The Whippingham Papers*: the tormentor, Swinburne specifies, is a 'beautiful' woman, but there is no *a priori* reason why she should need to be beautiful—anyone who would carry out the ritual as contracted ought to suffice. But Swinburne specifies beauty, and most readers would accept his specification as appropriate; this suggests

[26] 'Aesthete: 1881. One who professes a superior appreciation of what is beautiful, and endeavours to carry out his ideas in practice' (*Oxford Dictionary*). Whether this practice is only artistic, or extends into life is left unspecified. The date is significant: it was the *fin de siècle* that cared sufficiently to invent the word.

—but no more—an objective overlap between algolagnia and aestheticism.

Furthermore, it is not in Swinburne only that the coincidence between beauty and cruelty is to be found. Severin's 'ideal' in Sacher-Masoch's *Venus in Furs* is 'the cruel bliss of adoring a woman who makes a plaything of us, of being the slave of a lovely despot. . . .'[27] The same connection is implicit in Huysmans's essay on Gustave Moreau: Moreau's women, he says, give

> the impression of spiritual onanism, in chaste flesh; the impression of a virgin, with a body of solemn gracefulness, of a soul worn out by ideas in solitude, by secret thoughts; . . . of a woman . . . drivelling to herself . . . insidious calls to sacrilege and stupor; to torture and murder.[28]

Huysmans's comments on Moreau are paralleled by Swinburne's comments on the Pre-Raphaelite Simeon Solomon: his 'epicene figures' express the 'cunning and cruel sensibility' of de Sade.[29] The theme is sufficiently well-known: Praz has listed a significantly large number of Salome/Cleopatra figures, and it is clear that what characterizes them all is precisely the coincidence of beauty and cruelty. The problem is to provide an analysis of the connection, to establish that it is more than a passive contiguity. An explanation is to be found in Baudelaire.

In *Le Peintre de la Vie Moderne*[30] Baudelaire outlines what is effectively an aesthetic way of life: Dandyism. The heart of Dandyism, he specifies, is neither love, money nor elegance, even though these are all natural activities for those without productive occupations. They are merely marks of 'the aristocratic superiority of [the Dandy's] mind'. The heart of Dandyism is 'the burning need to create an originality for oneself within the limits of decorum', 'a cult of oneself' which can survive every disappointment; it is 'the pleasure of astonishing and the proud satisfaction of never being astonished'. Dandyism is beautiful, and its specific beauty 'consists above all in the Dandy's cold mien which comes from the unshakeable resolution to be un-

---

[27] *Venus in Furs*, tr. H. J. Stenning (London: Luxor Press, 1965), p. 34.

[28] Quoted by Praz, *op. cit.*, p. 390, n. 4. My translation.

[29] Quoted *ibid.*

[30] In *L'Art Romantique*, ed. Raynaud (Paris, 1931). Overtly the essay is an appreciation of the painter Constantin Guys; it is also—perhaps first and foremost—a presentation of Baudelaire's own predilections. The translations are mine.

moved'; its beauty is Baudelaire's motive for writing about it. In *Le Peintre de la Vie Moderne* he chooses to talk about three categories of people, the soldier, the Dandy and women; what they have in common is that each has its own specific way of being beautiful. Recognizing the specific beauty of Dandyism allows us to put its moral element in perspective. Dandyism, Baudelaire says, is the form of heroism appropriate to decadence.[31] Heroism is the exceptional, by definition; it is therefore, in some sense, a break with the natural order. In Baudelaire this is explicit: the order of nature is the order of self-interest, necessity and Evil, which are more or less conflated.[32] The good and the beautiful are artificial—hence Baudelaire's 'Eulogy of Make-Up'.

In Baudelaire's scheme women and male sexuality are ambivalent: his conviction that women drag men down into evil is well known— it is one of the recurrent themes of *Les Fleurs du Mal*— yet as the bearer of beauty, woman belongs to another realm. Whores, he says, 'sometimes find, without trying, poses so daring and so noble that they would enchant the most fastidious sculptor'; they are 'nobility in the gutter'. Women in general, Baudelaire argues, are not just 'the female of mankind':

> They are rather a divinity, a star, which presides over all the conceptions of the male mind; they are the shimmer of all nature's graces condensed into a single being; ... They are a kind of idol, stupid perhaps, but dazzling, enchanting, ... They are not, I say, animals whose limbs, correctly assembled, form a perfect example of harmony; they are not even the type of pure beauty, ... no, that would not be enough to explain their mysterious and complex enchantment.

And to underline the point, he stresses that women, their clothes, their jewellery and their make-up form an indivisible whole.[33] Correlatively, love is presented through the eyes of the Dandy: 'It is

[31] 'Le dandysme est le dernier éclat de l'héroïsme dans les décadences ...', p. 74. The elements of Dandyism, listed above, all in fact refer to components of the heroic ethic that was a central component of the culture of the Ancien Régime; for details, cf. J. N. J. Palmer, *Form and Meaning in the Early French Classical Theatre*, Ph.D. thesis, University of Southampton, 1972, ch. 3. But the references are distortions; for example, in the heroic ethic, it is considered appropriate to 'appear what one is'; in Dandyism one 'is what one appears'.

[32] pp. 78–9. This is one of the passages Praz quotes to show Sade's influence on Baudelaire. Out of context it has a Sade-ean tone; in context it bears more resemblance to Hobbes than to Sade.

[33] pp. 76–7.

unfortunately true that, without leisure and money, love can only be the common man's orgy or the accomplishment of marital duty. Instead of a burning or musing whim, it becomes a repugnant utility.'[34] In the case of the Dandy the focus is displaced from the relationship to the imagination.

Dandyism and the contemplation of female beauty are both, in essence, means of lifting the soul out of the everyday, the order of nature. They are thus an ecstasy, an ek-stasis, a snatching-up of the soul into an empyrean. Now this is also the function that Baudelaire elsewhere ascribes to algolagnia in a way that connects it with 'ennui':

> C'est l'Ennui! l'œil chargé d'un pleur involontaire,
> Il rêve d'échafauds en fumant son houka.

> (It is boredom! in his eye an involuntary tear,
> He is dreaming of scaffolds and smoking his houka.)[35]

Ennui' is badly translated as 'boredom', for it means much more: apathy, accidie, lack of energy and direction . . . . Accidie is also the subject of the short essay 'Le Mauvais Vitrier', in which Baudelaire analyses the bursts of energy that people find, against their normal natures, when they do something irrational—they are 'a form of energy that spurts out of accidie and dreaming; and those in whom it is so stubbornly manifest are in general, as I said, the most indolent and dreamy of creatures'. And he recounts an act of wanton cruelty he inflicted on a poor working man who happened to be passing his appartment. Such acts, he reflects, often get one into trouble, but 'what does the eternity of damnation matter to someone who has found in one second the infinity of pleasure!'[36] 'Ennui' is caused by immersion in the world of trivia, the world of daily banality; cruelty, Dandyism and the contemplation of beauty are all ways out of it, through ecstasy—the 'infinity of pleasure', with the emphasis on 'infinity'. To that extent they are equivalents.

[34] p. 72. I have translated as 'common man's orgy' Baudelaire's 'orgie de roturier'; I can find no adequate English rendering of the would-be aristocratic scorn of 'roturier'.

[35] 'Au Lecteur' in Les Fleurs du Mal, final stanza. This poem introduces the collection; the attention Baudelaire gave to the order of the poems within the collection is well known (cf. Enid Starkie's edition of Les Fleurs du Mal, 1956, Intro., p. xvii); the final stanza of the introductory poem is an especially emphatic situation. My translation.

[36] In Oeuvres, ed. Maulnier (Paris, 1948), Vol. III, pp. 27–31. Cf. G. Blin, Le Sadisme de Baudelaire (Paris, 1948), ch. 1.

It is not inappropriate to cite Baudelaire as an explanation of the isomorphism that has been traced here. One of the first reviews in English of *Les Fleurs du Mal* was by Swinburne, who insists both on its *fin-de-siècle* stylistic qualities and its algolagniac overtones:

> ... Languid, lurid beauty of close and threatening weather—and heavy heated temperature, with dangerous hothouse scents in it; ... Not the luxuries of pleasure in their simple first form, but the sharp and cruel enjoyments of pain, the acrid relish of suffering felt or inflicted, the sides on which nature looks unnatural. . . .[37]

And it is surely to the point that both Baudelaire and Swinburne had an enormous admiration for Gautier's *Mlle de Maupin*—Swinburne called it 'the holy writ of Beauty'[38] and Baudelaire dedicated *Les Fleurs du Mal* to Gautier—for the hero of the novel has an entirely aestheticist attitude towards life:

> I might see a beautiful woman, who I knew had the most wicked soul in the world, who was an adulteress and a poisoner, I admit that it wouldn't matter at all to me and wouldn't in the least stop me delighting in her, if I found the shape of her nose right.[39]

But fundamentally it is not literary history, in the conventional sense at least, that is of interest here. Even if the English decadents had not been acquainted with their French counterparts it would still be possible to establish themes which echo from one text to another, even though they may be taken up in individual fashion by each of the authors concerned.

The present essay has attempted two things: in the first place it has argued that the second half of the nineteenth century saw an increase in the number of people who resorted to algolagniac fantasies as a solution to the (universal) contradictions imposed by male gender-role training in modern Britain. In the second place it has been argued that these fantasies are connected with other literary themes, not normally thought of as specifically algolagniac, by an underlying series of shared perceptions of the world: disguised references to gender-role and the ek-stases of aestheticism. This does not mean to say that non-pornographic texts are pornography in disguise; nor does it mean to say that 'creative' readers could find in—say—the

---

[37] *Spectator*, 6 September, 1862. Edited by Edmund Gosse and printed for private circulation in 1913.

[38] Quoted in Praz, *op. cit.*, p. 318.

[39] Quoted *idem*, p. 158. My translation.

Jeanne Duval poems in *Les Fleurs du Mal* a starting point for, or an incarnation of, masturbatory fantasy—though no doubt an algolagniac reader would 'read' Swinburne's 'Dolores' in a very different way to any other reader. What is suggested is that on the basis of a simple relationship between literature and its social base—pornography and gender-role—may be constructed a moral and aesthetic edifice of considerable complexity, but one which may make much more sense if it is seen in terms of its (hypothetical) base than if it is seen in isolation. Thus—for instance—the aestheticist conception of beauty might make more sense if seen as part of an attempt to understand and cope with the contradictions imposed by male gender-role than it would if it was seen—for example—as a late outflowering of Platonism. In other words, the isomorphism should be seen as a mediation between literature and its social base.

Note

The seminal work for the study of the aesthetic issues discussed in this essay is Frank Kermode's *The Romantic Image* (1957). The same author's *Modern Essays* (1971) is also relevant, as is Richard Ellmann's *The Golden Codgers* (1973). Malcolm Bradbury's *The Social Contexts of Modern English Literature* (1971) is the best starting point for a study of the sociological dimension of the literature of this period, but I have also been much influenced by two studies of related areas, D. J. Gordon's 'Aubrey Beardsley at the V & A' (*Encounter* XXVII, October 1966) and John Stokes's *Resistible Theatres* (1972).

The theoretical bases of this article owe most to Walter Benjamin's *Charles Baudelaire: A Lyric Poet in the Era of High Capitalism* (1973). This and two other essays by the same author—'The Author as Producer' (in *Understanding Brecht*, 1973) and 'The Work of Art in the Age of Mechanical Reproduction' (in *Illuminations*, 1967)—make possible the materialist analysis of the literature of the late nineteenth century. Renato Poggioli's *Theory of the Avant Garde* (1968) is an invaluable discussion from a different point of view. T. J. Clark's *The Absolute Bourgeois* (1913), a study of the history of art in the era of the 1848 revolution, has relevance both as a model and as an argument. Two further important contributions to the problem of literary production are Pierre Macherey's *Pour une Théorie de la Production Littéraire* (1966), soon to be available in English, and Terry Eagleton's *Criticism and Ideology* (1976).

The distinction between organic and traditional intellectuals which lies at the heart of this analysis is Antonio Gramsci's, and his essay on 'The Intellectuals', *Prison Notebooks* (1971), is fundamental to any serious discussion of literary production.

N.B. In the footnotes to this article only the first reference to a text is annotated. Later quotations are indicated by a page number in parentheses which refers to the edition cited.

V

The Decadent Writer as Producer

JOHN GOODE

I

'WAS IT that we lived in what is called "an age of transition" and so lacked coherence, or did we but pursue antithesis?'[1] Yeats's question is still no easier to answer, even though it is generally recognized that the tragic generation foreshadows modernism: for modernism itself seems largely to inherit elitist and organicist tendencies which site it, if antithetically and problematically, within the late capitalist ideology.[2] Generally this essay makes larger claims for what I shall term, following Symons, the decadent movement: what I shall set up as a 'materialist' perspective reveals a 'break' with the hegemony (crucially restricted) that modernism only repairs by assimilation.

But to begin with, it is necessary to identify a negative answer to Yeats's question, and it is Sartre, I think, who makes it most significantly:

> Thus, whereas literature ordinarily represents an integrating and militant function in society, bourgeois society at the end of the century offers the unprecedented spectacle of an industrious society, grouped round the banner of production, from which there issues a literature which, far from reflecting it, never speaks to it about what interests it, runs counter to its ideology, identifies the beautiful with the unproductive, refuses to allow itself to be integrated, and does not even wish to be read.[3]

He sees possibilities in this spectacle: it constitutes the writer's transgression and fall; the excesses of its formal displacement might have been an adolescence out of which emerged not merely an open break, but a *déclassement* from below, a new content and virtual public. It never went beyond the antithetical assertion of autonomy because of

[1] Yeats, *Autobiographies* (1956), p. 304.
[2] Eagleton, 'Ideology and Literary Form', *New Left Review* 90, pp. 81–109.
[3] Sartre, *What is Literature* (1950), p. 108.

the danger of the writers becoming ' "a white collar proletariat" on the margin of the real proletariat, suspect to the workers and spurned by the bourgeois' (p. 89). The consequence was that Marxism, in a triumph without glory, became the Church, 'while the gentlemen writers, a thousand miles away, made themselves guardians of an abstract spirituality'. It is hard to resist this account of the transition from 'decadence' to modernism, 'autonomy' to 'abstract spirituality'. Especially in England, where a distinction between even 'the avant garde' and modernism proper can be made.[4]

If Sartre defines the spectacle, it is Poggioli who provides the concepts with which to explain it. The term 'avant-garde' itself, he argues, only becomes applicable to the arts as it begins to lose its political significance.[5] It is only from within a hermetic field that the arts enact analogous revolutionary moments. Notoriously, the most progressive artists have been at best naive in their descents into political actuality. Even Walter Benjamin, who goes further than most critics in understanding the political significance of technical change, argues that it is better to see Baudelaire not from the perspective offered by his appearance on the barricades, but as a 'secret agent in the enemy camp'.[6] Poggioli makes a further distinction between the 'intelligentsia', which, as Herzen realized, is capable of a proletarianization, and the actual public of the avant garde which he calls the 'intellectual elite' (pp. 84–8). Sartre's whole analysis stems precisely from the perspective of an intelligentsia which recognizes the irrecoverable *incorporation* of the intellectual elite. The domination of English intellectual history by the elite explains the containment of modernism. For the struggle to organize the traditional intellectual, as Eagleton has shown, ends in victory for the hegemony precisely because the whole concept of his alienation (stemming from Arnold) is based on the felt need of a totalizing unity (the State, tradition, culture, organic form, organic community, etc.) produced by the fissures in utilitarian ideology as it has to cope with a higher organization of the capitalist production process. Almost literally, the modern intellectual organizes himself on behalf of monopoly capitalism, becoming the guardian of an abstract spirituality duplicating the corporation of the imperial state, and actually making possible 'literature' as an ideological form—that is, as a canon avail-

[4] Kermode, *Modern Essays* (1971), p. 71
[5] Poggioli, *The Theory of the Avant-Garde* (New York, 1971), p. 12.
[6] Benjamin, *Charles Baudelaire: A Lyric Poet in the Era of High Capitalism* (1973), p. 104.

able to the academy for the intellectual training of the ideological managers.[7]

I wish to affirm the achievement of the decadent movement both on the basis and in the face of this analysis. For already a contradiction emerges: how, if modern literature offers the spectacle of a non-integrating, isolated form, can it become organic in Gramsci's sense? It can only do so if, in achieving its 'coherence' the transition has lost the main thrust of its antithesis. The decadence thus becomes important not in so far as it prepares the way for modernism, but in so far as it rebukes its betrayal. This is not a matter of overturning the analysis, but of reminding ourselves of another statement of Benjamin's which is not, like the first, a tentative footnote, but a firm principle: 'Sundering truth from falsehood is the goal of the materialist method, not its point of departure. In other words, its point of departure is the object riddled with error' (p. 103). The first stage of any analysis has to be the identification of what riddles the object, and in this case it is a principle of Benjamin that enables us to perceive it: that the first question we have to ask about a work of art is not what is its situation *vis-à-vis* the relations of production, but what is its situation *in* them. The analysis I have compiled from Sartre, Poggioli and Eagleton poses the question of the *ideological relationship* of the modern movement to social change. But if we pose the question of the *production relations*, we can see that the decadent movement in particular, if it frequently voices ideas that flow into the organicism of the intellectual elite, and if, as in Yeats's essay 'The Autumn of the Body', it can be subsumed into it, distinguishes itself by being a specific resistance to coherence, the resistance of the producer to the guardian. If this only emerges in restricted and distorted ways, it may be because it could be no more than a white-collar proletariat, but it nevertheless met that risk. The coherence of the transition may mask a *break* which demystifies the text.

II

'Decadent, decadent, you are all decadent nowadays. Ibsen, Degas, and the New English Art Club; Zola, Oscar Wilde, and the Second Mrs Tanqueray.'[8] Hubert Crackanthorpe thus neatly exposes the absurdity of the meaning of the word. Even within a single writer it had no

[7] Balibar and Macherey, 'Sur la Littérature comme Forme Idéologique—Quelques Hypothèses Marxistes', *Littérature* 13 (Février 1974), pp. 29–48.

[8] Crackanthorpe, 'Reticence in Literature', *Yellow Book*, Vol. I, 1894, p. 266.

stability: Symons, for example, sees it as an inclusive term in 1893, a marginal one in *The Symbolist Movement*. It embraces Henley and Pater in the magazine version of 1893, but not in the reprint of 1923; while in the interim, Symons has applied it to Meredith (again specializing its meaning from the term offered in 1893). Yet, even its bewildering semantic diversity, the fact that it needs to be used, acknowledges that if it is ridiculous to generalize the innovatory forms in art in the 1890s, it is also natural and meaningful. The most obvious variation is not so much one of meaning but one of levels of meaning. Symons sees it as the pursuit of *la vérité vraie* in 1893, but confines it to 'that learned corruption of language by which style ceases to be organic' in 1897.[9] It can thus be taken to signify a total ideological commitment or else a stylistic character, and it is notably as the former that the outstanding polemics against 'decadence' attack it, while its most notable defence assumes it is the latter. Le Gallienne sees literary decadence as a break with 'vital' literature:

> In all great literature, the theme great or small, is considered in all its relations, near or far, and above all in relation to the sum total of things, to the Infinite, as we phrase it; in decadent literature, the relations, the due proportions, are ignored. One might say that literary decadence consists in the euphuistic expression of isolated observations.[10]

And he goes on to cite the Arnoldian criterion of seeing life steadily and seeing it whole. Lionel Johnson, in his book on Hardy, also stresses the break with universality that decadence brings ('the great books and utterances tell all one story under diverse forms').[11] In decadent writing, literature becomes 'the private toy of its betrayers', and the universality it must lose, though it is not Le Gallienne's 'infinite', is still a totalizing conception, 'its humanity'. Both writers, in other words, see decadence as a break with some form of organic whole, with culture. On the other hand, not only Symons, but also Havelock Ellis, see this as a specific *stylistic* development—for Ellis, it is the inversion of the classical subordination of the parts to the whole.[12] These and other definitions may make it useless to define decadence as an idea, yet they make it clear that it is possible to identify a movement which can

9 Symons, *Studies in Prose and Verse* (1904), p, 149.
10 Le Gallienne, *Retrospective Reviews*, Vol. I, pp. 24–5.
11 Johnson, *The Art of Thomas Hardy* (1923), p. 2.
12 Ellis, 'Huysmans', reprinted in Stanford, *Critics of the Nineties* (1970), pp. 142–71.

be classified by its structural relation to the literature of the past—as a break with that past which disintegrates it from the reflection of ideology (that is, of an expressive totality, whether it is the Infinite or Humanity) and insists on the break-up of stylistic totalities, 'a revolt from ready-made impressions and conclusions, a revolt from the ready-made of language, from the bondage of traditional form, of a form become rigid'.[13] The precise importance of Symons's negations (and their negativity) can be seen if we see Crackanthorpe's essay as a whole. For although he rejects the umbrella word, he is nevertheless affirming a movement: not only is he envisaging the time when the 'battle for literary freedom will be won' but basing this on the fact that 'a new public has been created', one that has 'eaten of the apple of knowledge'—that is, understands the nature of artistic production.

But Crackanthorpe takes us a stage further. His polemic is directed not against the philistine, the moral objector, but against a new phenomenon, the artistic objector, the aesthetic philistine who opposes the innovatory in terms of the art of the past. Arthur Waugh, against whom the polemic is addressed, had tried to distinguish between 'nakedness' and 'nudity':[14] 'that universal standard of good taste that has from the days of Milo distinguished the naked from the nude.' Implicitly, at least, this escapes the utilitarian opposition by incorporating art within a totalized mode of seeing, and it is this that Crackanthorpe attacks in the name of productive excellence. In other words, he is concerned to expose the elite. Although it is right to see a break in the productive relations of literature in the 1860s, the concept of the artistic objector suggests that we must distinguish between kinds of break. On the one hand, Arnoldian hellenism, which constantly makes application to the hegemony (as Swinburne put it, David, son of Goliath); on the other hand, the paganism of the aesthetic movement which demystifies art and sets it resolutely outside the walls. The break at this level is best studied through Pater's major confrontation with romanticism, the essay on Coleridge. For in that essay, the intelligentsia and the intellectual elite oppose one another not as knowledge and art but as the knowledge of art and the ideology of art.

[13] Symons, 'The Decadent Movement in Literature' in Beckson, *Aesthetes and Decadents of the 1890's* (New York, 1966), p. 137. I have used this text because it is based on the magazine version of 1893.

[14] Waugh, 'Reticence in Literature', *Yellow Book*, Vol. 1 (1894), p. 218. The whole essay is an example of the kinds of arguments against decadence that I have been discussing. Unity, tradition, restraint are its keynotes.

The essay is usually cited as an example of modernist relativism, and relativism is very important to it, but not the liberalism of indecipherable pluralities. For Pater's relativism is linked again and again specifically to the positive method: 'The idea of the "relative" has been fecundated in modern times by the influence of the sciences of observation.'[15] And it is derived not from a helpless confrontation of idealism and empiricism (the rage for order whistling and smiling in the rich mess) but from an awareness of the material determinants of consciousness: 'The truth of these relations experience gives us; not the truth of eternal outlines effected once for all, but a world of fine gradations and subtly linked conditions, shifting intricately as we ourselves change'. It is not to a factitious totality that we resort to contest this: on the contrary 'to the intellect, to the critical spirit, these subtleties of effect are more precious than anything else'. To stress this is not necessary merely to rescue Pater from the capitulations of modernist ideology, but also to emphasize how much his theory of art depends not on a defensive elitism (the constitution of an abstract spirituality) but on an endorsement of the most advanced epistemology of his time. In fact, his critique of Coleridge's ideas bears a marked resemblance to Foucault's history of forms of knowledge.[16] The 'esemplastic power', for example, is seen to be more 'valid' because of the 'charm . . . in the clear image' than because of its ability to 'bear a loyal induction'. In the realm of poetry, therefore, Coleridge struggles against the coming of the relative with an epistemology of signification which Foucault sees as characteristic of the Middle Ages and surviving as literature. Equally, however, Pater is sceptical about what Foucault would term an epistemology of representation: 'Ancient philosophy sought to arrest every object in an eternal outline, to fix thought in a necessary formula, and types of life in a classification by "kinds" or "genera".' Both ways of knowing, the connecting sign and the fixating table, are rejected in the name of an understanding of natural laws and determinants—the epistemology of nineteenth-century science. It is this positive sense that underlies the total rejection of any attempt to explain men's activities and consciousnesses by anything outside themselves and the historical determinants of their lives.

The consequences for the theory of art are radical. Since there is no absolute, no expressive totality, art cannot embody any ideological

[15] Pater, *Essays on Literature and Art*, edited by Jennifer Uglow (1973), p. 2. Again I have used this because it reprints the 1867 version.
[16] See Michel Foucault, *The Order of Things* (1970).

function. Above all, it has to be dissevered from the romantic unity of art and the universe. Pater quotes Coleridge's famous comment on Shakespeare: 'The organic form is innate .... Such as the life is, such the form', and comments:

> There 'the absolute' has been affirmed in the sphere of art; and thought begins to congeal. Coleridge has not only overstrained the elasticity of his hypothesis, but has also obscured the true interest of art. For after all, the artist has become something almost mechanical; instead of being the most luminous and self-possessed phase of consciousness, the associative act itself looks like some process of assimilation. The work of art is sometimes likened to the living organism. That expresses the impression of a self-delighting, independent life which a finished work of art gives us; it does not express the process by which that work of art was produced.

It would be astonishing, if we didn't know the ideological necessity of it, that the notion of organic form has survived Pater's clear perception of its *mechanical* (i.e. in modern terms, *reified*) nature. But the passage not only points this out; it explains its persistence. Organic form expresses the *reader's* impression: that is, it explains an effect in the sphere of circulation (which Marx also termed 'realization') which precedes and follows the productive process. As in Marx, so in Pater, it is not a question of denying the phase of reception, but of not allowing the phase of production to be mystified out of existence. For it is production that creates value, and it is the historical determination of the mode of production which makes a work of art what it is. Coleridge thought beauty grew on trees, as capitalists think that money begets money. In the realm of theory, Pater accomplishes a demystification which would make it impossible for art to subserve the ideology that supports it. The most achieved moments of the decadence not only break with received ideas in ideological antithesis, but do so by affirming the productive source of value—I think primarily of Huysmans's railway engines, but also of a poem like *La Mélinite* where the mirror dislocates the dancer from the chorus, or Gray's *The Barber* where the produced beauty of the dream moves to an encounter with madness. Such texts are not mere antithesis, but make for a transition to the contradiction of the producer.

If this is the case, why is it that a theoretical revolution in art, not merely analogous to, but also with the same consequences as, the theoretical political revolution—the affirmation of the productive source of value—remains a series of moments that are betrayed? An answer must be speculative. But it is possible to argue that as in politics, so in art, the exposure of ideology is insufficient to effect a revolution in practice because the base is not motivated by the superstructure. What Poggioli neglects, in his brilliant distinction between the intellectual elite and the intelligentsia, is that art has a very definite situation in the economic base. Significantly, Pater is housed in Oxford, but even he found it necessary to censor himself. The 'actual' relations of production, however, not only retain a capitalist form but intensify it. Or to be more precise, the economic practices of book production demand an ideological commitment that runs so counter to the theoretical demystification that the latter has to site itself, in order to survive, in an elite within the elite.

III

I can best stress the extremity of the contradiction between the base and the superstructure by considering the case of the Society of Authors. It is not merely that the progressive thrust of the decadence grows up within an increasing commercialization of the kind indicated by Q. D. Leavis. It is rather that a more complex market situation demands a more mystified ideology of literary production. The Society, by its very attempt to clarify and rationalize the relationship of the writer to the economic realization of his work, offers the most obvious example of this mystification.

Founded in 1883, the Society[17] reached a membership of nearly a thousand within a decade. It quickly gained prestige and respectability. Tennyson became its first president, and Meredith succeeded him; Collins, Reade and Yonge were among its first vice-presidents. The Lord Mayor of London gave it a banquet in its first year. Seeking to obtain greater legal recognition for literary property, and to place the relations between authors and publishers on a basis of 'equity and justice', its activities were diverse and coherent. It issued information on the technicalities of publishing and distribution, to enable its members to form a realistic view of the value of their work (e.g. S. Squire Sprigge's *The Methods of Publishing*, 1890, and *The Costs of Production*, 1891). It arranged three conferences in 1887 on the grievances between authors and publishers, and drafted bills to consolidate the law of copyright. From 1891, it had its own journal, *The Author*. In

[17] The most accessible source on the Society's history is Walter Besant's *Autobiography* (1902), Chapter XII (written in 1892).

1894, it took a formal decision to oppose the continuation of the three-decker novel, bound for the circulating libraries. In addition to public activities such as these, it acted as an advice bureau to authors, and eventually began its own literary agency. In short, it worked as an organization to give secure professional standing to an occupation riddled with amateurism, romantic vagueness and apparent unpredictability. It is not insignificant that it is founded in the era of the New Unionism, that movement to provide a structure of industrial relations to the casualized labour of the unskilled. Walter Besant, its leading figure, wrote novels about the working class, and was indeed the brother-in-law of Annie.

And yet to make that connection is to see immediately how little the organization of the casual intellectual has to do with that of the casual worker. For fundamentally it inverts the recognition of his productive role. The 'leading principles' of the society, according to a declaration of 1889, were:

> First that literary property needs to be defined and protected by legislation, and the relations between author and publisher to be placed upon a basis of equity and justice. Secondly, that the question of copyright, especially between this country and America, is one which requires to be kept steadily in view and persistently attacked.[18]

Productive relations are thus made a function of the legal status of 'property', and this not only subordinates the concept of literary work, but even of professional service. Writing becomes the creation of a property which must not be 'used' without the owner receiving what he demands for it. Sprigge, the Society's secretary, began his book with a chapter entitled 'Literary Property', and wrote of the literary work in terms which reveal how far the mystification goes:

> A man's literary work is, though the fact is too often forgotten, his personal property, which he may use absolutely as he chooses, over which he alone has control, to sell, to lease, to lend or to give away.
>
> (p. 9)

[18] Reprinted in Sprigge, *Methods of Publishing* (1890), p. 113. The declaration reveals that subscriptions were a guinea a year, that the Secretary was available for advice Monday–Friday, and that among the council members were Edward Arnold, Alfred Austin, Augustine Birrell, R. D. Blackmore, Edward Clodd, Marion Crawford, Edmund Gosse, Rider Haggard, Hardy, Meredith, G. A. Sala, H. D. Traill and Edmund Yates. Haggard and Gosse were on the Committee of Management.

In order to make the literary work a property, Sprigge has to postulate a 'use value' (may use as he chooses) which a moment's thought will show to be non-existent. It is true that, as he says later, 'there is nothing illogical in the author's wish to benefit by his work', but he can clearly only realize this benefit by the exchange of his work as a commodity. He has no choice therefore in the disposition of a thing (his manuscript) since the only value this has is that of his objectified labour power, an objectification which only has exchange value as the means of production of a book. Significantly, Sprigge does not imply that the author has, among his choices, the power of witholding it from the process of production. The only 'choice' he has is in the kind of contract he accepts. Of course, this is more variable than the kind of choice open to all productive workers (because, unlike them, he is able to work without the aid of the owners of the means of production, though that is a useless privilege since without their aid the work must remain unproductive). The mystification is not one that is confined to Sprigge. Matthew Arnold, for example, in an essay on copyright, wrote that 'a man has a strong instinct making him seek to possess what he has produced or acquired, to have it at his disposal'.[19] Production and acquisition thus confer the same rights (and of course the copyright issue, as it has to do not only with the remuneration of the writer, but also with a value persisting beyond his death, is an index of the transfer of the value created by work into the object as an innate property). John Hollingshead spoke of the laws concerning dramatization explicitly in terms of the laws protecting land-ownership,[20] and Wilkie Collins called his article on American piracy 'Thou shalt not steal'. Thus, although literature is the product of work, and although, in the realm of aesthetic theory, the recognition of the productive role of the artist is the most important advance, here, in the realm of the actual relations of production, literature is seen, by those who seek an equitable status for it, not as a function of the productive process but as a property, protected by law, which in effect acts as a barrier to capitalist investment by demanding a kind of rent—in Marx's terms, a monopoly rent, subject only to the laws of demand. Clearly the Society would do little for the writer who had not the forces of the market to increase the exchange value of his commodity.

But the mystification goes much further. For since a literary manu-

[19] Arnold, *English Literature and Irish Politics*, ed. Super (Ann Arbor, 1973), p. 118.
[20] *Grievances between Authors and Publishers* (1887), p. 94.

script is not really like a piece of land, it has to be regarded as well as an equivalent for money capital exacting interest. When George Smith (of Smith and Elder) produced a suggested pro-forma account sheet, he was taken to task by the *Law Journal* (which was quoted as authoritative by the Society) because he had included in the account a five per cent charge for the advance of the publisher's capital, as well as a charge for risking bad debts and offering discounts. These charges were invalid, the *Law Journal* argued, because the cash advanced, the risks taken, the incentives offered, constituted the publisher's investment in the partnership between himself and the author and so he had no right to charge for what he had only undertaken to do. In this argument, the manuscript becomes an equivalent for money capital, although its money value is not realizable until the actual money capital has set in motion the productive process which will convert the book into a consumable commodity. The manuscript is thus given a magical ability to operate in in the phase of circulation before it becomes a commodity. Besant was to take this illusion to amazing lengths in a lecture at one of the 1887 conferences entitled 'The Maintenance of Literary Property':

> What would be said in the City, if, when two men had agreed on sharing the profits of an enterprise, the one who kept the books were to make a secret profit for himself by setting down the expenses as greater than those actually incurred. . . .
> What would be said in the City, when two men went shares in an enterprise, should the one who did the active part refuse to let his accounts be examined?[21]

Not only has the point of reference become the centre of mercantile speculation, the City, but so mystified into 'investment' has literary work become that the writer is seen as a sleeping partner, the publisher as the only one who does the active part. It is true that these points are being made about a phase after the completion of the manuscript; but that that should be the centre of attention reveals how ill equiped the Society, and their supporters, were to see the capitalist production of books as the confrontation of capital and labour.

When Flaubert was in the midst of writing *Madame Bovary* (a text in which both author and protagonist are seen to produce the 'reality' they need to expose), he wrote to Louise Colet that he detested the French equivalent of the Society of Authors, 'bédouin tant qu'il vous

[21] *Ibid.*, p. 25.

plaira; citoyen jamais'.[22] He added that he would like to inscribe in front of his books that reproduction of them is permitted. The concept of a literary property right, the role of citizen in that sense, is precisely what forces what I have termed the 'decadent' writer into the desert of his own autonomy. In 1895, Gissing made the same complaint to Edouard Bertz: 'The extent to which novelists are becoming *mere* men of business is terrible.'[23] He blamed Besant for this, but he also went on to praise him 'for his efforts to improve the payment of authorship'. The whole contradiction of nineteenth-century authorship lies in these letters. For the writer is no longer faced with a simple market situation, as Byron and Scott and Dickens were. They could be professional writers by being capitalist writers. They made the market their works reflected. Once the writer is a producer—not the secretary of reality (nature or society)—he is confronted either with total isolation from the productive relations of his society, or the possibility of becoming the deviser of a form of capital. There is no way for his *work* to be integrated into the capitalist process. When Hardy was asked whether he thought that writers should receive national recognition, he replied, with characteristic irony:

> I daresay it would be very interesting. . . . But I don't see how it could be successfully done. The highest flights of the pen are mostly the excursions and revelations of souls unreconciled to life, whilst the natural tendency of a government would be to encourage acquiescence to life as it is. However, I have not thought much about the matter.[24]

This shifts the discussion into another area, the relation between the writer and the state, but it is deeply bound up with the analysis we have been considering. For what Hardy is saying is that the writer by his very nature has to oppose ideology (that is, the apparatus for enabling the free subject to subject himself to 'reality'). We have seen how, on the one hand, this break is at the very centre of the progressive theory of art at the end of the century, and how although this most significantly expresses itself as the recognition of the productive role of the artist, the very form in which that productiveness has to realize itself is one which remystifies the literary process for a market economy. There is a real

[22] Flaubert, *Correspondance*, 4e Série, p. 17.

[23] Gissing, *The Letters of George Gissing to Edouard Bertz*, ed. Young (1961), p. 204.

[24] Hardy, *Life of Thomas Hardy* (1965), p. 240. The question was put to him by Robertson Nicoll in November 1891.

connection between Coleridge's organicist displacement of art into the realm of realization and Besant's spiriting away of the writer's work into an equivalent of money capital. We have to produce the state at this point because the way out of the difficulty in real terms is to re-organize the writer, not for the market, but for the institutions of social control, to make the work in other word's the means of production for another production, literary criticism. Hardy is relevant here because in his own practice he recognizes the contradiction of the decadent producer in its class implications.

IV

Jude the Obscure was published in 1895: the boom novel of the mid-nineties is Du Maurier's *Trilby*. *Trilby* is an appropriate context for Hardy's novel in the terms of this essay, not only because of its success, but also because it is about the nature of artistic success in itself; and it offers a clever version of what Crackanthorpe identified as aesthetic philistinism. The bohemian idyll, history of the lily bred of corrupt soil, of the artistic vision bred of unrequited love and resistance to 'philistine hate', is cleverly distanced, so that what in fact is a lucid portrayal of the conditions of artistic production is presented at once as something belonging to a world richer than the reader's (and author's) tame normality ('The present scribe is no snob. He is a respectably brought up old Briton of the higher middle class—at least he flatters himself so. And he writes for just such old philistines as himself'),[25] and at the same time as belonging to a very definite past and so placed as an adolescence ('and now having really cut our wisdom teeth' (p. 447)). So that if we are, like Billee's mother, incapable of entering that world, we can also love it, as she does Trilby, on its deathbed. It is a classic instance of the best-seller having it both ways: the world of value displaced into nostalgia and therefore enclosable within the 'real' world: the flower of the dunghill, in Renan's image, entering the drawing room on promise of an early death.

Nevertheless, Du Maurier is knowledgeable enough to understand that the Parisian world of art is more than a world of vision. If Billee's inspiration is a romantic memory that reproduces itself through him, as though his canvases had been made with Trilby's foot, the other version of art, that presented through Svengali, is that of beauty produced against nature. Honorine, whose voice is naturally talented, is

[25] Du Maurier, *Trilby* (1896), pp. 151-2.

ruined by his training: Trilby is tone deaf. The art that he trains in her is an art of acute transformation, of a trivial ditty made to bear tragic passion, of an impossible Chopin piano piece vocalized ('And there is not a sign of effort, of difficulty overcome' (p. 318)). To achieve this, Svengali has to make another Trilby—'an unconscious Trilby of marble' (p. 441)—who reflects back 'as from a mirror' his own love of himself. Against this, Billee's 'old cosmic vision of the beauty and sadness of the world' (p. 311) is a tired romantic cliche, acceptable on precisely the same terms as Waugh's distinction between nakedness and nudity—'all beauty is sexless in the eyes of the artist at his work' (p. 95).

It is, of course, precisely because Billee's sexless naturalism reflects the sad reality that it can be accommodated. Svengali, who changes his material through a productive process (significantly manifest as theatre), is evil, poor without pathos, a visitation destroying innocence. It is such a clever novel because Svengali's power is repressed in the story itself: it is only after the story is over, when Svengali has shown himself as destructive and is safely dead, that we actually learn about what he has been doing. So it never challenges the romanticism of Billee, and the Paris world can be forgiven in a vale of tears because the actual process of artistic production is placed as a strange gap within it. Trilby is the myth of aesthetic philistinism.

Hardy's novel, which is the very opposite kind of sensation from Trilby, can also be seen as its mirror image. For Jude is also an artist who tries to emerge from his utilitarian field to materialize his aesthetic image—the impression of a halo in the light of Christminster, the photograph of Sue. But, unlike Billee, this is no contained nostalgia, and, unlike Svengali, there is pathos in his poverty. The Jew is a deliberately contrived absence ('Nobody knew exactly how Svengali lived' (p. 52)), whereas Jude is at the very centre of his own experience, which is the novel itself. So that the struggle to materialize a vision is not mystified. And Jude is no strange pariah, but a member of a class— 'the voice of the educated proletarian' as The Saturday Review put it (Critical Heritage, p. 283). The whole of the Christminster episode is the ordeal of Jude confronting his own proletarianization, knowing his real place according to the terribly sensible advice of the Master of Bibliol, but knowing also the reality of his productive role, as when he realizes that the mechanistic bits of reproduced masonry are probably no more factitious than the weather-worn originals, or when he recognizes the greater centrality of working-class Christminster.

Equally the sexlessness of the beauty that he desires, the impenetrable walls of Christminster and Sue, is not a condition of his achievement but the annihilation of it.

A. J. Butler's review of *Jude* was entitled 'Mr Hardy as Decadent', and in the terms of this essay he was surely right, The decadence of the novel for him lay in its denial of the law which the earlier novels affirmed, and which is at 'the base of social existence',[26] that 'you can't have everything'. He rightly sees the novel as an explicit exposure of ideology itself (all the terribly sensible advice, the 'perception' of contradictory truths), seen in terms of what Althusser[27] has called 'the ideological couple' of the capitalist state, the family and education. The protagonist is not only displaced from the totality (the buried organic continuity of the brown field), but is forced by this both to seek to reconstitute it for himself as a secret mystery he can journey towards and to confront the implications of his failure (the grammar books foreshadow the whole process: the access to the privileged world of vision that they promise is replaced by the repressive insistence of the letter, a rote learning that will keep him in his place). The only access offered by the series of repositories of cultural value is that of emulation, repairing the crumbling masonry of its exclusivity. The aesthetic image, the hazy light in the distance, materializes itself only as denial. The nearest Jude gets to self-realization is modelling Christminster in cake. 'You can't have everything', the base of social existence, is denied because Jude in his obscurity cannot have anything that corresponds to that light.

The original notes for the novel were made in 1887, the scheme laid down in 1890, the detailed writing began in 1893. It can be no accident, surely, that the most vital work to emerge from Oxford in those years was that of Pater. *Marius* was published in 1885; and not only does the syntax of Hardy's title (which is so unlike any of his previous titles) echo Pater's but Lionel Johnson's description of *Marius* (in a review of 1894) might also do as a description of *Jude*: 'Youth, confronting this very visible world, yet upon a quest for some interpretation, harmony, absolute truth, which should make the vision, if not beatific, yet somehow divine.'[28] Equally, the Conclusion to *The Renaissance* was restored in 1888, and it is surely this that is echoed in Hardy's

[26] Cox, *Thomas Hardy, The Critical Heritage*, p. 287.

[27] See 'On The Reproduction of the Relations of Production' in *Lenin and Philosophy* (1972).

[28] Johnson, *Post Liminum* (1911), p. 26.

preface: 'Like former productions of this pen, *Jude the Obscure* is simply an endeavour to give shape and coherence to a series of seemings, or personal impressions, the question of their consistency or their discordance, of their permanence or their transitoriness, being regarded as not of the first moment.' To give shape to impressions that have *in themselves* no shape or value—this is surely decadent production as we have defined it: the preface might almost have been written in defiance of Lionel Johnson's book. But not only is the organic coherence disavowed, and thus the novel programmatically disengaged with the totality, but it reflects a historical determinism. The serial version, of course, appeared in *Harper's New Monthly*, which in November 1893 printed Symons's 'Decadent Movement', in which he quotes a phrase of Ernst Hello's to define decadence which accounts for one dimension of Jude's obscurity: 'desire without light, curiosity without wisdom'. The novel is thus a 'decadent' production, and its protagonist the hero of a 'decadent' displacement. We find many incidental features of the decadence incorporated into the text: Jude's time-travelling appreciation of Christminster, Sue's paganism (she buys the statues of Apollo and Venus, and later declares that she is not modern but older than medievalism) and her androgyny, even her final retreat into ritualism, Father Time's Schopenhauerian pessimism ('the coming universal wish not to live'), the text's massive allusiveness, particularly the double quotation from the 'Hymn to Proserpine'. If, on the one hand, it is the first truly working-class novel in English (not the first novel about the working class, but the first to articulate a working-class voice), it is also this because it confronts the world of value with a decadent disaffection. In more than one way, Jude is of the white-collar proletariat.

And this is not merely a matter of portrayal. If Jude's dream is materialized as an excluding totality, he has also the possibility, which is the basis of decadent art, of producing that dream as an opposing materiality. When he returns to Christminster, Sue tries to remind him that it has done nothing for him, but he replies that 'it is the centre of the universe to me because of my early dream'. What we have in the last section is not a helpless spectatorship but a theatrical production of the ironies and dislocations. Jude in this sense is outside his own predicament. He enjoys the irony of living in Mildew Lane; he announces his failure and celebrates it in a speech to the Christminster crowd. And if Father Time theatricalizes his superfluity by suicide, and Sue theatricalizes her theoretic unconventionality by mortifying the flesh, Jude, who may seem to take another decadent way out by getting drunk, goes further by reciting Job to an audience that cannot hear him, bent on cheering the festivities. More than this, however, that last section is not only Jude's theatre (ultimately the mirror theatre, opposed to the audience like La Mélinite), but Hardy's too: his farewell to the novel, that 'scientific game' whose organic realism his text despises. For here, in this last part of the last novel, his most offensive assaults on the reader's credulity, particularly the grotesque joke of Father Time's death, are made. The proletarian hero and the literary producer make an alliance to affirm their autonomy, but in order to do so take their place in a cultural struggle. For true autonomy, the completeness of dislocation, cannot rest content with an independence.

V

Hardy's novel offers a perspective on the whole situation of the writer in the late nineteenth century, and it also marks a point beyond which it would be necessary to make literary production revolutionary in more than an *analogous* way. That point is never moved beyond. Henley, Gray, Davidson and Symons all in their way shared Jude's obscurity and the best of their work stands opposed, as form of production, to the hegemony. But none of them cross the barrier reached in *Jude*—on the contrary, for all of them there is an expressive totality —Imperialism, Catholicism, vitalism, mysticism—in which to take refuge. More importantly, the journey from decadence to modernism is no road forward. On the contrary, the way out of literary production and its contradictory identity, is literature—the text for an ideological practice, education, the training of the agents of social control. Let me end by suggesting the way this happens in a seminal work such as Symons's book, *The Symbolist Movement in Literature*.

Most critics would agree that this text represents a radical development in Symons's work that can best be expressed by saying that he got to know Yeats.[29] It may be less acceptable to assert that this development represents more of a loss than a gain. 'The Decadent Movement in Literature' really has the sense of a movement, a sense of a new phase of consciousness embodied in various, but related forms. By the time 'Symbolism' has come to replace 'Decadence' as the comprehensive

[29] See the excellent essay by Richard Ellmann, 'Discovering Symbolism', *Golden Codgers* (1973), pp. 101-12. Reference to Symons's book is to the edition introduced by Ellmann (New York, 1958).

E

word, this sense of a movement, the change in the relations of literary production signalled by the word 'revolt', is dissolved in a vaguer assertion of continuity—all poetry is symbolic, symbolism is merely the self-consciousness of the symbol. The key concept is no longer revolt but 'ancient lights'. In 'The Autumn of the Body' (1898), Yeats had seen the decadence as a faint light on a transcendent world denied by positive science: it was in other words a seasonal return to an abstract spirituality. Symons hovers uneasily between this— which is affirmed by the overall argument, beginning as it does with Carlyle's organicist definitions of the symbol and reaching a climax with the essay on Maeterlinck with its blurring of the lines between symbolism and mysticism—and a residual grasp of the specific new movement. This latter feeling emerges, for example, in the realization of the cult of the actress and its implications in Nerval, of the strategic pose of aristocracy in Adam, of the function of travesty in Laforgue and above all of the programmatic and *logical* research of Mallarmé. All these points recognize the specific productive nature of Symbolism, whereas the presence of mysticism, the assertion of the eternal quality of symbolism, together with the sentimentalization of Verlaine (the poet as child) and the total failure to come to terms with Rimbaud, all these have to do not with the production of the symbol but with the realization of the symbolic as the sign of an expressive totality, 'the once terrifying eternity of things about us' (p. 95). Thus, in however bizarre a way, Symbolism becomes not a movement, but a Romantic continuity. Symons travels an inverse journey from Jude. Beginning with the recognition of the separation of the producer, the need for him to produce his own revolt, he comes to rest in the aesthetic image as vision: 'We find a new, an older sense in the so worn out forms of things' (p. 74). It is because Symbolism came to England not as the making of new forms, but as a new light on an organic, if occult, tradition that modernism could site itself within the ideology. We could pinpoint the whole issue by reminding ourselves that Symons has to write off Baudelaire, and when Eliot comes to embrace him it is merely as the ideologue of damnation.

Symbolist—symbolic; aesthetic—occult; autonomy—abstract spirituality. These are the terms of the transition, but they constitute a reversal—the dislocation becomes a relocation. Of course, such terms only locate an ambiguity. No one would want to claim, for example, that Yeats makes himself the scribe of a vision: on the contrary, he invents a vision to provide material for production. But ambiguity, irony, mask, if they make for an exposed margin, and enable us to treat modernist writers as secret agents in the enemy camp, also form part of the specific condition of the insertion of the writer in that camp. I have argued that aesthetic theory, which is above all a theory of production, is in contradiction with the ideology demanded by the market, an ideology necessarily of realization in which literary work becomes capital. But we must go further. With very few exceptions (the major instance is Bennett) there is no way back into the market for the writer, but there is a back road through the occult, an expressive totality which, however eccentric, can oppose itself to positivism (I think of Eliot and Bradley, Lawrence and Haeckel, Joyce and Aquinas as well as Yeats and Swedenborg), can become independent (because it is a thousand miles away from capitalism) but not autonomous (because like capitalist ideology it reflects the transcendent creation of value, whether through the Golden Dawn, tradition or the phallic consciousness). And this back road leads to the University which neither Jude nor Symons entered, and of which Pater, though he worked within it, saw the walls (see *Emerald Uthwart*). It makes possible, that is, literature at the point beyond which literary production must confront the terms of its possibility. Yeats's flirtation with Gentile is not a local event—it represents the claim of the writer on the hegemony to be housed within its institutions as an abstract spirituality whose coherence mirrors the mysteries of the capitalist state, opposed to science, to historical relativity, to, in the end, literary production. If we have to demystify literature, to rescue it from its role as realizable value, the constant capital of critical practice, we must begin by recognizing that it expelled itself from the market not, in the first instance, to enter the cloister, but to expose the market and its bases. The tragic generation lived, to be sure, in an age of transition, but that they lacked coherence is not their limitation but their very potentiality, for it is a transition, not to modernism, but to the new forms that wait to be made.

METHODOLOGICAL NOTE

This paper has been usefully criticized on two grounds, both of which relate to its apparent Althusserianism. I don't think I am an Althusserian, and though I borrow ideas both from Althusser and Macherey it is because I find them useful for specific purposes. This is not eclectic: the sources for a materialist account of literature are, I believe, Benjamin (and to some extent Brecht) and Gramsci. Althusser and Macherey seem to me to be elaborating a theology based largely on a system of analogies. But I think that to deny their contribution of usable vocabularies and unavoidable negations is foolish.

The first ground of criticism is of my use of the term 'production'. The point is made that I use the term in three different ways—as a concept of aesthetic theory, as a material fact (the production of books as commodities) and as a form of generalized social description (the mode of production which Jude encounters). The connections between these levels are not made clear. I hope I have improved the matter a little by deleting from my text any suggestion of a fourth use, 'ideological production'. This term seems to me to be entirely analogical: education and 'communication' are not 'productive' except peripherally though their forms are determined (in a highly complex way) by the demands of a mode of production (the need of a class domination, the need of managerial and bureaucratic supervision of developed phases, etc.). The literary text, however, is different. What differentiates a poet or a novelist from other types of intellectual is precisely that he makes an object which can be consumed. You can be an intellectual without producing a book: but a poem is not written until it is written, and does not function until it is readable. Therefore, although the connection between a Paterian sense of production and the actual production of commodities is difficult (that is precisely the subject of this essay), it has to be made. I wrote this essay precisely to find a concrete way of elaborating the problems of that connection. Furthermore, in any mode of production, except one in which there is no surplus, or possibly in which the surplus is consumed by the producers (this is not so impossible as it might appear), there will be many nonproductive people, and their social membership will be defined precisely by the manner of their non-productiveness, that is, their relations to the mode of production. Priests, professors and prostitutes, in Marx's phrase, are all consumers of an appropriated surplus, but if they had no function then they either would not exist, or their existence would not have to depend on their specific roles (they could simply be consumers). Writers belong to that category precisely by making certain objects which are seen to have a use value. The whole problem is historically specific, because it is not until the development of a literary market, in which the writer can insert himself into society as the producer of *commodities* (that is, use values that are distributed as exchanged values, that realize themselves ultimately as the universal value, money) that the literary text as a production, as the object of a determinate productive process, becomes truly visible. As Marx points out in *Theories of Surplus Value*, Milton produced *Paradise Lost* not really for £5 but as a silkworm 'produces' silk. But the form and tendency of that poem is not natural all the same: it is generated by the social situation of the writer who *works* at it. So there is a gap between the writer's activity (which resembles productive labour) and his effectivity (which lies outside the actual mode of production). As soon as the market becomes dominant, it is possible to make an equivalent between a writer and a piece of cheese: *The Corsair* equals *x* pounds of cheese in a way that, in its time, *Paradise Lost* does not equal it. Once you have the concept of the text as commodity, the question of its use value then becomes crucial since the gap opens up between use value (measurable by its necessary labour) and its exchange value. Baudelaire, Flaubert and Pater, among others, are so important because the problems they expose are not merely abstract. From them, any theory of literature which is not ideological has to begin. There is then every need to relate the theory of production to the actual relations of production within a social totality, the mode of production. The present essay only tries to get to the problematic that faces us. This problem is interestingly treated by Nicole Gueunier in 'La Production Littéraire: Métaphore, Concept ou Champ Problématique', in *Littérature* 13.

The second criticism was of my use of 'expressive totality'. It is argued that I merely oppose to this a negation: the break-up of totalities. Obviously this is partly the limitation of the decadent movement. But I am trying to argue that behind such an antithesis is an attempt to make a totality which is not expressive but effective. The expressive totalities opposed by decadent art the mystified systems that lie beyond it: but the displacing mirror of decadent art has itself as a total commitment, and in *Jude*, at least, tries to relate that commitment to the possibilities of a more advanced mode of production. I see the decadence as leading not to Dada or mere self-consciousness, but to the possibilities of proletarian art, Tatlin's dream and Brecht's theatre. This probably seems wayward, but I have the example of Benjamin, and Trotsky's attack on the Futurists ends with seeing it as 'a necessary link'.

Note

Editions of works cited or referred to:

Arnold Bennett, *A Man from the North* (first published 1898, re-printed 1973); Joseph Conrad, *Heart of Darkness* (1899); E. M. Forster, *Howards End* (1910); George Gissing, *New Grub Street* (first published 1891, re-printed 1968, ed. Bernard Bergonzi); *The Odd Women* (1893); George Moore, *A Modern Lover* (1883), *A Mummer's Wife* (1885), *A Drama in Muslin* (1886), *Modern Painting* (1898); Arthur Morrison, *A Child of the Jago* (1896, re-printed by Panther in 1971, ed. Peter Keating); Arthur Symons, *The Symbolist Movement in Literature* (1899, 1958); W. B. Yeats, *Autobiographies* (1955), *Essays and Introductions* (1961).

Relevant studies:

George J. Becker, ed. *Documents of Modern Literary Realism* (Princeton, 1963); Ernst Fischer, *The Necessity of Art* (Harmondsworth, 1963); Ian Fletcher, ed. *Romantic Mythologies* (1967); F. W. J. Hemmings, ed. *The Age of Realism* (Harmondsworth, 1974); David Howard, John Lucas and John Goode, *Tradition and Tolerance in 19th Century Fiction* (1966); Maurice Larkin, *Man and Society in Nineteenth Century Realism* 1977); A. G. Lehmann, *The Symbolist Aesthetic in France, 1885–1895* (Oxford, 1950); John Lucas, *Arnold Bennett: A Study of his Fiction* (1975); J. P. Stern, *On Realism* (1973); Roland N. Stromberg, ed. *Realism, Naturalism, and Symbolism* (1968); Philip Wheelwright, *The Burning Fountain: A Study in the Language of Symbolism* (Indiana, 1968).

VI

From Naturalism to Symbolism

JOHN LUCAS

I

NATURALISM came to England at the end of the nineteenth century. It flourished in a pallid sort of way for a few years, and was more or less dead by the turn of the century. In what follows I want to comment on these facts and also suggest why naturalism brought about the rise of the symbolist movement. I am not concerned with anything like an exhaustive account of the two: we have the documents and we have quite enough monographs to be going on with. The reader who wants to enquire more deeply into the nature and causes of naturalism and symbolism may be referred to—among others—Becker's *Documents of Modern Literary Realism*, Stromberg's *Realism, Naturalism and Symbolism*, Stern's *On Realism*, Powers's *Henry James and the Naturalist Movement*, and Lehmann's *Symbolist Aesthetic in France, 1885–1895*. In this brief essay I shall largely concern myself with four writers: George Moore and George Gissing, and Arthur Symons and W. B. Yeats.

We start, however, with a French novelist. Zola is the undisputed father of naturalism, and his preface to *Thérèse Raquin*, added to the second edition, 1868, is a key text for an understanding of the movement. Zola sets down there his ideas of the artist's role and responsibility:

> I had only one desire: given a highly-sexed man and an unsatisfied woman, to uncover the animal side of them and that alone, then throw them together in a violent drama and note down with scrupulous care the sensations and actions of these creatures. I simply applied to two living bodies the analytical method that surgeons apply to corpses. ... The human side of the models ceased to exist. ...

It is a highly contentious statement and one that begs a number of crucial questions. But it would be beside the point to quarrel with

Zola's account of his task. All that need concern us here is the serious-
ness with which he insists on dispassionate observation, and the fact
that this is bound to imply some crippling limitations (though it is
only fair to add that the limitations often don't apply to Zola himself,
simply because he is frequently more than a naturalistic writer). Once
you decide to see human beings or a social situation in the manner
which Zola describes, they become exotic, strange, and not fully known
at all. The naturalist programme is immensely ambitious: the novelist
acts as a kind of Baconian scientist, recording, reporting, listing. Yet
the end result of the enterprise is to make the whole add up to less than
the sum of the parts. It must be so. For the novelist who follows Zola
is reduced to working with the strictly contemporary, which at the
very least means not understanding, or not seeing as relevant or taking
account of, the complicated meshings in which human beings and
social situations gain their identity, and which have a great deal to do
with the past and perspectives onto the past. These matters are closed
to the naturalist writer since observation and reportage have to be of
the present. History shrinks to now.[1]

This is not to say that the naturalist programme has no concept of
history. It has one all right, but unfortunately it is a hopelessly reductive
one. Unwavering, gimlet-eyed scanning of the contemporary world
will reveal or find clues to the important truth that individuals are
determined by environment and circumstance. Whatever socio-economic process there may be indifferently condemns the vast majority of
human beings to lives of pointless suffering. These are the beliefs on
which a naturalist concept of history is built.

Naturalism: pessimism: determinism. The three terms go together
and between them they provide a defeatist, glumly pessimistic fiction
(optimistic naturalism is a contradiction in terms). The struggle for
survival, the reduction of a person to his elemental, 'animal' level,
success or failure depending on how well adaptation is made to given
circumstances: this is the very stuff of the naturalist novel, and its
terms spread wide. In William Hale White's *Revolution in Tanner's
Lane*, the hero, Zachariah Coleman, finds himself in the alien world
of Manchester:

These men treated him not as if he were a person, an individual soul,
but as an atom of a mass to be swept out anywhere, into the gutter—

[1] In his essay on Zola in *Studies in European Realism*, Lukacs shows how
Zola's 'reporting' inevitably limits his achievement, and at its worst makes
him anti-realistic.

into the river. He was staggered for a time. Hundreds and thousands
of human beings swarmed past him, and he could not help saying
to himself as he looked up at the grey sky, 'Is it true then? Does God
really know anything about me? Are we not born by the million
every week, like spawn, and crushed out of existence like spawn?'
(ch. IX)

Zachariah does not finally lose his dissenting faith(this part of the novel
is after all set in the early years of the nineteenth century). But Hale
White was writing in the 1880s and the language of atoms and spawn
has much more to do with that decade than with any earlier one.

Grant the possibility of being crushed out of existence, like spawn,
and you are faced with an account of the historical-social process
which invites you to set aside all moral considerations in the interests
of survival. One of the most rigorous expressions of this in English
fiction is to be found in Gissing's *New Grub Street*. Characters may be
presented as apparently bad in a conventional sense (to call someone
Jasper is certainly to invite your reader to think badly of him), yet
moral judgement is warded off, or made irrelevant. Consider the
account of Mrs Edmund Yule:

> She kept only two servants, who were so ill paid and so relent-
> lessly overworked that it was seldom they remained with her for
> more than three months. In dealing with other people whom she
> perforce employed she was often guilty of incredible meanness; as,
> for instance, when she obliged her half-starved dressmaker to pur-
> chase material for her, and then postponed payment alike for that
> and for the work itself to the last possible moment. This was not
> heartlessness in the strict sense of the word; the woman not only
> knew that her behaviour was shameful, she was in truth ashamed of
> it and sorry for her victims. But life was a battle. She must either
> crush or be crushed. . . .
> But whilst she could be a positive hyena to strangers, to those
> who were akin to her, and those of whom she was fond, her affec-
> tionate kindness was remarkable. One observes this peculiarity
> often enough; it reminds one how savage the social conflict is, in
> which these little groups of people stand serried against their
> common enemies, relentless to all others, among themselves only
> the more tender and zealous because of the ever-impending danger.
> (ch. 18)

At first glance it might look as though Gissing is being ironical: Mrs
Yule's defence of herself—crush or be crushed—could be mere
sophistry. But Gissing's own underlining of the savagery of the social

conflict makes it plain that as far as he is concerned Mrs Yule isn't to be condemned as a moral hypocrite. And her struggles to survive are matched by others in this grim novel of London life in which the ultimate winners are those who fight meanest, understanding the need to do so, and having the right kind of toughness for the battle.

Yet here it is important to note that a particular kind of complacency underlies Gissing's bleak account of contemporary life, and I think it is one that inevitably belongs to the naturalistic movement. It surfaces in an early description of Mrs Yule:

> Mrs Yule's speech was seldom ungrammatical, and her intonation was not flagrantly vulgar, but the accent of the London poor, which brands as with hereditary baseness, still clung to her words, rendering futile such propriety of phrase as she owed to years of association with educated people. In the same degree did her bearing fall short of that which distinguishes a lady. The London work-girl is rarely capable of raising herself, or being raised, to a place in life above that to which she was born; she cannot learn to stand and sit and move like a woman bred to refinement, any more than she can fashion her tongue to graceful speech.
>
> (ch. 7)

One notes here the entirely spurious use of terms derived from evolutionary biology, as though to suggest that class is immutable and that refinement is more than the name for a blood sport of arbitrarily framed rules. ('We see Blood in a nose, and we say "There it is! That's Blood!" It is an actual matter of fact. We point it out. It admits of no doubt. 'But Dickens's wonderful satire didn't kill the sport off.)

The naturalistic writer in England relies heavily on assertions about 'types', as though he is providing scientifically exact observations. We may place beside the passage from Gissing one from Moore's *A Mummer's Wife*:

> The hearts of the people change but little—if at all. When rude work and misery does not grind and trample all feelings out of them, they remain for ever children in their sentiments, understanding only such simple emotions as correspond to their daily food . . . in the woman of the people there is no intellectual advancement; she never learns to judge, to discriminate. . . .
>
> (ch. 8)

There are similar passages scattered about Moore's 'Realistic' trilogy (the term is his own choice).

Moore and Gissing are without doubt the most important naturalistic writers in England. Frank Swinnerton remarks that they 'alone, or almost alone were trying in the published novel to tell the world something about life at first hand'; and he considers that the success of their efforts was such that they gave rise 'towards the end of the nineties, to a new school of naturalistic writers'. Yet Swinnerton later calls this school 'a vogue for tales of mean streets', in which the 'very poor [were used] as literary material'.[2] That gives the game away with a vengeance. To speak of a movement as a vogue is to imply that in the final reckoning it simply isn't authentic. And in one respect at least Moore and Gissing are every bit as vogue-ish as their imitators. They work from stock assumptions which are hardly ever put to the test, and this is especially true for what they have to say about class.

This brings us to a crucial point, The naturalist differs absolutely from the realist in believing that class is somehow a given fact of—well, of nature. People *naturally* belong to one class or another. It's a matter of genes, or blood, of evolved characteristics: of anything but money. The possibilities of class mobility are therefore outlawed. You find your natural place, and you stay there (the exceptions only serve to prove the rule). In which case the very poor can be treated merely as literary material. And of course it is material which illustrates the naturalistic writer's proper pessimism. Or so it is assumed. The poor are doomed to suffer and there is nothing much that anyone can do about it. It's the way, not of the world, but of nature. When Gissing remarks that the accent of the London poor still clings to Mrs Yule's words, 'rendering futile such propriety of phrase as she owed to years of association with educated people', he doesn't simply mean that those educated people recognize that she is no lady, but that she is doomed to eventual defeat, that she'll go under. For in the world of Gissing's novels if someone isn't capable of raising herself, or being raised, to a place in life above that to which she was born then she must fall into the limbo world of the scarcely human. (And of course such raising is finally impossible. Mutimer in *Demos* cannot sustain his marriage with the gentle Adela because he is too near the condition of beast.)[3] In the struggle for survival 'the people' and the 'London poor' will always lose.

[2] Swinnerton, *The Georgian Literary Scene* (1938), pp. 132–3, 152. Arthur Morrison's *Tales of Mean Streets* was first published in 1894.

[3] For fuller account of this, see my essay on 'Conservatism and Revolution in the 1880s' in *Literature and Politics in the Nineteenth Century*, ed. J. Lucas (1971).

II

London is very important. By the 1880s it had become the City of
Dreadful Night, grinding out 'death and life and good and ill; / It has
no purpose, heart or mind or will'. (Thomson's poem was first published in 1878.) The city is an appalling, oppressive fact of modern life,
an uncontrollable growth which feeds on millions and to whom all
but the strongest are thrown as victims. In *Mark Rutherford's Deliverance*
(1885), Mark and his journalist friend, M'Kay, try to relieve the
meaningless lives of people who exist in and around Drury Lane. But
it is a hopeless task, and Mark reflects that:

> To stand face to face with the insoluble is not pleasant. A man will
> do anything rather than confess it is beyond him. He will create
> pleasant fictions, and fancy a possible escape here and there, but this
> problem of Drury Lane was round and hard like a ball of adamant.
> The only thing I could do was faintly, as I was about to say, stupidly
> hope—for I had no rational, tangible grounds for hoping—that
> some force of which we are now not aware might someday develop
> itself which will be able to resist and remove the pressure which
> sweeps and crushes into hell, sealed from the upper air, millions of
> human souls every year in one quarter of the globe alone.
>
> (ch. V)

Hale White is not a naturalist novelist, but he is writing at the same
time as Gissing and Moore, and his feelings about London are shared
by Gissing at least. Hopelessness is the keynote; and it is echoed by
Arthur Symons, walking along the Edgware road in the 1890s,
wondering at the people he passes, wondering:

> why these people exist, why they take the trouble to go on existing.
> As I passed through the Saturday night crowd lately, between
> two opposing currents of evil smells, I overheard a man who was
> lurching along the pavement say in a contemptuous comment:
> 'Twelve o'clock: we may all be dead by twelve o'clock.' He seemed
> to sum up the philosophy of that crowd, its listlessness, its hard
> unconcern, its failure to be interested. Nothing matters, he seemed
> to say for them; let us drag out our time until the time is over,
> and the sooner it is over the better.[4]

London is the fact and the type of what existence means in the last
decades of the nineteenth century. Its growth, size, complexity, all

[4] Arthur Symons, *London: A Book of Aspects* (1909), p. 66. The passage was
written in the 1890s. I owe my discovery of it to Martin Wood's as yet un-
published thesis on *Darwinism and Pessimism in Late-Victorian Life and Literature*.

indicate that the majority of men are unable to control their own fates. Individuals triumph, but at the expense of shared humanity. This is undoubtedly the view that Gissing takes from *Demos* onwards, and it marks something of a departure from the argument put forward in the 'Hope of Pessimism', an essay which he had written in 1882. There, he had presented the struggle for survival as an unacceptable concept with which to identify, a fact to be resisted. He imagines its champion claiming that:

> the competitive system, depend on it, is the grandest outcome of civilization. It makes us robust and self-reliant: we expect no mercy in the battle, and accordingly give no quarter; the strong man will make his way; for the weak are there not workhouses and prisons? We are a growing population; our great problem is, how to make the food of two keep three alive; it is patent that we cannot stand upon ceremony, must e'en push our best to get us a place at the board. Does not science—the very newest—assure us that only the fittest shall survive? If we tread upon a feeble competitor and have the misfortune to crush the life out of him, we are merely illustrating the law of natural selection. A man must live we suppose?

To which rhetorical question Gissing returns the answer, but not by bread alone. And he asks us to give our approval to the pessimist, the man whose habit of life is the conquest of instinct. 'Life is no longer good to him; he is a Pessimist. And this is the final triumph of mind, the highest reach of human morality, the only hope of the destruction of egotism.'[5]

Variations of this form of pessimism abound in the literature of the period, but what matters to us is the fact that by the time Gissing came to write *The Odd Women* and *New Grub Street* he had more or less abandoned it. Instead, he creates his heroes out of those who are determined to save themselves. Admittedly, he preserves an ambiguity of tone towards those heroes: there is a saving irony in the way in which he writes about Rhoda Nunn and Jasper Milvain. But it is a protective irony. What else could they do? It isn't *their* fault if triumphant survival requires unscrupulous behaviour. Pessimism is now directed at history—history according to a naturalistic reading, that is. The individual or small group of individuals is pitted against society at large, 'the common enemy'. If you belong to the middle-class, so much

---

[5] George Gissing, *Essays and Fiction*, ed. Coustillas (1970), pp. 90–1.

the better for you. You have more chance of surviving, not because of economic factors, but because nature has created certain breeds to be middle-class and hence more likely to succeed (economic advantage is the effect, not the cause). In *The Odd Women*, Rhoda and Miss Barfoot are quite clear that their status as middle-class women gives them an advantage they would be fools to throw away. Which means that they feel contempt for weaker—lower-class—women who cannot find ways to survive. In *New Grub Street* Reardon and Biffin throw away their advantages and so inevitably go down.

I realize that this may look like the grossest parody of Gissing's position, and yet it is not really unfair to him. For Gissing is in the tradition of nineteenth-century English thought whose typical expression is melioristic humanism; only for him the tradition has turned sour. The humanism I have in mind had found its most eloquent expression in positivistic ideology, with its idea of historical progress from which any serious possibility of conflict has been excluded, and its thoroughly decent but mistaken insistence on the doctrine of altruism. (Gissing's hope for pessimism is a last despairing flare-up of the doctrine.) As all commentators have recognized, positivism and liberalism run parallel courses in the nineteenth century, so far at least as their theories of history go. In both cases progress is seen as fundamentally evolutionary and unilinear; it is not to be marred by radical upheaval or conflict, and it will promote the general good of humanity. But by the late 1880s matters seemed not to be working out that way. The result was that as it became increasingly apparent that progress didn't guarantee an improvement in the general good, positivism ceased to be a vital force in British thought.[6] The hope for altruism passed into its opposite: a belief in the necessity or inevitability of egotism. George Eliot had been sustained by her belief that history steadily unfolded possibilities, realized promises and potentialities. A later generation of writers took over her belief in history as an unfolding, but they saw no promise in it. Pessimism replaces optimism, ardour gives way to cynicism: realism turns into naturalism.

In 1896 John Jacobs noted that:

It is difficult for those who have not lived through it to understand the influence that George Eliot had upon those of us who came to our

[6] As far as I know, W. H. Mallock was the only man of opinion to think that Positivism was still alive and well and to be attacked in the 1890s. In 1895 he published a volume of essays, *Studies of Contemporary Superstition*, an attack on Positivistic ideas.

intellectual majority in the seventies. Darwinism was in the air, and promised, in the suave accents of Professor Huxley and in the more strident voice of Professor Clifford, to solve all the problems of humanity. George Eliot's novels were regarded by us not so much as novels, but rather as applications of Darwinism to life and art. They were to us *Tendenz-Romane*, and we studied them as much for the *Tendenz* as for the *Roman*. Nowadays . . . their *Tendenz* is discredited. . . .[7]

Jacobs's remarks hint at the fact that by the 1890s the typical 'applications of Darwinism to life and art' were in no sense offering to solve all the problems of humanity. It is the opposite. Only the most cynical solutions were on offer. Survival is for the few. For the rest: 'Let us drag out our time until the time is over, and the sooner it is over the better.' This is the essence of English naturalism.

III

Four years after Jacobs's regretful account of the discrediting of melioristic humanism, W. B. Yeats asked himself, 'How can the arts overcome the slow dying of men's hearts that we call the progress of the world, and lay their hands upon men's heart-strings again, without becoming the garment of religion as in the old times?'[8] Yeats is the greatest spokesman for the symbolist movement in English literature as it developed at the end of the nineteenth century, just as he is its greatest (some would say only) practitioner; and it is no accident that he should set symbolism up as the supreme antagonist of naturalism. 'The scientific movement', he wrote in the essay from which I have already quoted, 'brought with it a literature which was always tending to lose itself in externalities of all kinds, in opinion, in declamation, in picturesque writing, in word-painting, or in what Mr Symons has called an attempt "to build in brick and mortar inside the covers of a book".'[9] Symons may well have derived his figure from a memory of Clough's famous championing of high-Victorian novels as ones that give us 'a real house to be lived in'; but Yeats's grandly vague reference to the 'scientific movement' serves to remind us that Symons's

[7] *Jewish Ideals and Other Essays*, quoted by V. Cunningham, *Everywhere Spoken Against: Dissent in the Victorian Novel* (1976), p. 281.

[8] 'The Symbolism of Poetry', in *Essays and Introductions* (New York, 1968), pp. 162–3.

[9] *Ibid.*, p. 155.

remark was directed at Zola himself,[10] and that both men were on the attack against the naturalism of their own day.

Yeats sets his face against an art which deals in 'externalities'. It is more than probable that when he used the word he was recalling George Moore's *A Modern Lover*, in which the art we are asked to approve of is concerned with the painting of 'housemaids in print dresses, leaning out of windows, or bar girls serving drinks to beery-looking clerks'. On the studio walls of one of the approved artists are canvases filled 'not with the softness of ancient, but with the crudities of modern life' (*A Modern Lover*, ch. 7).[11] Yeats hated such art. 'I was in all things a Pre-Raphaelite,' he famously remarked, and he mourned his father's readiness to take up the cause and practice of realist painting,

> its defence elaborated by young men fresh from the Paris art schools. 'We must paint what is in front of us,' or 'A man must be of his own time,' they would say, and if I spoke of Blake or Rossetti they would point out his bad drawing and tell me to admire Carolus Duran or Bastien-Lepage.[12]

It was precisely this art for which Moore had beaten the drums in *A Modern Lover*: an art 'of truth, unpopular and created by men of integrity'.[13] But Yeats would have none of it, and by the 1890s Moore had also withdrawn his approval. Indeed, in an essay called 'Our Academicians', he does a complete about-turn and belabours the very art which he had earlier both championed and professed. In this extraordinary performance he picks out 'Mr Stanhope Forbes, the last elected Academician, and the most prominent exponent of the art of Bastien-Lepage', for particular criticism. According to Moore, Stanhope Forbes 'continues at the point where Bastien-Lepage began to curtail, deform, and degrade the original inspiration'. And then he goes on:

> Mr Stanhope Forbes copied the trousers seam by seam, patch by patch; and the ugliness of the garment bores you in the picture,

[10] The phrase comes from the introduction to Symons's *The Symbolist Movement in Literature*, published in 1899 and dedicated to Yeats, who 'will sympathize with what I say in it, being yourself the chief representative of that movement in our country'.

[11] For a fuller discussion of this and the other novels in the trilogy see my *Arnold Bennett: A Study of his Fiction* (1975), pp. 31–40.

[12] *Autobiographies* (1955), p. 115.

[13] Milton Chaikin, 'George Moore's Early Fiction' in *George Moore's Mind and Art*, ed. Graham Owens (1968), p. 26.

exactly as it would in nature. . . . A handful of dry facts instead of a passionate impression of life in the envelope of mystery and suggestion.

Realism, that is to say, the desire to compete with nature, to be nature, is the disease from which art has suffered most in the last twenty years. . . . Until I saw Mr Clausen's 'Labourers' I did not fully realize how terrible a thing art becomes when divorced from beauty, grace, mystery, and suggestion. . . .

Mr Clausen has seen nothing but the sordid and the mean, and his execution in this picture is as sordid and as mean as is his mission. . . . Mr Clausen seems to have said, 'I will go lower than the others; I will seek my art in the mean and the meaningless.' But notwithstanding his very real talent, Mr Clausen has not found art where art is not, where art never has been found, where art never will be found. . . .

The mission of art is not truth, but beauty. . . .[14]

As the language of that passage sufficiently reveals, Pater has replaced Zola as Moore's lawgiver. In Chaikin's words, 'It was Pater who convinced Moore that repose and evenness were in tune with his genius rather than the dynamism of Zola . . . and that it served the cause of Art better to wander in the flowered field than to roll in the mud. Naturalism was putrid; Zola was vulgar; and it came to him that the artist preferred the refined to the vulgar.'[15] It is worth noting that after his conversion Moore used the word 'externality', as did Yeats and Symons, to define and damn naturalism. For example in an essay on Turgenev, written in 1888 and collected in *Impressions and Opinions* (1891), Moore complained that Zola 'was too much concerned with the externalities of life.'[16]

I cannot take Moore's conversion very seriously—he seems to me nothing if not unserious—but it least it shows that symbolism is the reverse side of the coin from naturalism. Moore trivializes the matter by setting 'truth' and 'beauty' in opposition, but his sudden and spectacular rejection of the naturalistic mode offers at least initial comparison with Yeats's much more serious criticism of *A Doll's House*. 'I was divided in mind, I hated the play; what was it but Carolus Duran, Bastien-Lepage, Huxley and Tyndall all over again? I resented being invited to admire dialogue so close to modern educated speech that

[14] *Modern Painting* (1898), pp. 116–19. [15] Chaikin, *op. cit.*, p. 26.
[16] Chaikin, *ibid.*, p. 26. cf. Yeats's complaint against literature which 'was always tending to lose itself in externalities of all kinds'. Behind both statements is Pater's phrase about 'the flood of external objects'.

music and style were impossible.'[17] Yeats's concern with music and style may be linked to some remarks of Symons's in his Introduction to the *Symbolist Movement in Literature* (who knows but that they came from Yeats?):

> after the world has starved its soul long enough in the contemplation and the re-arrangement of material things, comes the turn of the soul; and with it comes the literature of which I write in this volume, a literature in which the visible world is no longer a reality and the unseen world no longer a dream.

For in the art of the symbolist may be found:

> an attempt to spiritualize literature, to evade the old bondage of rhetoric, the old bondage of exteriority. Description is banished that beautiful things may be evoked, magically. ... Mystery is no longer feared. ... We are coming closer to nature, as we seem to shrink from it with something of horror, disdaining to catalogue the trees of the forest. And as we brush aside the accidents of daily life, in which men and women imagine that they are alone touching reality, we come closer to humanity, to everything in humanity that may have begun before the world and may outlast it.

As I imagine is clear from these passages, Symons's language owes a good deal to Pater, but it would be quite wrong to think that he is therefore championing a literature of escapism—such as Pater may well look to be championing at the end of *The Renaissance.* On the contrary: Symons makes no break between 'truth' and 'beauty'. But he does insist that the more true-to-fact art is the less truthful it becomes, because it is then less able to penetrate beneath accident and casual phenomena ('exteriority') to the 'essence' or 'soul' (favourite words of his and of Yeats).

The point needs some stressing, I think, because we may otherwise be tempted to dismiss Yeats's concern with 'music and style' as mere sterile aestheticism. This is not to deny that the concern can and does sometimes lead in that direction, as Yeats's own early verse amply reveals. But there is a good deal more to it than just that. We need to recall and to take seriously Yeats's insistence that the arts should be 'the garments of religion' and to link the phrase with a famous and crucial pasage in the *Autobiographies* where he remarks that:

> I was unlike others of my generation in one thing only. I am very religious, and deprived by Huxley and Tyndall, whom I detested, of

[17] *Autobiographies*, p. 279.

the simple-minded religion of my childhood, I had made a new religion, almost an infallible Church of poetic tradition.... I wished for a world where I could discover this tradition perpetually....[18]

He is properly wry about this youthful attempt to overthrow the dominant presence of the 'scientific movement'; but there can be no doubt that in this passage we have the seeds of Yeats's deep and abiding concern with symbolism. For he sees in symbolism a way of reading the universe that will discover permanences and, by extension, purpose and design. It provides for an unfailing recognition of mysteries that once again bring alive the possibility of religious faith. This is made absolutely clear in his note on 'The Body of the Father Christian Rosencrux', written in 1895, and published in *Ideas of Good and Evil*:

I cannot get it out of my mind that this age of criticism is about to pass, and an age of imagination, of emotion, of moods, of revelation, is about to come in its place; for certainly belief in a supersensual world is at hand again; and when the notion that we are 'phantoms of the earth and water' has gone down the wind, we will trust our own being and all it desires to invent; and when the external world is no more the standard of reality, we will learn again that the great passions are angels of God, and that to embody them 'uncurbed in their eternal glory', even in their labour for the ending of man's peace and prosperity, is more than to comment, however wisely, upon the tendencies of our time, or to express the socialistic, or humanitarian, or other forces of our time, or even 'to sum up' our time, as the phrase is; for art is a revelation, and not a criticism....[19]

Such a passage makes plain the reasons for Yeats's hatred of naturalism. Naturalism, dwelling on the surface of things, is anti-visionary, whereas for Yeats the true function of art is to be visionary. The externalities of the world are to be rejected. They spread a thick crust of accidentals which prevent the artist from seeing into the underlying structure of things. Of course naturalism has its own structure of things: the scientific movement means progress of a kind, means reducing human beings to jostling atoms in an unending fight for survival. But Yeats fiercely rejects the adequacy of such a structure, for 'I am deeply religious'. It will take him a lifetime's effort fully to develop his own reading of the universe—*A Vision* is its most elaborate expression— but already, in the 1890s, he finds it natural to identify with such

[18] *Autobiographies*, pp. 115–16.   [19] *Essays and Introductions*, p. 197.

system builders as Blake and Shelley, and he writes magnificently of both. What he says of Blake in particular applies to himself. 'He was a symbolist who had to invent his symbols. . . . He was a man crying out for a mythology, and trying to make one because he could not find one to his hand.'[20]

Yeats's genuinely religious temperament explains his need to create his own mythology. It also explains why he found it impossible to take socialism seriously. He flirted with it, largely because he fell under the influence of Morris's writings, but he soon abandoned it. He attended a number of meetings at which Morris was in the chair (presumably they were meetings of the Socialist League), but:

> gradually the attitude towards religion of almost everybody but Morris, who avoided the subject altogether, got upon my nerves, for I broke out after some lecture or other with all the arrogance of raging youth. They attacked religion, I said, or some such words, and yet there must be a change of heart and only religion could make it. What was the use of talking about some new revolution putting all things right, when the change must come, if come it did, with astronomical slowness, like the cooling of the sun, or it may have been like the drying of the moon? Morris rang his chairman's bell, but I was too angry to listen, and he had to ring it a second time before I sat down. . . . I never returned after that night. . . .[21]

It is hardly surprising. For a symbolist reading of history can have little in common with a socialist one. Yeats's own version was not of course fully elaborated at this time, though both its inevitable assertiveness and its necessary indifference to fact are implied in his claim that 'certainly belief in a supersensual world is at hand again'. But the point to make is that Yeats the symbolist is at one with Gissing the naturalist in rejecting a socialist interpretation of history. For both a 'change of heart', either through a realized pessimism or acceptance of belief, will accomplish social change. Nothing else will do. In the 'Trembling of the Veil' Yeats asked rhetorically, 'Had not Europe shared one mind and heart, until both mind and heart began to break into fragments a little before Shakespeare's birth?'[22] The mission of the true artist is to restore the fragments to a condition of wholeness (at least among his own people).

[20] *Essays and Introductions*, p. 114.   [21] *Autobiographies*, pp. 148–9.
[22] *Ibid.*, p. 191.

IV

The symbolist says that art cannot be 'criticism'. The naturalist agrees. The naturalist writer is, after all, necessarily debarred from doing anything other than record the facts: he has to tell it as it is, or as the Marxist critic, Ernst Fischer, puts it:

> Naturalism revealed the fragmentation, the ugliness, the surface filth of the capitalist bourgeois world, but it could not go further and deeper to recognize those forces which were preparing to destroy that world and establish socialism.
> That is why the naturalistic writer, unable to see beyond the patchwork shoddiness of the bourgeois world, was bound—unless he moved towards socialism—to embrace symbolism and mysticism, to fall victim to his desire to discover the mysterious whole, the meaning of life, behind and beyond social realities.[23]

I do not know what writers, if any, Fischer may have had in mind when he came to write that passage. But Moore obviously fits the case and Fischer could point to Yeats as an example of the writer whose hatred of naturalism led him 'to embrace symbolism and mysticism'.

One can hardly think of naturalism as a powerful literary moment in England, and as I have said by 1900 it was more or less a spent force. The only novels that we can reasonably put beside those of Moore and Gissing already mentioned are Arthur Morrison's *A Child of the Jago* (1896) and Bennett's *A Man from the North* (1898).[24] In both novels London is presented to us in terms that strictly echo Gissing's fiction: it is vast, menacing, indifferent to the lives it feeds on. Indeed, as Peter Keating has pointed out in his introduction to *A Child of the Jago*, Morrison was to endorse a proposal by the Rev. A. Osborne Jay 'for the establishment of Penal Settlements which would solve the problem of heredity by wiping out the entire strain [of Jago Rats]'. Keating comments:

> At first it seems incredible that so humane a man as Jay could advocate building Penal Settlements in isolated parts of the country where the inmates would be well treated but 'actually sentenced to remain there for life, and will not under any conceivable circumstances be allowed to propagate their species and so perpetuate their

---

[23] *The Necessity of Art* (Harmondsworth, 1963), p. 80.
[24] Maugham's *Liza of Lambeth* is not so much a genuine naturalistic novel as one that 'took its place in the fashion' in Swinnerton's apt phrase (*The Georgian Literary Scene*, p. 153).

type'. But the seemingly contradictory mixture of profound humanity and unbelievable inhumanity or stupidity, was a common characteristic of many late-Victorian slum workers; an ambivalence created by their fear of failing at the vast work of character trans- formation they had eagerly undertaken.[25]

Keating has put his finger on a crucial matter, but without properly understanding its cause. For it is surely the fact that a naturalistic writer, such as Morrison, comes up against a hopeless contradiction: if he is right about society, then only the exceptional individual escapes from the abyss, that nether world in which the 'very poor' and the 'people' dwell? Morrison shares with Gissing and Moore a complacent assertiveness about the immutability of class. And since that is so he, too, has to rule out 'character transformation' or a 'change of heart' on any large scale.

Now in writing his novel Morrison relied heavily on Jay's *Life in Darkest London* (1891). Jay had concentrated his attention on the Old Nichol, one of the worst London slums (Morrison's Jago); and the sardonic title of his work alerts us to the fact that he sees London as containing life at jungle level: nature red in tooth and claw. And it may also perhaps remind us that *Heart of Darkness*, written some eight years later, is about London, at least in part. As Conrad's story opens we are on board a cruising yawl, at anchor in the Thames. It is even- ing and our narrator tells us that:

> the air was dark above Gravesend, and farther back still seemed condensed into a mournful gloom, brooding motionless over the biggest, and the greatest, town on earth.

The sun finally sinks, and as it does so the narrator fancies that it is about to go out, 'stricken to death by the touch of that gloom brooding over a crowd of men'. And then Marlow speaks. ' "And this also," said Marlow suddenly, "has been one of the dark places of the earth." ' Has been? Still is.

Heart of Darkness is a symbolist tale. It uses language as a way of evok- ing terrible and final truths that lie somewhere beneath the surface of things. (The word 'dark' in particular threads through its pages, con- necting London and Africa, past and present.) For Conrad as for Morrison there can be no large-scale 'character transformation', but in Conrad's case pessimism is not confined to a single class of men. It applies to all. The heart of man is dark.

[25] *A Child of the Jago*, ed. P. J. Keating (1971), p. 21.

Most commentators have felt that there is something evasive in Conrad's persistent use of this word. It is as though he is about to deliver some final truth, but cannot or will not do so. I share the feeling, but am surprised that nobody—to my knowledge—has suggested that the explanation for Conrad's evasiveness can be traced to the same source as the naturalistic pessimism which saw London as a place of final darkness. History is reduced to a set of timeless absolutes —'the horror, the horror'—freed from any sense of complex actuality and presented with the symbolist's characteristic concern for evocation rather than argument. Conrad's reading of history is as absolute as Yeats's.

It was left to Forster to lighten the darkness by showing London as grey. The London of *Howards End* spreads uncontrollably and with no concern for individual lives:

> bricks and mortar rising and falling with the restlessness of the water in a fountain, as the city receives more and more men upon her soil. Camelia Road would soon stand like a fortress, and command, for a little, an extensive view. Only for a little. Plans were out for the erection of flats in Magnolia Road also. And again a few years, and all the flats in either road might be pulled down, and new buildings, of a vastness at present unimaginable, might arise where they had fallen.
>
> (ch. 6)

Leonard Bast belongs to this world, just. He is poised perilously above the abyss, knowing of people who had 'dropped in, and counted no more'. Above him are the Schlegels, 'still swimming gracefully on the grey tides of London'. Forster comments:

> To speak against London is no longer fashionable. . . . Certainly London fascinates. One visualizes it as a tract of quivering grey, intelligent without purpose, and excitable without love; as a spirit that has altered before it can be chronicled; as a heart that certainly beats, but with no pulsation of humanity.
>
> (ch. 13)

Forster clearly knows all about late-Victorian attitudes to London— he could hardly not have known. But, decent-minded and liberal by persuasion, he cannot bring himself to see it as a heart of darkness, or as providing the raw material for a blackly apocalyptic reading of history. Grey, yes it is grey all right; and at the end of the novel its advancing tide is moving steadily nearer to Howards End itself. Yet the

Note

Eleonora Duse (1858–1924) toured throughout Europe and America, visiting London in 1893, 1894, 1895, 1900, 1903, 1905 and 1923. Her performances were extensively reviewed in the papers—a good early example is *The Pall Mall Gazette* of June and July 1895.

Between 1895 and 1904 she was deeply involved with the Italian poet Gabriele d'Annunzio and there are innumerable joint biographies, many of them little more than exercises in hagiography. Among the better known books are: Jeanne Bordeaux, *Eleonora Duse. The Story of her Life* (1924), E. A. Rheinhardt, *The Life of Eleonora Duse* (1928, trans. 1930), Betita Harding, *Age Cannot Wither* (1947), Francis Winwar, *Wingless Victory* (1956), Eva Le Gallienne, *The Mystic in the Theatre* (1966), Jean Stubbs, *Passing Star* (1970). Two books by Olga Signorelli can be recommended: *Eleonora Duse* (trans. 1959), a splendid picture-book, and *Vita di Eleonora Duse* (1962); as can Henry Knepler, *The Gilded Stage* (1968). The latest biography of d'Annunzio is by Phillipe Jullian (1971, trans. 1972).

The sensational Paris season of 1897 is most usefully surveyed by Victor Mapes in *Duse and the French* (1898, reissued 1969), who makes extensive use of the doyen of French critics, Francisque Sarcey. Among other important French critics there are Jules Lemaître in *Revue des Deux Mondes* (July 1897, repr. *Impressions de théâtre* X, 1898) and Gustave Larroumet, *Nouvelles études d'histoire et de critiques dramatiques* (1899).

Typical descriptions of Duse can be found in Willa Cather, *The Kingdom of Art. 1893–1896* (1966) and *The World and the Parish. I. 1893–1902* (1970); in Anon., *Anonymous 1871–1935* (1936); in James Huneker, *Iconoclasts* (1906). Hugo von Hofmannsthal's essay on Duse is in *Selected Essays*, ed. Mary E. Gilbert (1955), and is referred to by Michael Hamburger in 'Art as Second Nature', *Romantic Mythologies*, ed. Ian Fletcher (1967). Interesting late commentary is provided by the film director Rouben Mamoulian (*Theatre Arts*, September 1957) and by Luigi Pirandello (*Theatre Arts*, December 1954, repr. *The Theory of the Modern Stage*, ed. Eric Bentley, 1968).

In 1926 Arthur Symons collected his essays on Duse together with some other material into a single volume, *Eleonora Duse* (reissued 1969)—but where possible reference is given to their first book publication.

The seminal discussion of the image of the dancer is Frank Kermode, *Romantic Image* and 'Poet and Dancer before Diaghilev' in *Puzzles and Epiphanies* (1962, repr. *Modern Essays*, 1971).

The Legend of Duse

JOHN STOKES

DECADENT THEATRE

To fix the last fine shade, the quintessence of things; to fix it fleetingly; to be a disembodied voice, and yet the voice of a human
soul. . . .

This famous definition of the Decadent ideal, from Arthur Symons's
'The Decadent Movement in Literature' (1893),[1] was of course composed to suit its moment. But in an article which served a double
purpose—to propose 'Decadence' as a literary term subsuming both
'Impressionism' and 'Symbolism', and to introduce the latest wave of
French Symbolists and link them with Walter Pater and his English
followers—Symons left the role of the Decadent largely hypothetical.
His prototype was Des Esseintes: 'the effeminate, over-civilized,
deliberately abnormal creature who is the last product of our society:
partly the father, partly the offspring of the perverse art that he adores.'
Exhausted after his debauches, the imaginative explorations of his
artificial paradise, Des Esseintes, Symons tells us, 'is left (as we close the
book) with a brief, doubtful choice before him—madness or death, or
else a return to nature, to the normal life'.[2] Symons's characteristic
unwillingness to distinguish between cause and effect (as between
nature and society) would have serious repercussions, especially in the
light of subsequent developments—though these he could hardly
have anticipated. The Paterian paradox, 'to be a disembodied voice,
and yet the voice of human soul', while responsive to the efforts of
the Symbolist poet and the prose stylist, was to become an intolerable
ideal, a contradiction even, once the Decadent was given the opportunity of assuming a public presence, an identifiable and vocal personality.

---

[1] *Harper's Magazine* (November).
[2] Symons is here presumably modifying Barbey d'Aurevilly's famous
comment that after writing *A Rebours* Huysmans would have to chooes
between 'the muzzle of a pistol and the foot of the Cross'.

That prominence was no sooner reached than it was made untenable: by the scandals surrounding the publication of Nordau's *Degeneration* and Hardy's *Jude*, by the competing allegiances of feminism, Ibsenism and Socialism, above all by the Wilde trial. By the late nineties a wider acquaintance with Nietzsche, and Symons's own elevation of Symbolism to an all-embracing category of literature, replacing the earlier function that he had attributed to Decadence, made it clear that a moment had passed, along with the opportunity for a literary tactic that, however precarious and insubstantial, had had its rationale.

So long as he had stayed poised at a tangent to the official culture, the Decadent artist could claim to reflect its opposing tendencies and be enigmatic about his own origins at the same time; he might be type or deviant, he might belong to the past or to the future: his own uncertainties about himself asked to be exploited to his own advantage. In a more central position he could be exploited by others in return—the fate of Wilde was, after all, only the worst that could be known. A need for anonymity prohibited the full demonstration of his innately theatrical nature. Mirror and mask were his emblems, illusion and disguise his techniques; but the Decadent normally kept a marginal position; the mask was rarely heroic, more often it was that of Pierrot, and the mirror was primarily for observing the minutiae of his own behaviour. The true Decadent remained dark, inward, reclusive.

One important and continuing response to the pressures of public discourse upon the artist was involvement in what Frank Kermode has named the *topos* of the dancer.[3] What might equally be called the *topos* of the actress, although closely allied, had its own distinctive set of concerns. The solitary dancer aspired to and perhaps achieved a much desired unity of being, and her isolation and self-regard offered an hermetic image that included both artist and work. The actress, conscious of her audience, interpreter of many roles, and contributor to a corporate activity (both of which distinguished her from the *chanteuse* or music-hall performer), offered a more flexible image, a way of keeping social and aesthetic relationships unresolved. This could have a special appeal because it reflected the artist's own irresolution towards the problems of participation and personality. But interest in the actress could still be risky, particularly if she were a star, for stars sometimes succeeded to the degree that they had private

[3] *Romantic Image*, p. 72.

lives, real or invented, on which to capitalize. The Decadent had his mirror, but the star gazed out from a hoarding and he could hardly pretend that in her case there was no exploitation, no paying public. The answer was to idolize from a distance: a voyeuristic position that enabled him to preserve his separateness from both performer and performance.

In any case, like his precursor the Dandy, who had maintained the rigid elegance of his body, a perfect male silhouette, to protect himself from the mutability of woman (Baudelaire was epitome), the Decadent, although more willing to confess openly to all kinds of physical weakness (thereby disclosing all that the Philistine might want to conceal), was also sensitive to the treachery of the female form. Spellbound by a performance that he dared neither imitate nor approach, he knew that the vibrant actress, posing and exposing in her bright exterior world, was best observed from the dark safety of box or wings. The great actress joined then those Fatal Women who were to be possessed only vicariously, through the imagination.

More generally the rise of the star actress was a commercial process, a sign of an aesthetic and social imbalance in the theatre. She drew more attention to herself than to either play or role: she was more than the part that she played, more than the whole in which she appeared. Yet as an artist her development was restricted. Her very success inhibited order and growth; that she could sustain it was a further indication of the fallen state to which the theatre had come; but to celebrate it, knowingly but from a distance, could suit the Decadent purpose. By acknowledging the debased nature of the beguiling object, the Decadent could still preserve the ambiguity of his own relationship to culture and of culture to society. A connoisseur of the debased, he could after all exalt the meretricious surface of the commercial theatre, confident that it would end up by faithfully reflecting the decaying world that it attempted, absurdly, to idealize; a world to which he himself may or may not have belonged. But for the uncertainty of his own position this admiration would of course have been merely complicit. And because he was sensitive to the ambiguities of surface, the Decadent was drawn alike to the commercial theatre which displayed them and to the Symbolist theatre which explored them. Both Wilde and Symons felt this double attraction: Wilde attempted a synthesis when he invited Bernhardt to appear as Salome. Symons could finally reconcile his divided appreciations only through mysticism and an organic theory. An alternative solution lay in the propagation of the Symbolist marionette, in metaphor or in practice. The marionette was the star's gross parody: wooden as she was plastic, manipulable as she was predictable. But more provoking even than the marionette and certainly more credible was the star's palpable opposite, the anti-star, who arrived with the distinctive claim that, despite everything, the pressures and conditions of her profession, her own performance was natural and spontaneous, and she was free.

If Bernhardt was the type of the star, Eleonora Duse was the type of the anti-star, and her career seemed to offer a way of resolving the Decadent's public dilemma. Duse seemed to fulfil Symons's early definition of the Decadent. She attempted to 'fix the last fine shade, the quintessence of things' and to do so 'fleetingly'; she wanted (extra-ordinary ambition for an actress) to be a 'disembodied voice', yet she also wanted to be 'the voice of a human soul'. Symons later explicitly identified Duse as 'the type of the artist', and compared her, on a more personal level, with himself: they were both like gypsies—she the wandering actress, he the rootless artist. In the eyes of the world, however, Duse—an Italian who succeeded in a *métier* dominated by the French—was firmly identified with Decadence as an international phenomenon. She played the Ibsen heroines who were thought to be typical of the *fin-de-siècle* woman, there was the liaison with d'Annunzio —her virtual retirement after 1909 preserved her association with an earlier period. But although the strict cult of Duse was a Decadent affectation, her performances were of focal importance for a much wider audience, and a fascination with her art joins Arthur Symons with as disparate a figure as Shaw or the many others who found their own feelings mirrored yet challenged by her personality.

The 'legend' of Duse is unique. It tells of renunciation, austerity, desperate ambitions combined with desperate integrity. Duse's most recorded pronouncement was: 'To save the theatre the theatre must be destroyed, the actors and actresses must all die of the plague: they poison the air, they make art impossible.' Symons and Edward Gordon Craig quoted it continually; Craig even made it an epitaph for his essay on the *über-marionette*. The legend is true in the way that legends can be: a testimony to emotions achieved in her art beyond the bounds of what seemed, given her conditions, to have been possible. Indeed Duse herself reputedly sought not just to deny her conditions but to destroy them. She once described her ideal theatre as 'quite small, quite simple, with plain white-washed walls—no ornamenta-tion. Very little scenery. The things that matter are that one should

be heard clearly, and be able to create a genuine communication
between audience and player.'[4]

THE THOUGHTS AND EXPERIENCE OF THE WORLD

This is how Symons described Duse in 1900:

> Her face is sad with thought, with the passing over it of all the
> emotions of the world, which she has felt twice over, in her own
> flesh and in the creative energy of her spirit.[5]

Behind the evocation there lay, of course, the shadow of Pater: 'all
the thoughts and experience of the world have etched and moulded
there . . .' If Duse could express all the emotions, of the past and of the
present, it had to be because in some sense or other she contained them.
Her means of expression was, as Symons suggested, the exercise of
spiritual energies upon the body. The head of the Mona Lisa, Pater had
written, had 'a beauty wrought out from within upon the flesh, the
deposit, little cell by cell, of strange thoughts and fantastic reveries and
exquisite passions'. The art of Duse, wrote Symons, aligning her with
his own Symbolist theory and with Paterian ascêsis, was suggestion and
renunciation rather than statement; it sought to 'escape from the
bondage of form, by a new, finer mastery of form, wrought outwards
from within, not from without inwards'.[6]

Pater's Mona Lisa and Symons's Duse were both process and result:
they created selves out of selves, their material was the whole of history. Yet this somehow left them untouched: for the Mona Lisa the
innumerable experiences were 'but as the sound of lyres and flutes' and,
whatever her emotive power, Duse retained a private self: 'When she
has thrilled one, or made one weep, or exalted one with beauty, she
seems to be always holding back something else.'[7] The Mona Lisa had
'learned the secrets of the grave'; Duse, said Symons, had 'an art
wholly subtle, almost spiritual, a suggestion, an evasion, a secrecy'.[8]

Pater thought that the Mona Lisa 'might stand as the embodiment
of the old fancy, the symbol of the modern idea': the old fancy was
that of perpetual change and eternal life; the modern idea was Darwin-
ist, life summing up past modes because it developed out of them.

[4] Eva Le Gallienne, *The Mystic in the Theatre* (1966), quoting in translation
Edouard Schneider, *Eléonora Duse. Souvenirs, Notes et Documents* (1925).

[5] 'Eleonora Duse' (1900), *Studies in Seven Arts* (1906), p. 333.

[6] *Ibid.*, p. 346.   [7] *Ibid.*, pp. 342–3.   [8] *Ibid.*, p. 346.

The image became an instance of itself. The picture could be proposed as a symbol of continuous development because, paradoxically, a painting is unchanging, an arrested moment, and it is only by fixing the moment that the process can be observed. That paradox became more demanding when the image was embodied in a living actress; Symons nevertheless did his best to meet it.

Although neither of them were to satisfy Symons, there were in fact two fairly obvious ways in which an actress could be seen to combine the individual and the universal, the one and the many—not including that of simple admiration for her ability to play many different kinds of part, which would have been self-defeating anyway because her own special presence would have become diffused and lost. The first was for the critic to accept that she adapted all her parts to fit within the bounds of her own, albeit multiple, personality. (It was a commonly held view that Duse accurately represented herself by misrepresenting the characters that she played: she turned Marguerite Gautier, for example, into a dignified woman, simply and deeply in love, ignoring the fact that she was a courtesan, and even Symons could not accept her efforts to make a tragic heroine out of Pinero's Mrs Tanqueray.) The other way was to emphasize the emotional range which the actress created within each part, and it was unanimously agreed that Duse was extraordinary in this respect.

The real legend of Duse went much deeper than that and was less obviously open to manipulation. It was a response to the largely historical yet seemingly intractable dilemmas that confronted her as an artist and as a woman; and it was on those terms that she engaged the more thoughtful members of her audience. Yet it is not surprising that for many her talents stood merely as a rudimentary touchstone for the mystery and integrity of art. Edward Garnett, writing in 1898:

> ... the astonished spectator loses sight of the individual life altogether, and has the entrancing sense that all life is really one and the same thing, and is there manifesting itself before him. He feels that, for example when he watches Duse at her best, or when he stands before Leonardo da Vinci's 'Joconda' in the Louvre and is absorbed by it.[9]

HER BLUSH

As a metaphor for art as a whole the use of cosmetics contained all the favourite Decadent paradoxes. Symons often classed it as an art in

---

[9] *The Academy* (17 December 1898), repr. *Friday Nights* (1922), p. 207.

itself, because it not only concealed but improved upon nature; it was thus, following a traditional line of reasoning, an art whose processes imitated those of nature, so that ultimately it was a part of nature. This rapprochement allowed elsewhere for him to put forward another ancient proposition, which was that the art of the theatre reflects the workings of nature, for theatre is above all transient.

But for the Decadent the real point of interest lay less in identifying the painted object than in exploring its relationship to himself, the onlooker. Naturally the actress, who specialized in illusion, figured as a most compelling instance, as Symons makes clear:

> Maquillage, to be attractive, must of course be unnecessary. As a disguise for age or misfortune, it has no interest. But, of all places, on the stage, and, of all people, on the cheeks of young people; there, it seems to me that make-up is intensely fascinating, and its recognition is of the essence of my delight in a stage performance.[10]

Delight in illusion was part of the moral and sexual game in which the onlooker saw a beautiful young woman showing signs of a corruption that was probably not there. The options were usually left open and the onlooker was given the freedom to speculate according to his own needs without having to test them against another. In his poem 'Maquillage', for instance, Symons uses pathos to forestall alternative commitments: the juxtaposition of the rouged cheeks of the concubine, shielded from time, with the untouched but fading complexion of the natural woman, implies a familiar quandary: art and nature are equally ephemeral, equally treacherous. This paradox was to be found quintessentially in the mystery of a woman's blush. In Symons's poem 'At the Cavour', for example, the observer is undeceived by the blush:

> Wine, the red coals, the flaring gas,
> Bring out a brighter tone in cheeks
> That learn at home before the glass
> The flush that eloquently speaks.

While in 'Pastel', the blush momentarily persuades him:

> And then, through the dark, a flush
> Ruddy and vague, the grace—
> A rose—of her lyric face.

---

[10] *London: A Book of Aspects* (Minneapolis, 1909), pp. 55–6, repr. *Cities and Sea-Coasts and Islands* (1918), pp. 205–6.

F

So the capacity to create an artificial blush became a test case in the aesthetics of make-up, for all Symons's bland apologia:

> Is there any 'reason in nature' why we should write exclusively about the natural blush, if the delicately acquired blush of rouge has any attraction for us? Both exist; both, I think, are charming in their way; and the latter, as a subject has, at all events, more novelty.[11]

Although 'novelty', within the terms of the Decadent ideal, could be an end in itself, Symons was on the defensive even here, and by withholding distinctions he was carefully limiting his own responses—a vital precaution when the behaviour was as potentially compelling and revealing as a blush can be.

It was not Symons, however, but Max Beerbohm who sourly noted that 'Signora Duse has inspired much awe through her contempt for the art of making up'.[12] Duse's insistence on performing without make-up was a fundamental part of her legend, and was seen as evidence of her firm refusal either to disguise her own personality or to involve her art in any deception whatsoever.

Her unadorned complexion alone might have been sufficient challenge to the sensibilities of Decadent and Dandy. But Duse went even further. She turned what might have been a technical disadvantage to remarkable use and displayed on her naked face, of all things— a blush. The *coup* was most famously achieved in the name part of Sudermann's play *Magda*.

In an 1895 review Shaw describes the moment when Magda, a provincial girl turned opera singer, confronts her former lover; and the elaborate care with which he records his observations of Duse at this point invites speculation about the complicated feelings that she activated within him:

> He paid his compliments and offered his flowers; they sat down; and she evidently felt that she had got it safely over and might allow herself to think at her ease, and to look at him to see how much he had altered. Then a terrible thing happened to her. She began to blush; and in another moment she was conscious of it, and the blush was slowly spreading and deepening until, after a few vain efforts to avert her face or to obstruct his view of it without seeming to do so, she gave up and hid the blush in her

[11] Preface to *Silhouettes* (1896).
[12] Max Beerbohm, *More Theatres* (1969), p. 475.

hands. After that feat of acting I did not need to be told why Duse does not paint an inch thick. I could detect no trick in it: it seemed to me a perfectly genuine effect of the dramatic imagination. In the third act of *La Dame aux Camélias*, where she produces a touching effect by throwing herself down, and presently rises with her face changed and flushed with weeping, the flush is secured by the preliminary plunge to a stooping attitude, imagination or no imagination; but Magda's blush did not admit of that explanation; and I must confess to an intense professional curiosity as to whether it always comes spontaneously.[13]

The blush signals Magda's sexuality, and possibly her shame—her past life must now be confronted, her present life brought into question; but equally it signals her essential innocence—as either an admission of guilt or of natural reticence. These ambiguities are intensified by Duse's delayed awareness of what is happening to her and intensified even further by her attempts to conceal it. In the end she replaces the blush with her famous hands: hands that are expressive but, in comparison with the blush, impersonal. What Shaw must have seen, or thought that he had seen (an uncertainty he also allowed for), was a moment of supreme dramatic eloquence, an illumination of her beauty that was all the more moving because of the part that Duse was playing: Magda is herself a performer, tempted by glamour. And this dimension, reminding him as it does that he is a member of an audience, raises the pitch of Shaw's own self-awareness.

Shaw's account mingles the professional and the personal. He knows the professional trick when he sees it, and he makes certain that we recognize it too, by explaining to us how Duse managed to blush in *La Dame aux Camélias*. The difference is between a 'trick' and a 'perfectly genuine effect of the dramatic imagination', but it is not until the end of the passage that he refers directly to the blush coming 'spontaneously'; and that is something about which he 'confesses' and has 'an intense professional curiosity'. The language may betray him here or may be intended to suggest a yet closer involvement: it is of course erotic. In this remarkable appreciation the professional and the personal amplify each other, neither distancing nor sublimating, if ultimately patronizing, but forming together a full, if particular, response.

For all that, Shaw was predisposed to admire Duse's Magda because he could make her suit his own views about women in general; he could make her representative. 'Every woman', he asserted, 'who sees

13 *Our Theatres in the Nineties*, Vol. I (1948), pp. 153–4.

Duse play Magda feels that Duse is acting and speaking for her and for all women as they are hardly able to speak and act for themselves.' Magda achieves the power of self-expression. Writing elsewhere about the problems that actresses faced, Shaw said that 'most educated women have been trained to fight against emotional expression because it is a mode of self-betrayal'.[14]

Even for Shaw the blush had not demonstrated simple spontaneity; it had retained some degree of technical mystery. The residue of curiosity about that had fed his interest in her as a woman and as an actress. Indeed the blush, with all its uncertainties, does not forestall involvement so much as make it possible. The visible embarrassment on stage touches the audience much as it might do in everyday life, by pre-empting their own embarrassment, thereby freeing them to engage more fully with the other person or performer. The stage blush appeals to certain theatrical conventions and, as always, the theatre is at its most seductive, its most involving, not when its conventions are overruled but when they are deepened and humanized —always stopping just this side of complicity. This was an aspect of Duse that drew Shaw and others into the otherwise predictable situations that she acted out, obliging them to reveal themselves as she, seemingly, revealed herself.

It can hardly have been an accident that the blush and the non-existent make-up became so significant a part of the legend. The *fin de siècle* was fascinated by cosmetics because they symbolized the barriers between spectator and object, art and life. Duse's attempts to rupture these touched on many sensitive areas, and involvement with her art required that both artist and critic draw upon his essential beliefs. True to form Shaw made his own admiring response evidence of Duse's prophetic talents, and always endeavoured to promote both Duse and himself as harbingers of an evolving future.[15] In the case of Symons, an appreciation of Duse as a natural and changing phenomenon was in dialectical opposition to the attraction he also felt to static painted art: the two sides of his *fin-de-siècle* dilemma.

[14] *Our Theatres in the Nineties*, Vol. II, p. 113.

[15] In an 1895 review of Duse in *La Dame aux Camélias* Shaw analysed her performance in terms of 'points' and 'strokes' which were built up to form a complex whole or continuum. Artistic technique could thus be allied with natural process and Duse could be credited with a creative psychology that was able to apprehend a whole out of what to a less evolved intelligence would still appear as parts (*Ibid.*, Vol. I, pp. 146–8).

FEMME FATALE/MATER DOLOROSA

Duse's portrayal of the type of 'modern woman'—Hofmannsthal's 'Our Lady of the quivering nerves'—was again based as much on the actress as on the part that she played. The aged Ristori paid her the backhanded compliment that she was 'ill, neurotic, like our century'.[16]

Ibsen was principal medium; and Duse's interpretations of Nora, Hedda and Mrs Alving were widely debated. But the record of a theatrical performance permits at least three levels of ideological intervention: first that of playwright, who mediates his subject matter; then that of performer, who brings or finds his own interpretation; finally that of specatator, who is in part free to see and remember whatever he chooses. It is particularly necessary to keep these various levels in mind when thinking about Duse and feminism.

Laura Marholm was only one of many to take Duse as example. In her *Modern Women* (1896)[17] she put forward a Schopenhauerian thesis typical of the *fin de siècle*: the neurotic, who seeks freedom through independence, 'is generally one who desires to escape from a woman's sufferings. She is anxious to avoid subjection, also motherhood, and the dependence and impersonality of an ordinary woman's life, but in doing so she unconsciously deprives herself of her womanliness.' By 'womanliness' Marholm means female urges to be both child and mother, a definition which conditions every aspect of her book. Duse is dependent on men and 'a martyr of circumstance'; she acts out of intuition rather than rationality, with a 'quiet indifference'. Throughout her acting a sense of surprise that she should have to suffer coexists with the knowledge that is has to be so; her capacity for love is part of her need to give and to receive sympathy. Every one of her interpretations can be accounted for in these terms: from the start of *A Doll's House* her Nora is resigned rather than capricious, and she surmounts the notorious problem of Nora's apparent character change by expressing surprise, then disappointment, then contempt when Helmer reproaches her—a sequence of emotions that is apparently instinctive to women. When Duse's Nora leaves, 'she is a woman in the moment of woman's greatest ignominy—when she discovers she

---

[16] Henry Knepler, *The Gilded Stage* (1968), p. 244.

[17] Laura Marholm, *Modern Women: An English rendering of Das Buch der Frauen by H. Ramsden* (1896). The book deals with four women: Sonia Kovalevsky, George Egerton, Marie Bashkirtseff and Duse.

does not love'. Yet she is *not* 'nervous', because Duse's own soul is 'too full of harmony'. She, is in fact, Marholm reiterates continually, 'a complete woman', an indissoluble unity. Her Marguerite Gautier fails because 'a superabundance of good spirits is foreign to her nature, which is as sad as life itself'.

Duse's acting style relies on the creation of suspense but only because she recognizes that life is ruled by chance. Even her appearance is fatalistic; no make-up of course (disclosing her age but also the 'woman's tragedy' engraved on her features), the loose gowns worn without stays ('nothing to hinder the slow, graceful musical movements of her somewhat scanty figure'), the dark velvet and silks ('an air of mourning'), the infrequent hats ('sober ... such as a widow might wear'). When Duse is required to die (Marguerite was the most famous example) she dies quickly, 'out of instinct'. When she is called upon to tell a lie she does so naturally, like a child, although she is conscious that lies are a woman's weapon (and this was apparent, Marholm tells us, in spite of the language barrier).

It emerges that the career of the average actress is typical of the life of the average modern woman, composed as they both are of 'impulses of short duration'. The stage partly satisfies a craving for myriad sensations, but can never fulfil it, which parallels female experience in life: only disillusion can follow. This makes Marholm pessimistic even about Duse's powers of endurance. The burden of re-enacting your own hopelessness must, it seems, eventually result in the weariness that typifies the female condition as a whole.

Certainly there is throughout the 1890s, among women writers in particular, an almost unanimous agreement about the type that Duse stood for:

> ... the modern actress, the *fin-de-siècle* woman par excellence, with her hysterical maladies, her neuroticism, her anaemia and all its consequences. For this reason, and with much sagacity, Eleonora Duse's repertoire largely consists of a collection of these abnormal types whom she renders with all their weaknesses, their paradoxes, their fantasies, their languors, their fascinations.[18]

Reports of Duse's Nora are unusual in that they vary rather considerably;[19] but Marholm's thesis was obviously more than a simple projection of her own preconceived ideas. Duse certainly tamed Nora,

[18] Helen Zimmern, 'Eleonora Duse', *Fortnightly Review* (June 1900), p. 983.
[19] See for example William Archer, *The Theatrical World of 1893* (1894).

much as she had domesticated Marguerite and emphasized Magda's bourgeois background: she cut the scene in which Nora hints at suicide and all but omitted the tarantella.

Marholm's idea of the female 'receptive faculty' was confirmed by Duse's acting style. Most unusually for a star she made unobtrusive entrances and frequently kept to the back of the stage. Her great discovery was probably to have found that hysteria, paradoxically, is best rendered by keeping unnaturally still. By organizing her performances so that they depended mainly on reactions to events and characters, she created an air of resignation that appealed to exponents of the female psychology and to Symbolists alike. For Symbolists in particular her representation of passive suffering united her with the sacred image of the Madonna, and moreover passivity itself lay deep within the antinomies of the Fatal Woman.

The indivisibility of Fatal Woman and Symbolist-inspiring woman is demonstrated in d'Annunzio's turbid symbolist dramas: *La Gioconda* and the highly Maeterlinckian *La Città Morta*. But it was in his delirious novels *Il Piacere* and *Il Fuoco* that d'Annunzio exploited most voluptuously the connection between actress and Fatal Woman. Taking his cue from Pater (according to Symons) but sensationalizing it beyond all bounds d'Annunzio repeats the same basic idea in page after endlessly tumescent page.

In *Il Fuoco* the ageing La Foscarina (based of course on Duse) is mistress of a young poet, Stelio (d'Annunzio). She is by turns violently tyrannical and pathetically submissive: her most frequent emotion is jealousy, but at times she remains motionless and enigmatic—a chimaera, and she is often compared with Cassandra, with Clytemnestra and with Medusa. Her smile is constantly referred to: it is 'inextinguishable' and 'infinite'. Her past roles are equated with her previous lovers and some sort of climax is reached in a particularly brutal passage when Stelio imagines taking La Foscarina after a performance. Mutability implies Dionysiac promiscuity, and the sexual superman proves his own superiority by taming the woman whose implicit wantonness has already enraptured a multitude.

A more sober point of reference for the mutuality of suffering and seduction lies in Pater's juxtaposition of the Empress Faustina with Saint Cecilia in *Marius the Epicurean*. Marius sees Saint Cecilia as a Madonna—'with a certain antique severity in the gathering of the long mantle, with coif or veil folded decorously below the chin, "gray within gray"'—but is simultaneously reminded of other female images, of the 'serious and virile quality of the best female statuary of Greece. Quite foreign, however, to any Greek statuary was the expression of pathetic care, with which she carried a little child, at rest in her arms.' Cecilia is to all intents and purposes a vision, and a vision reminiscent of a statue at that. Moreover, with ineluctable irony, she seems to threaten to exact the price of all Fatal Women:

> Might this new vision, like the malignant beauty of pagan Medusa, be exclusive of any admiring gaze upon anything but itself? At least he suspected that, after the beholding of it, he could never again be altogether as he had been before.

In Marius's consciousness the vision inevitably crystallizes into art —'some matter of poetry, of another man's story, of a picture on the wall'—an external object that can be possessed, so that with a final twist she becomes, at least potentially, the victim of his own image-making faculty.

It would be pointless to expect Pater's descending ironies in d'Annunzio; but it is clear that Duse's later image developed in traditional ways, over which she had little control (indeed she showed few signs of having wished it), and was, for all it belonged in the mainstream of Italian culture, essentially a matter of emphasis within an international composite. What d'Annunzio had realized to the full was that although only an actress could literally embody Nora and Marguerite and countless others, her multiplicity would always be bounded by parts and by plays, and within those choices by what she might wish to become and what her audiences might conceive of her becoming. She was finite after all. Indeed her whole range can be seen to be covered by an overall concept: passivity. The actress who reincarnates other women becomes prey to the men who make their own image out of her; and because she performs her trick of reincarnation professionally, it can be insinuated that there is little that need be said in her defence.

So it becomes clear that Duse, who seems to have sought a more equal involvement between actress and audience through the naked expression of feelings, was doomed from the start—held together by suffering, the circle of *nerveuse*, *femme fatale* and *mater dolorosa* was complete.

SYMBOLIST SURVIVALS

The face of the actress is the 'mirror of her soul';[20] it is 'wonderful to watch the changes of her face';[21] for Symons, the face is a 'mask for the tragic passions' which he modulates into a sculptural analogy:

> ... a mask which changes from moment to moment, as the soul models the clay of the body after its own changing image. Imagine Rodin at work on a lump of clay. The shapeless thing awakens under his fingers, a vague life creeps into it, hesitating among the forms of life; it is desire waiting to be born, and it may be born as pity or anguish, love or pride; so fluid is it to the touch, so humbly does it await the accident of choice. The face of Duse is like the clay under the fingers of Rodin. But with her there can be no choice, no arresting moment of response; but an endless flowing onward of emotion, like tide flowing after tide, moulding and effacing continually.[22]

All observers found the secret of Duse's expressiveness to lie in the movement of emotion across her face, the endless sequence of her changing moods, which Symons celebrated as proof that she achieved, though with a less equal balance, the same duality that Pater had found in the face of the Mona Lisa: stasis (experience has 'etched and moulded there') and process (it has 'moulded the changing lineaments'). Symons thought too that 'her supreme distinction comes from the kind of melancholy wisdom which remains in her face after the passions have swept over it'—leaving a kind of after-image—and he noted her way 'of looking as if emotion has left her face expressionless, as it often leaves the face of real people'. Hence Symons's concept of the mask was of an artefact that captured the floating essence of the human spirit behind it, which the actor shared with the character that he was playing. The mask fixed the moment of coming into being, of energy coming into form, and it had distinctly organicist overtones.

Symons also thought that Duse, by embodying all history, including her own, and all past effort, including her work as an actress, functioned on a level at which, most deeply expressive of herself, she became most wholly impersonal. And indeed in her later Symbolist repertoire this most physical of actresses did attempt to become pure spirit—but she managed it only by becoming passive, and her audience had to match her passivity with pity and, in the case of the Symbolist, gratitude for

---

[20] James Huneker, *Iconoclasts* (1906), p. 321.
[21] A. B. Walkley, *Drama and Life* (1907), p. 259.
[22] *Studies in Seven Arts*, pp. 340–1 and *passim*.

its redeeming powers. Some found an excuse for the implicit senti-mentality in the failure of any playwright to use her talents creatively. Pirandello was among them: he thought d'Annunzio's static and sensational plays to have distracted Duse from her great opportunity—Ibsen. And at the same time her acting could still appear superbly naturalistic in a way that won the admiration of Stanislavsky and Chekhov, although later theoreticians have disapproved of it.

Naturalism is nothing if not paradoxical. Symons's application of Donne—'her whole body thinks'—was perhaps automatic but Symons clearly viewed Duse's performances as the creation of an organic entity, which united all the old antinomies, whose structural complexity as a living work of art partook in the complexity of nature and thus signified a higher truth.

Naturalism and Symbolism were significantly alike in their appeal to a concept of time measured by organic development. Hofmannsthal for instance wrote of Duse:

> She acts the transitions; she fills the gaps of motivation; she re-constructs the psychological novel in drama. With a pursing of the lips, a movement of a shoulder she portrays the maturing of a decision, the passing of a thought through the mind, the whole psycho-physiological occurrence which precedes verbal expres-sion.[23]

This is an organic notion of psychology, which the audience understands by identifying with natural patterns of behaviour. Even the descriptions of her as an empty vessel (Symons's 'a chalice for the wine of the imagination') still assumed identification, by virtue of the contributory act that the spectator was always required to make in the presence of the Symbolist drama, a contribution that was made primarily by responding to form and gesture.

Because it drew on the interlinked traditions of naturalism and Symbolism the legend of Duse confirms that the difference between the two was frequently only a matter of style, that both amounted to sets of suggestions, and that consequently Symbolism transcended its own conditions only when it too had an audience that was willing to react to what it saw with the requisite contribution. Symbolism involved an adulation of surface that could in turn lead to the objecti-fication of surface; and when that progression took place the results could be either ridiculous or dangerous.

[23] As quoted in translation by Henry Knepler, *The Gilded Stage*, p. 189.

Yet when T. S. Eliot attacked realism he used an inherently conser-
vative metaphor and asked for something that sounds very much like
the Symbolist drama:

> There has been no form to arrest, so to speak, the flow of the
> spirit at any particular point before it expands and ends its course in
> the desert of exact likeness to the reality which is perceived by the
> most commonplace mind.[24]

And Eliot's dislike of realism should be set alongside that of Yeats:

> Realism is created for the common people and was always their
> peculiar delight, and it is the delight today of all those whose minds,
> educated alone by schoolmasters and newspapers, are without the
> memory of beauty and emotional subtlety.[25]

These attitudes were closely joined to ideas of the performing artist.
It's worth remembering that Eliot's demand for 'impersonality' and
his famous analogies arose out of a discussion of acting, and that he
effectively made the actor the whipping boy for his general assertion:

> The advantages of convention for the actor are precisely similar to
> its advantages for the author. No artist produces great art by a
> deliberate attempt to express his own personality. He expresses his
> personality indirectly through concentrating on a task in the same
> sense as the making of an efficient engine or the throwing of a
> jug or table-leg.

Moreover Eliot had previously involved the actor in a derogatory
comparison with the dancer, citing Massine as the greatest actor then
in London:

> Massine, the most completely unhuman, impersonal, abstract
> belongs to the future stage . . . the difference between the con-
> ventional gesture, which is supposed to *express* emotion, and the
> abstract gesture of Massine, which symbolizes emotion is enormous.
> The former is usually untrue, and always monotonous. . . .[26]

This is very like Symons and the high estimation of the dancer
aligns Eliot still further with the dancer's greatest mythologizer. Yeats,
Eliot and Symons, all three, considered that theatre was at its most

[24] 'Four Elizabethan Dramatists. I. A Preface', *The Criterion* (February 1924).
It is not suggested that this was always Eliot's position. For a later opinion see
'Gordon Craig's Socratic Dialogues', *Drama* (Spring 1955).
[25] 'Certain Noble Plays of Japan', *Essays and Introductions* (1961), p. 227.
[26] 'Dramatis Personae', *The Criterion* (April 1923).

powerful when it was closest to dance, which is to say when, at its most 'impersonal' (Symons too uses the word), it could by gesture alone invoke universal response.

Whether 'impersonality' could ever actually unite an audience was to be the dilemma that dogged Yeats throughout his theatrical career. Nevertheless his antithetical system allowed him to ask, within a single essay, for both a specially qualified elite (albeit possibly a vanguard)—'a feeling of exclusiveness, a bond among chosen spirits, a mystery almost for leisured and lettered people'—and for a popular theatre that

> ... should grow always more objective; more and more a reflection of the general mind; more and more a discovery of the simple emotions that make all men kin, clearing itself the while of sentimentality, the wreckage of an obsolete popular culture, seeking always not to feel and to imagine but to understand and to see.[27]

The acknowledged division shows how the doctrine of 'impersonality' rested on the assumption that an audience must be created before it can be honestly moved (unless the playwright is fortunate enough to find an audience composed only of primitives), and yet no audience has anything to give without what Yeats called 'memory' and Eliot thought of as the capacity to respond to 'convention'. As Frank Kermode has shown, 'impersonality' was the name that modern artists sometimes gave to an aesthetic ideal that confirmed their own sense of isolation, although an alternative account of that ideal might stress the historical circumstances that produced it, riddled with myth and nostalgia.

Organicism played a major part in the construction of 'impersonality' (as Kermode has also demonstrated) just as Symbolism and naturalism had coincided in their appeals to its principles; and the insufficiency of organicism to form by itself a basis for theatrical representation is clearly revealed in the legend of Duse. 'Impersonality' preserved a double difficulty.

The obvious problem with naturalism is that the artist sets out single-handedly to reveal the moral structure of the world while denying his own moral contribution and his own structuring presence: this contradiction was concealed within the admiration for Duse's reticence, within the eager acceptance of her ability to identify with her parts, and within what some feminist critics made of her. Sym-

[27] 'A People's Theatre', *Explorations* (1962), p. 257.

bolism contained a parallel challenge: Duse, the extreme type of the subjective artist, was said to represent generalized experience. Both theories tried to resolve the possible discrepancies between actress and role (her Nora, her Marguerite); between role and play (the star-vehicle, the heroine artificially placed at its centre); between play and circumstance (the paying public, the regularity of performance)—which shows that the really crucial distinction between the two modes may have lain beyond their mutual organicism in the audience relationships that they respectively assumed. And there in fact the differences become more evident: because Symbolism is participatory only an elect or elevated state of mind can recognize the true nature of what is being shown; whereas because naturalism is seemingly objective recognition is available to anyone who applies common procedures of understanding.

The modernist denigration of the actor was a response, surely an extreme one, to these dichotomous audience relationships, rather than just to the two superficially opposed modes of representation. There was an initial failure on the part of modernism to moderate between the undesirability of the actor as the type of the artist— all personality, and the possibilities of his art—a responsible and direct relationship with a contemporary audience. The skills of the actor, although they are traditionally based on disguise and illusion, are also to do with responsiveness to an audience, with self-control and self-awareness: serious matters requiring generosity and tact, if capable of alienation too. 'Impersonality' was a despairing ideal when it attempted to exclude rather than confront these reserves, and when it presumed the absolute dominance of the playwright so that the actor would be nothing more than a projection of the writer's own aesthetic purity. Modernist 'impersonality' was by its very nature on the defensive, but it betrayed its origins when it took the Symbolist revelation to the point where it became a potential coercion.

The further origins of 'impersonality' lay in the Symbolist notion of world as ballet, ordered and ecstatic—rather than in the Decadent variation which Symons also sometimes proposed: world as music-hall, urban, vulgar, immediate. Yet in 1893 the issue had been partly one of finding suitably ironic styles and roles; and partly one of finding the right contemporary subject matter. The definition of Decadent literature had had a broad reference which related to style in that it incorporated the minor categories of Symbolism and Impressionism which were said to be coterminous, working on the same stylistic hypothesis ('not general truth merely, but *la vérité vraie*, the very essence of truth'); but which also related to subject, with the claim that all Decadent styles reflected their time. In his introduction to *The Symbolist Movement* (1899), where these categories were reshuffled, Symons did not however choose to make the relevant point that Symbolism often resembles the transcendent aspect of Decadence. Instead he decided to denigrate Decadence as a descriptive term, saying that it should be applied to style alone; and the Decadent movement as a whole he dismissed as a 'straying aside from the mainroad of literature'. The most vital point that he had made in 1893—that the Decadent style was 'certainly typical of a civilization grown over-luxurious, over-inquiring, too languid for the relief of action, too uncertain for any emphasis in opinion or in conduct', which 'reflects all the moods, all the manners of a sophisticated society'—disappeared altogether, to be replaced by concepts of art and style that although mystical were also more conventional and not always more construc-tive.

Yet even the 1893 definitions had been tacit acknowledgement of a deadlock: the rhetoric had been tautological, and the lost classicism had been given all the moral weight but allowed none of the artistic possibilities. Reconsidered from this standpoint it becomes more obvious why Symons had been unable to develop his notion of the Decadent as the product of a stagnant society. The Decadent may have been allowed ubiquity, he may have been free among 'all the moods of choice', but he was still, in Symons's definition, firmly restricted to the present, his own particular moment. Later still the increasing organicism of his aesthetic reduced Symons's application of the word Decadent to instances of the frank pursuit of artificial sensation in the cult of personality (as when he compares d'Annunzio with Poe and Baudelaire) and to the waning stages of creative energy when all that remains is method or 'mechanism'. A converse movement can be traced in his tributes to Duse, who is more and more seen as a life-giving force who communicates through a personal electricity that overcomes her resistance to her own profession.

In some respects Symons had forgotten the lessons of his master throughout. In the essay on Style Pater, after endless qualification, had resolved that the matter of literature was 'the transcript, not of mere fact, but of fact in its infinite variety, as modified by human preference in all its infinitely varied forms'; although the grounds for that 'human preference' were always to remain extremely elusive. That Symons should have later spoken so resignedly of Duse as lacking the power of choice (and that this should have become synonymous with the tedious oxymoron 'the accident of choice') shows how both the Paterian precedent and Symons's own Decadent ideal had been reduced.

For an actor the equivalence of literary style is part a matter of feeling, part a matter of technique—both are directed toward maintaining a consistent characterization. Symons saw Duse as trying to go beyond technique by relying entirely on feeling, meaning perhaps that she did indeed lose the 'power of human preference'. She could display some integrity within the self—the whole beyond her many parts—but only by becoming a passive personality, another stereotype; she failed, inevitably, to express a transcendent self—the whole beyond the single part—despite her use of gesture and silence. As one who may have aspired to become a 'romantic image' of internal cohesion and to engage with an audience but who could never escape the time-bound world of discourse, her whole career is a salutary failure. Yet ironically it was by her desperate attempts to achieve unity in the conventional drama that Duse best expressed what had earlier been the Decadent impasse of fragmentation and marginality. For although her attempts to redress the balance between performer and performance, character and play, rarely worked even on the level of dramatic illusion and were probably born of professional wisdom, her striving to reconcile herself to her roles through feeling alone certainly had the effect of re-opening questions about formal and psychological relationships at the very moment of performance. It was never denied that her presence was variable, difficult and painful: an authenticity achieved despite the factitious wholeness of her later productions.

It is as a counterpoint to Decadent withdrawal and to modernist 'impersonality' that the legend of Duse, the anti-star, should be set: a failure in that she reinforced passivity and cultivated mystery, but valuable then and since in that she reminds us that the ultimate reconciliation of artist and audience lies not in the metaphysics of part and whole, nor in the dominance nor in the absence of feeling, but rather in a conscious understanding of present feelings together with the re-examination of present means.

Note

Extensive though not total listings of the numerous little magazines published during the last decade of the nineteenth century are C. N. Pondrom, *English Literary Periodicals 1885–1918* (University Microfilms, Ann Arbor, 1966), and J. R. Tye, *Periodicals of the Nineties* (1974). There is no substantive study of the magazines as a group; Ian Fletcher deals with several in *Union and Beauty: An Examination of Certain Minority Periodicals, 1850–1905* (unpubl. Ph.D. thesis, Univ. of Reading, 1965); also see T. D'Arch Smith, *Love in Earnest: Some Notes on the Lives and Writings of the English 'Uranian' Poets* (1970).

The Germ has been reprinted several times, most recently with an introd. by R. M. Hosman (1972); this also contains W. M. Rossetti's preface to the 1901 repr. identifying pseudonymous contributors, and James Ashcroft Noble's critical essay. For an account of discussions leading to publication, and of sales and finance, see W. E. Fredeman (ed.), *The P.R.B. Journal: W. M. Rossetti's Diary of the Pre-Raphaelite Brotherhood* (1975).

The Century Guild Hobby Horse and *The Hobby Horse* were repr. in 1969. Studies are Lilian R. Block, *The Pursuit of Beauty: The Background and Creators of 'The Hobby Horse'* (unpubl. M.A. thesis, Columbia Univ., 1941), incl. correspondence about the periodical between Mackmurdo and the author, and Loraine R. L. Hunt, *'The Century Guild Hobby Horse': A Study of a Magazine* (University Microfilms, 1966); also see S. E. Ticknor, *Selwyn Image: His Life and Art* (unpubl. Ph.D. thesis, Univ. of Reading, 1972), on Image's connection with the magazine. On Herbert Horne, see Ian Fletcher, 'Herbert Horne: The Earlier Phase', in *English Miscellany* (1970); his connection with the magazine is explored in Ian Fletcher, *Herbert Horne* (1979).

The Yellow Book has been repr. several times in selection; the entire 13 vols. were reproduced in 1968. Beardsley's dismissal is explored in J. B. Townsend, '*The Yellow Book*', in *Princeton Library Chronicle* (1955). Also see Katherine L. Mix, *A Study in Yellow: The Yellow Book and Its Contributors* (1960); J. G. Nelson's excellent *The Early Nineties: A View from the Bodley Head* (1971), on financing and sales; A. Brisau, 'The *Yellow Book* and its Place in the 1890s', in *Studia Germanica Gandensia* (1966); G. Glastonbury [Aline Harland], 'The Life and Writings of Henry Harland', *Irish Monthly* (April 1911), pp 210–19, pious, but useful; and K. Beckson, *Henry Harland* (1978), the most complete biographical and critical account, though with little new on the *Yellow Book*.

The Savoy is repr. in 5 vols. (1967); there is a useful selection with introduction by S. Weintraub (1966). Also see T. J. Garbaty, 'The Savoy, 1896: A Re-Edition . . .' (University Microfilms, 1966); Wendell V. Harris, ' "Innocent Decadence": The Poetry of the *Savoy*', in *PMLA* (1962); Robert M. Booth, 'Aubrey Beardsley and the *Savoy*', in *Aylesford Review* (1966); and Marguerite Strehler, *Der Dekadenzgedanke in 'Yellow Book' und 'Savoy'* (1932).

The Dome is studied in two useful articles: Paul West, '*The Dome*: An Aesthetic Periodical of the 1890s', in *Book Collector* (1957), and Arthur P. Zeigler, '*The Dome* and its Editor-Publisher', in *The American Book Collector* (1965).

as it needed to include more and more, to become eclectic. The little magazine was an ideal decadent paradox.

Decadence always negotiated between evanescence and stabilization. Object and self being alike corrupt and dissolving, it called for style, dandyism, the substitution of carapace or mask for self, and the replacement of lost metonymic objects by metaphor or word separated from thing. But evanescence needed—as in the short story, the wavering lyric, the minute whimsical essay, the nocturne or impression—an endeavour to stabilize; and these scenes and impressions made up the stuff of the decadent periodical. Dissolving space needed to be enfolded within total art: the House Beautiful of the Aesthetic movement, the ideal total building implied in the title of *The Dome*. But not too much stability; hence the Mallarméan suite of blank pages, infinitely interpretable, in the notoriously empty second issue of the *Equinox*; or the popularity of the pseudonym, most manifest in the *Pagan Review*, where William Sharp wrote everything—short story, prose poem, travel impression, poem, etc.—under different masks. Fragmented individualism and multiplicity pervade the decadent magazines; the problem was to relate it to a programme, to move from subjectivism to group art ideals. Many of the magazines—most are notoriously short-lived—foundered on the contradiction; others, like *The Century Guild Hobby Horse*, the first English magazine to aspire to total art, changed totally, in editorial control and format. The failure of *The Yellow Book* and the early collapse of the *Savoy* arose from like contradictions. John Lane planned *The Yellow Book* to match Wilde's extreme version of decadence, based both on collusion with and hostility to press and populace. The frontiers that broke with his trial broke the magazine too. Decadence, after all, enacted the fall that was prelude to necessary regeneration; the magazines did much the same. But they were essential foci, and movements and tendencies after all depend on collective effort, concerted actions, campaigns and acts of publicity. The magazines therefore acted out much of the cultural politics of arts and crafts and decadence. It is possible to argue that the 1890s were the founding period of that most crucial form of modern artistic action: the small magazines, 'often an analogue or extension of the manifesto formula', which 'represented a privatization of the publishing process', and, often by dialectic and antithesis, generated much Modernist publication.[1] But, before examining the scene in the 1890s, it is worth recalling that these ventures have a pre-history from the 1850s.

[1] *Modernism*, ed. Malcolm Bradbury and James McFarlane (1976), p. 203.

II

THE GERM (1850)

This Pre-Raphaelite monthly was the first secessionist if failed model for British and American 'little' magazines. The contrast remains patent between, say, the static architectural space implied in Goethe's *Das Propyläen* and the *Germ*, seemingly programmatic but suggesting a possible organic uncertainty. Contributions were mostly anonymous or pseudonymous, contrasting with early twentieth-century use of strident manifestos set alongside unreverberating names. The *Germ* had only a gnarled sonnet by the younger Rossetti tepidly restating Romantic 'sincerity'; several attempts at producing a manifesto came to nothing. The impression of the four issues remains amateurish. A penumbra of non-Brethren, some of an older generation, some non-painters, influenced the initial discussions; their disparate voices can be distinguished under the pagoda of sixty-five proposed titles. It remains difficult to identify the magazine's rejection of a current model, the Royal Academy, guardian of ideal generalized nature and pyramidal compositions. The Brothers' knowledge of medieval art was vestigial (F. G. Stephens excepted); contributors might well have been abolishing the past rather than reverting to purer, more primitive sources. And, though the Brotherhood had been founded in revolutionary 1848, for them that barely represented a future trans-figuring the past (as 1830 had for the circle round *L'Artiste*). Only W. M. Rossetti was republican, democrat, agnostic and—civil servant. As reviews of poetry by the younger Rossetti indicate, attempts there were to isolate and praise symptoms analogous to Pre-Raphaelitism both in its 'modern' and 'medieval' aspects. But the final coherence of the *Germ* remains one of personality, almost fortuitously grouped, welded by the warm mythologizing gestures of youth into those mystic initials 'PRB'. That 'mystery,' however, had only to be glossed for the centrifugal, not the aesthetic, millennium to assert itself. In their uncertain association, their uneasy stance between past and future, the Brothers' role is altogether predictive of their end-of-century counterparts.

The *Germ* also dimly anticipates the 'golden decade' of illustration, the 1860s; art and craft and the movement toward the total book (Hunt, Millais and Rossetti were all to be involved in the Moxon Tennyson (1857); Rossetti's book designs begin in 1861 and have a powerful influence on Ricketts, L. Housman and others in the 1890s). But it is an inauspicious overture. The *Germ's* title page, Humphrey

House observed, with Gothic type and traditional rectangular frame, recalls a Puseyite parish magazine. Borders were from stock; the etchings in each issue, examples of artists illustrating their own texts, are feeble, even if attempts to work the plate themselves look forward to art and craft. The letterpress is angular and costive: the monthly cycle proved too strenuous a rhythm for those more facile with brush than pen. Though some of the better contributions appeared in the third and fourth issues, there was also infilling material, chiefly by John Tupper, member of the printing family which had taken over as proprietors; all the issues contain a severe amount of Tupper's loweringly facetious verse and lumbering aesthetics (his interpretation of 'nature', a word occurring elusively in the *Germ*, is whether still-life painting makes one salivate).

'Nature', the central word in the PRB programme, emerges in the realist psychology of Patmore's essay on *Macbeth* or the phrasal minutiae of his lyric 'The Seasons', where April 'dots' the sombre thorn; there are pods and the cycle of the season plastically rounds the peach, while during winter 'the frozen rut / Is bound with silver stars'. Such cyclic rhythm is introduced to stabilize the tendency of early Pre-Raphaelite verse to flake into segments (compare the early Pre-Raphaelite habit of composing a painting by segments). Patmore remarked that Woolner's 'My Beautiful Lady' (stunning though it was) struck him as 'sculpturesque', each stanza freestanding. Naive minutiae and seasonal rhythms appear also in W. M. Rossetti's sequence 'Fancies at Leisure', in the Keatsian 'bardic trance' tradition. The macabre, 'the lank dead hairy dog', is distanced through trance—recalling the younger Rossetti's verse narrative 'Mrs Holmes Gray', intended for the projected fifth issue of the *Germ* but not published until 1868, a hint of that species of Pre-Raphaelite verse that rarely got itself written: low-key, urban, thick with quotidianly sensuous reportage.

The medieval barely concerns us: whether as primitive, 'nature', or whether mediating debased sentimental typology from Tractarian sources in James Collinson's 'Child Jesus', partly unified also by seasonal sequence. But D. G. Rossetti's 'Hand and Soul', though its central narrative is medieval, should be touched on for decadent prefigurations. The influence of its cadenced prose and 'comely' hero on Pater's 'Imaginary Portraits', and its undercutting of the Brethren's Ruskinian notions of art, have often been remarked. Chiaro dell' Erma—brightness of the herm or the hermetic, perhaps—passes through an early phase of art conforming to Stephens's essay on early

Italian art (direct transcription from nature, artist linked through nature to God as priest) to discover that he has lost that 'feeling of worship and service ... the peace offering ... made to God and to his own soul for the eager selfishness of his aim'. Attempting to resolve the difficulty by painting cold and laboured moral allegories, Chiaro witnesses a brawl which sends blood running down one of his own frescoes, ironically an allegory of Peace. So much for public, didactic art. Passing through an aesthetic dark night of the personality, Chiaro experiences an epiphany, the figure of a woman preceded by 'a pulse in the light, and a living freshness like rain. The silence was a painful music.' The lonely, constricted room (we may compare the agoro-phobic space of Rossetti's early drawings and watercolours) is trans-formed into *locus amoenus*; but the lady's eyes reflect the content of Chiaro's soul in spite of the elements of *numen*, of 'living' water in a narrowing circle of consciousness: vision as death. 'What he hath set in thine heart to do, that do thou.' The religion of art: Chiaro kneels: the lady's hands knit in a gesture of prayer, as she tells Chiaro to paint his own soul. However, the frame round the story is contemporary; Chiaro's 'figura mystica' is rediscovered and temporarily hung next to a Raphael, the target of many copiers, where it is ignored, or dis-missed as uncouth. Yet for the narrator it clearly possesses an iconic quality since, by gazing at it, he experiences a numinousness similar to Chiaro's. Art becomes in this story both subject and object. The 'visible embodiment', the unfinished painting, is the climax but also the inevitable finale to Chiaro's art.

'Hand and Soul' is deeply autobiographical and, like Chiaro, Rossetti, waking from trance, was to find himself in a meaningless natural world described more in terms of ennui than horror. In 'From the Cliffs: Noon', which appeared in the third issue of the *Germ*, nature's particulars are not the ladder to any immanental radiance but to a sad subjectivity: the sea's

> Painful pulse is on the sands
> Lost utterly the whole sky stands
> Gray and not known, along its path.[2]

A landscape God cannot enter; or is excluded from. 'Sea' and 'time's self' in this poem act as deconstruction of the phenomenal world and anticipate further deconstruction in the later nineteenth century—

[2] *The Germ*, A Pre-Raphaelite Little Magazine, edited with an introduction by Robert Stahr Hosman, (1972), p. 129.

loss even of metaphoric relationship, the collapse of inscape in Hopkins; the parsimonious, even arid surface of Lionel Johnson's verse. There can be no recourse to subject relation as a centre of affirmation. The consequence is pursuit of significance in 'utterance', language rather than 'thought': yet language, art itself, was to be found incapable of furnishing such a centre.

A further stratagem is deployed in the six sonnets on works of art Rossetti contributed to the fourth issue. Rossetti attached sonnets to the frames of his own pictures, modulating the votive and inscriptional elements of this iconic genre. The two sonnets on Ingres's 'Angelica rescued by Ruggiero from the Sea Monster' have a direct relation to Yeats's 'Leda and the Swan'. Angelica's knowledge is not physically or intellectually derived: 'She does not hear nor see—she knows of them', coinciding with extreme experience. As in 'Leda and the Swan', the sestet of the second sonnet recedes into future perspective, but asserts that Angelica has lost the condition of knowledge through undergoing the crisis of 'imminent death', expressed in terms of religio-sexual metaphor, a reaction to Angelica's erotic bondage in the Ingres; she becomes 'Again a woman in her nakedness', dramatizing an anticlimax, the epiphanic moment revealed as disingenuous, counterfeit. Rossetti's other sonnets for pictures are closer to his later practice as defined by a note: spectatorial refining of a *tertium quid* through dialectic of image and word, defined as male and female beauty in congress. The mode may be a perfect moment stabilized, as in the sonnet on Giorgione's 'Fête Champêtre', where synecdoche fuses an unnamed woman and musicians into a totality of landscape and ideal present-tense instant. Death, 'et ego', in this Arcadia, become irrelevant for time has been gathered, suspended, abolished, so that the 'moment' of the painting remains as eternally present experience of the spectator.

Rossetti's work generates themes and modes of treatment that will be recurrent in the little magazines. The sonnets for pictures obviously predict *symboliste* union of the arts, as well as initiating the genre of the baroque 'Galeria' or imaginary museum culminating in Michael Field's *Sight and Song* (1892). As for the *Germ's* own afterlife, that was one of squalid settling up. Its progenitors forgot it, but it lived on in Morris's *Oxford and Cambridge Magazine* (1856); while from the 1860s on essays on the Brotherhood mentioned it with increased frequency as the first literary and artistic focus of Pre-Raphaelitism.

THE CENTURY GUILD HOBBY HORSE (1884–92)

The aesthetic movement, though it had its literary expression, was never expressed through a single magazine devoted to the arts; *The Century Guild Hobby Horse*, though often described as 'aesthetic', belongs as much to the Art and Craft movement, has connections with proto-Art Nouveau, and is tinged with Decadence. The centrality and influence of the magazine comes from its *fin-de-siècle* concerns and its disciplined eclecticism; so that its associates included some of Stewart Headlam's *Church Reformer* circle, the disciples of William Morris, the Rhymers' Club, and even stringent figures from the world of bibliography. The two principals in the conduct of the periodical were Arthur Heygate Mackmurdo (1851–1942) and Herbert Percy Horne (1864–1916), with assistance from Selwyn Image (1849–1930), rebellious Anglo-Catholic, associate of Headlam, calligrapher, book-designer, designer of stained glass, poet and art critic, the closest of one of eight or so associates in various fields. When in 1889, Mackmurdo bought 20 Fitzroy Street, it became a focus of turn-of-the-century preoccupations. It was studios and rooms for Horne, Mackmurdo, Lionel Johnson, later Victor Plarr; early meetings of the Rhymer's Club were held there; many distinguished figures were frequent visitors right up to the First World War—Wilde, Dowson, Sturge Moore, Roger Fry, Augustus John, and others.

Mackmurdo and Horne were architects, enterprising though minor. Beginning his training in 1869, Mackmurdo was influenced early both by Ruskin and positivism, though Italian travels in the 1870s left him with an enthusiasm for Renaissance architecture that could hardly have been agreeable to his master. His *Wren's City Churches* (1882), produced in response to threats of demolition, is his first essay in the unity of arts; its bold cover—the pillars anticipating the Century Guild's stress on the Renaissance rectilinear in their graphics; the stylized flames and phoenixes indicating *art nouveau*—can be read both as illustration and pure design, while the symbolism announces the decadent motif of regeneration through destruction. His pupil, Herbert Horne, though his work in decorative art is derivative (he has nothing as bold as Mackmurdo's *art nouveau* chairs), was as versatile; more distinguished as designer of books and typographer, he was also poet, collector of eighteenth-century English water colours (an early enthusiast for Alexander Cozens), and the first scientific art historian in this country (his *Sandro Botticelli* remains authoritative).

The Century Guild was founded either in 1882 or 1883; but its nucleus was certainly the architectural partnership of Mackmurdo and Horne formed in the latter year. It was the first of the artistic guilds flourishing from the 1880s, though the word was adopted by several nineteenth-century organizations, spiritual and secular: Ruskin's Guild of Saint George (1871); Stewart Headlam's Guild of Saint Matthew (1877); the Church and Stage Guild; the Art Workers Guild of 1884, the most important in the Art and Craft movement. The Pre-Raphaelites of the first and second generation constituted a loose personal relationship of artists rather than a fraternal association governed by a concept of the intrinsic unity of arts, and Morris strikingly did not form a Guild; nonetheless, both Pre-Raphaelites and Morris, Faulkner and Co. constituted paradigms.

The *Century Guild Hobby Horse* was its organ, though later it developed beyond the limits of a 'house' journal; but the attention it devoted to calligraphy, the revival of woodcut, old music and instruments, is part of a significant, Morris-influenced programme. As for the 'hobby horse' of the title, Horne's explanation was Shandy-ish: 'each writer is supposed to utter only his sincerest opinions and such opinions affect only the writer, . . . "there is no disputing about hobby-horses".'

The first issue was in April 1884. Mackmurdo was responsible; the mediocre quality of the letterpress resembles the issues of 1892 he also superintended. A quarto (9" × 11", slightly smaller than later numbers), it was set up at 'Sunnyside', Orpington, Kent, in the garden shed of George Allen, a former pupil of Ruskin at the Working Men's College (where Brown and Rossetti also taught) in the 1850s. Printing was entrusted to Chiswick Press, which had a reputation for quality work, using Caslon type on handmade paper; the reproduction of drawings and graphics was the responsibility of Emery Walker, associate of Morris, later to found the Doves Press. Aylmer Vallance observed that 'never before had modern printing been treated as a serious art, whose province was to embrace the whole process, from the selection and spacing of type and the position of the printed matter on the page, to the embellishment of the book with appropriate initials and other decorative adornments'.[3] Mackmurdo was to claim, perhaps justly, that the production of the *Century Guild Hobby Horse* strongly influenced the foundation of the Kelmscott Press.

Unlike the format of the *Germ*, the *Hobby Horse* challenged the

[3] 'Mr Arthur Mackmurdo and the Century Guild', *The Studio* XVI (1899), p. 187.

reader at the outset with a design emblematically mediating the Guild's aims and the content. Selwyn Image, who played some part in the preparation of the first issue, furnished a pen and ink drawing, engraved on wood by W. H. Hooper for the prospectus, later, in enlarged version, the central portion of the cover and title page. Square, it carries a design of two knights on decoratively caparisoned prancing horses; the mounted figures, appearing legless, cannot be considered as standing behind their steeds, so that the ambiguity of design constitutes an intentional visual pun or rebus on the name of the magazine with its dual meanings—literally, that draped horse-headed wicker framework traditionally worn by morris-dancers and, figuratively, the concept which decided the title, an *idée fixe*, a balance of stasis and quest. Outside the central square field, a white rectangle carries the lettering: an idiom repeated in later book designs by Image and Horne. This area is surrounded by a landscape border, where the thorny stems of tangled brambles swing across the lower half of the design in rhythmic curves which half conceal a coiled serpent concealed in the fungous undergrowth. (The swinging brambles are found also in Beardsley's *Morte D'Arthur* cover design of 1893.) Image's design, though complicated, is firmly organized with interplay of black lines and white masses in a manner both decorative and illustrative, fulfilling Image's criteria for woodcutting. Most remarkable of the visual illustrations is Mackmurdo's vignette on the back cover: a monogram consisting in a stylized long-stemmed flower (or seed-head) with two leaves, the leaves entwined with the initials 'C. G.' Two other *art nouveau* images may be mentioned: the waving headpiece on page 1 of the 1884 issue which Lisa Ticknor on stylistic grounds assigns to Mackmurdo; the highly formalized rhythmic design of trees and a river on page 20 of the 1886 assigned to Image.

Unlike the *Germ*, the *Century Guild Hobby Horse* did have a manifesto, Mackmurdo's 'The Guild's Flag Unfurling', to which Image added a lecture resisting narrow Aestheticism and attacking naturalism in illustration. After sharp reviews of the first issue, the second, with Horne's influence growing dominant, did not appear until January 1886. The magazine's tendency to abstract line is there, but still advocated in terms of Pre-Raphaelite idealism; Art, though based on Nature and 'forever returning to Nature for inspiration, is not imitation of Nature, but a coexistent world . . . a storehouse, so to say . . . of symbols'.[4] Pre-Raphaelite connections were stressed up to 1889, with

4 *The Century Guild Hobby Horse* III (1888), p. 120.

reminiscences of Rossetti, the printing of James Smetham's remains, poems by W. B. Scott and Christina Rossetti, etc. Blake and his 'Shoreham' followers were a related concern: the magazine reprinted Blake's *Marriage of Heaven and Hell* and first printed, in July, the *Book of Los*. Thus by the issue of October 1886 the pattern down to 1891 was established: the main themes were Pre-Raphaelite continuity, art and craft revival of woodblock, printing and other hand-arts, polemic against Impressionism conceived as naturalism, Blake's way of uniting the arts through the symbol, and, finally, Horne's ideal of severity and repose as a basis for the union of the arts. Image attacked the Royal Academy, now virtually synonymous with the Royal Society of Oils (though a few sculptures and architectural drawings were admitted to its annual exhibitions). By 1886, polarization between an Academy dedicated to exclusiveness and the Guilds was total. In 1886 came the New English Art Club, tepidly reflecting French advanced painting; the secretary, Francis Bate, expressed the club's aims in another magazine, the *Artist and Journal of Home Culture*. Image, reformist with regard to the Academy, was hostile to the New English, attacking Bate, in the July 1888 issue, as a representative of false science masquerading as art. Image theoretically was poised between Ruskin and expressionism. But his effect on the *Hobby Horse's* illustrations was restrictive. Largely through Horne, the impressionist Charles Shannon, of the *Dial* circle, did twice contribute lithographs. But these were not admired by Horne's associates, though Shannon marked the stone himself.

Two of these associates in particular influenced the magazine's direction: A. H. Galton, a disciple of Arnold who induced the master to contribute, and Lionel Johnson, an enthusiast for Pater. Galton and Horne were in fact in continuous conflict over the tone and range of the periodical, with Galton trying to remove all traces of direct affiliation with the Guild and establish an improved academic-literary periodical, less concerned with general principles, more with personalities. (Galton was an elderly Oxford undergraduate; with Johnson, an undergraduate also, he ensured a university audience.) Horne's resistance came from the conviction that return to high Victorianism was not possible, and that a personal, perhaps eccentric note was precisely the point of the magazine. Johnson, on the other hand, supported Horne's admission of decadent and symbolist material: Wilde on Keats in the July 1886 issue; two sonnets by J. A. Symonds on Narcissus and Baldur in 1887. Decadent themes never predominated in the

Century Guild, but they were not infrequently present, especially in the form of the Uranian theme (though Symonds's preference was for the mature and muscular male), which entered six months before the first 'Uranian' poems in the *Artist and Journal of Home Culture*. But Horne's preoccupations grew increasingly scholarly. Meanwhile Image established in January 1888 that key form of end-of-century minority culture, the short story, with his 'In the Days of the Philistine', the first of four stories to appear in the run of the magazine.

By April 1888 financial crisis—that classic threat to the little magazine—was added, as we can see from some notes of cost and sales which survive in Horne's hand:

Cost of No. IX.
Kegan Paul for printing etc.   25.   6.   9.
Paper   15. 12.   0.
Illustration on the average   17.   0.   0.

Sales of No. IX.   287.
              X.   271.
              VII. 307.
              VIII. 277.
Sales of 600 to July cover costs (100)[5]

This covers the period from April 1887 to January 1888. Sales, if not slipping, were not improving. In a letter to Lilian Block, Mackmurdo stated that 'the H. H. was sold only to annual subscribers, it never quite reached 500'.[6] All through its career the magazine, though circulating considerably more widely than the subscription figures suggest (via Oxford Common Rooms, for example), continued to cause concern; finances were the major cause of the later quarrel between Horne and Mackmurdo. The immediate outcome of the crisis was (as with the *Germ*) an agonizing reappraisal of title. Horne defended the existing title as expressive if grotesque; Galton even proposed a new cover that would certainly have represented Horne's increasing emphasis on the Renaissance rather than the medieval: 'A beautiful human figure, and the countenance of Image's Leonardo, he is to be in an Italian garden with statues and Renaissance architecture and a book with a rising sun or moon.'[7] In February 1887, John Gray

---

[5] Archives of the Museo Horne, Florence.
[6] 'The Pursuit of Beauty . . .', p. 145.
[7] Holograph letter. Collection of Mrs T. C. Dugdale, London.

of the Scottish National Portrait Gallery had written to Horne, pointing out that one detail only was required to mark the periodical as a total art production: 'Mr Image or some other of your artistic contributors should design a cloth cover with gold or other appropriate decoration (say something in the manner of Rossetti's poems) for binding the volumes of the *Hobby Horse*. The whole of the book inside and out, would then be harmonious and "all of a piece".'[8] The cover was changed; Horne, though, disliked gold blocking, and the binding was the blue-grey ingres paper characteristic of his own bindings, with vellum spine. By 1888, then, each issue was planned so that letterpress no less than format furnished an example of architectural unity.

By the end of 1888, partly as a consequence of the crisis of the spring, Horne decided that a restatement of principle was in order. Zola appears as villainous representative of modern materialism, posed against a Carolean age of 'manners and beauty', in the editorial of January 1889. Puritanism is the source of commercialism and naturalism; Pater is the antidote. Both Johnson and Galton violently disapproved of Horne's statement, though it attempted to embody some of their own notions; further editorial differences smouldered in the early part of 1889 between Horne and Galton.

I shall focus on the increasing contributions of a 'decadent' cast and the critical discussion of decadence and symbolism from this point on, though the art and craft accent and connected antiquarianism persist. In October 1890 Symonds contributed a translation of Bion's pastoral elegy, the *Lament for Adonis*, in which Horne considerably assisted; the most felt passages relate to the beauty of Adonis in death. Johnson, who approved of Symonds's version, contributed to that same issue a poem 'In Praise of Love' 'which touches, I trust, with delicacy upon Greek virtue and Greek vice. Have you seen Symonds's article on Platonic Love?'[9] This had recently appeared in the *Artist and Journal of Home Culture*: 'It is barely decent: the man is an absolute Priapus, a very Satyr.' Both Symonds and Johnson subscribed to the important but rationalizing distinction between Uranian (physical) and Pandemian homo-erotic love (though in Symonds's case this was mostly observed in the breach). The ideal might refer to an ascending ladder of love, from sight of the beloved to union with the supersensual beauty of the One; but this notion could readily be used as a rhetoric of

[8] Holograph letter. Collection of Mrs T. C. Dugdale, London.

[9] Holograph letter. Copy in the possession of Professor A. W. Patrick, Hamilton, Canada.

seduction, down the ladder of love from sight and touch to taste. That point is made in Percy L. Osborn's 'Echelle D'Eros' contributed to *The Spirit Lamp* (1892–3) where the last step of the ladder is described as 'l'union complète; / L'extase des corps et des cœurs, / Et je ne sais quelles langueurs'. The *Spirit Lamp*, however, was a private Oxford periodical in a university now distinctly secularized and accustomed to —without approving—the language of the 'new chivalry'. Johnson's poem is more discreet and with some irony dedicated to Lord Alfred Douglas (the dedication was prudently omitted in the 1915 edition of Johnson's poems). Suitably generalized references to 'full lips' and 'shapely limbs' there are; but the young men of the poem, like a bunch of Hippolytuses, strike one as athletic and pious, even though their religion seems to owe more to Saint Aloysius, Oxford, than to any Attic fane. Still, the question of whether this ladder of pleasure leads 'del goia al goia all ultimo diletto' is left usefully open. At night, in the one stanza not precisely muffled with delicacy: 'Their eyes on fire, their bright limbs flushed, / They dominate the night with love: / While the stars burn and flash above, / These kindle through the dark such flame, / As is not seen, and hath no name: / Can night bear more? Can nature bend / In benediction without end, / Over this love of friend for friend?'[10] The final question is perhaps not resolvable, but the vocabulary of 'no name' and 'friend' certainly derives from the homosexual half-world.

In the following issue, the first of volume VI (1891), an uncharacteristic painting by Watts, 'A Roman Lady in the Decadence of the Empire', is reproduced; however, Horne's note[11] concentrates on its architectural accessories and as usual deplores the state of contemporary art, appealing for a return to the classical spirit of 'repose and severity'. Johnson's poem *In Honorem B. V. M. de Winton Martyrumque Wiccamicorum* is in early Latin Christian style (Ambrose, Sedulius, Venantius Fortunatus), in four-line stanzas of accentual iambic dimeters, a metre of acute monotony, without full rhymes. The practice of Latin Christian metres is symptomatic of the decadence; Baudelaire's *Franciscae Meae Laudes* was followed by Des Esseintes's distinctly naturalistic and documentary account of late Latin literature; the hero of George Moore's *A Mere Accident* (1887) prolongs the cult, which finds more scholarly vent in Remy de Gourmont's *Le Latin*

10 *The Century Guild Hobby Horse* V (1890), pp. 141–3.
11 Holograph letter. Copy in the possession of Professor A. W. Patrick, Hamilton, Canada.

Mystique of 1892. Such stress on earlier Christian poetry connects with historical self-consciousness about contemporary 'decadence': the literary decadence, as innovation, renewal, on the model of the rise of medieval Latin verse from its first 'stammering beginnings'.

Image indeed concludes a note on Gluck's *Orfeo* with paradoxical confirmation: 'The world is very old and tired; it has been through so many experiences, and found them vanity. The world is very young and expectant; so many fresh emotions come upon it unaware; and it is full of hope.' In April 1891, Dowson contributed the famous 'Non Sum Qualis Eram Bonae Sub Regno Cynarae', and Johnson wrote to say that he admired Horne's daring in extending the frontiers of permissible publication. 'A Case of Conscience', Dowson's casuistical short story, is characteristic of its author: the present is rarely held in bold relief; mood rather than narrative is the idiom, and a set of impressions confirms the notion that the will is either powerless to effect their course or, if asserted, is disastrous. Like the typical lyric of Dowson's circle, the short story is autobiographical: the drifting hero is in love with a girl-child, innocent, inaccessible. Johnson's 'Upon the Practice and Theory of Verse at the Present Time Obtaining in France —the long titles have an antique flavour and assist the typographer in his refined patterning—introduces the readers of the magazine to 'the schools, to which belong, not it may be thought too happily, the names of *décadence* or of *symbolism*'. Johnson's summary is based on a French critic's account, and the range involves Wagner and colour audition; but vertical correspondences and Schopenhauer's influence are unmentioned, while the dialectical relationship of naturalism and decadence to symbolism is not boldly isolated, as in Symons's *Harper's Magazine* article of 1893. Nonetheless, it is an early account, and aligned to the Guild's general doctrines in its distrust of 'facile' talk about uniting the arts.

Then, at the close of 1891, tension between Horne and Mackmurdo resulted in the paper passing out of Horne's hands. Johnson informed Galton: 'Mackmurdo is, technically and financially, sole editor and proprietor; but one half of the paper will always be literary, under the informal management of Image and myself. . . . But I do not prophesy long life to the *Hobby Horse* under so vague a scheme.' The general standard of the 1892 volume is lower than that of its immediate predecessors, returning to the model of the 1884 and 1886 issues. Morris is the most distinguished of the new contributors, with a paper on 'The Influence of Building Materials upon Architecture'. Two members of the Rhymers' Club make a first appearance: Richard Le Gallienne and Ernest Rhys. Le Gallienne's essay attempts to define Decadence in general terms, though the immediate occasion was Churton Collins's notorious edition of Tennyson, with its elaborate display of sources, suggesting that Tennyson was Alexandrian, if not Decadent. Unusually for a Rhymer, Le Gallienne defends Tennyson. For Le Gallienne, decadence is more than a matter of style; it is one of ignoring proportion in treatment. In one passage he prefigures Nordau's association of artists with degenerates and imbeciles: disease as a theme does not necessarily imply decadent sensibility, only 'where it is studied apart from its relations to health, . . . To notice only the picturesque effect of a beggar's rags, like Gautier; the colour-scheme of a tipster's nose like Mr Huysmans; to consider one's mother merely prismatically, like Mr Whistler—are examples of the decadent attitude'.[12] Le Gallienne is playing his familiar trick of claiming intimate acquaintance with what he is attacking. And to illustrate the magazine's impartiality, Charles Sayle's 'New Poet' celebrates John Gambril Nicholson's 'Uranian' sonnets, though Sayle polemically asserts them to be 'natural' and 'healthy'. Similarly, though Johnson and Horne were committed Paterians, Symonds had been allowed to doubt Pater's notion of all the arts aspiring to the condition of music.

Early in 1893, Elkin Mathews and John Lane issued a circular for prospective subscribers to a new series of the *Century Guild Hobby Horse*. The first number of the now entitled *Hobby Horse*, edited by Horne, appeared in that same year, with a subscription to four issues, including postage and packing, of one pound; sheets of the English issue were published in the USA by Copeland and Day, Boston. Horne produced a new cover design, printed in black on blue-grey binding, and a title page where a knight in left profile carries a quiver and a swirling banner which occupies the upper portion of the design. He is mounted on a Hobby Horse; the cloth bears the device of a blindfold Eros and the motto 'Amor Vincit Omnia' repeated in initials. The ornaments were also designed by Horne, and the general impression of the *Hobby Horse* is quiet and austere, due in part to more disciplined management of type. Arnold Dolmetsch's 'Consorts of Viols, the Viola d'Amore, the Lyra Viol and the Viola da Gamba' takes the late sixteenth and early seventeenth century as the 'golden' moment of English music. (Horne had arranged for Dolmetsch to

[12] *The Century Guild Hobby Horse* VII (1892), p. 80.

give five concerts at the Guild's London centre, 20 Fitzroy Street; this is the only return to the Art and Craft tradition of the *Hobby Horse*'s predecessor.) The only 'decadent' items are three poems and a short story by Dowson, and one of Verlaine's later inferior religious poems (but Dowson can be readily aligned with Horne's classical and Renaissance enthusiasm: of the 1890s poets, he is the most delicate metrically and the most verbally refined). The remainder of the contributions reflect Horne's archival, architectural and typographical concerns.

The third issue of the *Hobby Horse* (1894) was its last. It expired without explanation, though the ending of the partnership between Lane and Mathews in about July 1894 and the first appearance of the *Yellow Book* in April 1894 may be relevant. Like the *Germ*, its immediate afterlife was financial sordor: as late as 1900 Mackmurdo was still trying to recover money he claimed Horne owed him in connection with the *Century Guild Hobby Horse*. 'Decadence' was only part of its programme; the unifying factor in its production was Horne, but by 1894 he was already simplifying his interests in the direction of severe art history. The magazine had some progeny in the United States: *The Knight Errant* (1892) similar in format and concerns, the first of a number of the small magazines of the 'mauve decade': *Moods*, *The Lotus*, *John-A-Dreams*, *Mlle New York* and others.

THE ARTIST AND JOURNAL OF HOME CULTURE
(1888–94)

Founded in 1880 as a journal for practitioners of painting, with its phrase 'Home Culture' as evident gesture to the House Beautiful spirit of the 1880s, *The Artist and Journal of Home Culture* was a truly minority periodical only between 1888 and 1894, when it was edited by Charles Kains Jackson (1857–1933), lawyer, antiquarian, minimal poet, and the pope—or more precisely the ombudsman—of both the London and Oxford groups of homosexuals. This resulted in his discreet use of the *Artist* as a vehicle for 'Uranian' propaganda, embracing both boy-love and Symonds-type passion for the brawnily mature. The editor's sexual brinkmanship finally failed soon after he published pseudonymously 'The New Chivalry' (2 April, 1894), where he argued (rather than discreetly praising in poetry) for a new type of ideal love that replaced traditional exaltation of women with that of male youth, on Malthusian grounds. This Hellenism was matched by a disgust with women, for instance in Gleeson White's contribution of

1 November, 1889, where women are seen as biologically unsound. Uranianism, however, was only one of the 'decadent'—meaning 'modern'—features of the magazine. Kains Jackson intensified the use of literary material, drawing on contemporary minority authors, though drawing them into the often trivializing context of his art material. Thus Pater is praised; the Rhymers' Club poets and their associates are discussed at the outset of their careers; there are articles and translations from the contemporary French, all of decadent cast: Verlaine, Mendès, Rachilde. Articles on topics popular with *fin-de-siècle* men of letters are frequent: the Poster; black and white illustrations; Impressionism and Photography; the Child Actress; Ballet and Music Hall; *Symboliste* artists like Khnopf and the *Rose Croix* school; Schopenhauer (1 October ,1888); Zola (1 December, 1888). Other periodicals such as the *Hobby Horse, Artistic Japan, Pagan Review, Dial* and the *Yellow Book* are, normally sympathetically, reviewed. But it is—with the exception of John Gray, taken up here before he was by Wilde—the less prominent and more provincial versions of the decadent poets who actually appear: Charles Sayle, 'Corvo', J. G. Nicholson, Wratislaw.

The word 'decadent' is frequently used, either neutrally or in laudation. John Gray and Pierre Loüys are described as young decadents; articles dwell on topics and express opinions of decadent interest, like 'Pastel', which speaks to the tune of Baudelaire about the charms of faces made haggard by nightly applications of cosmetics. Beardsley is recognized as a master of the 'eccentric' and 'fantastic', appealing always to an 'exotic' nature; the love of Des Esseintes for a refined art is identified as that of 'the age'. The transition from Aestheticism to Decadence is duly if superficially recorded in terms of sunflowers replaced by green carnations (1 April, 1892). There are even prescriptions, in the style of recommendations on artist's materials, on how to manufacture a green carnation, or a blue rose: malachite green, an aniline dye, will suffuse a flower with the proper absinthe hue. In typical gossipy tone we are told that Edgar Saltus's books are to be bound in a peculiar shade of pale green suggestive of absinthe, the green witch. *The Artist* wrily apologizes for using approvingly words such as 'unmanly' and 'effeminate', explaining that historical evidence shows that only yesterday to take a daily bath, and a little further back to drink claret rather than port, registered effeminacy.

'Realism' is found to be a feature connecting the Alexandrian and modern periods, though not surprisingly, in view of Kains Jackson's vulgarized Platonism, realism is not really approved (1 November,

G

1889). In the issue for October 1, 1890, comes the first (but in fact unique) offering of a series on Les Décadents mentioning Verlaine, Mallarmé, Mendès, Pater, Burne-Jones, Wilde, Moore and Eugene Lee-Hamilton: the phrase Decadence has, we learn, 'obviously no reference to a failure of technical ability, or of aesthetic insight'. But the author does not condescend to quotation and his discussion is virtually limited to Greek antiquity. There are reviews of *Meleagre* by 'one of our younger decadents' Pierre Loüys (2 December, 1893), of Wratislaw's *Caprices* by C. J. Hiatt (1 January, 1894). James Stanley Little (1 March, 1894), commenting on the detached intellectualism of Sargent, suggests that the painter 'may be with the advance guard of that androgynous age into which we seem to be gliding . . . such work . . . lacks the red blood of a noble vigour'. The ambiguously decadent note of Beardsley's Salome image is fittingly defined in Wratislaw's article of 2 April, 1894: of the artist's obsession with the monstrous and the grotesque he observes that Beardsley 'is fond of laughing at his self-created terrors and as though in mockery he draws a strange figure throwing out a showman's hand towards the titanic wife of the tetrarch'. 'Modernity of taste' is stressed in Kains Jackson's appreciation of Donne, an article strangely overlooked in discussion of that poet's afterlife. Kains Jackson admires the whole range of Donne's work; he calls attention to 'a modernity of expression and metre', recognizes the libertine element in *Songs and Sonnets*, and praises a line from Donne's lyrics as being 'of a wholly decadent fashion'. By this time we may suspect that the word has become so general a shorthand for 'modern' as to be meaningless.

After May 1894, the *Artist* changes format, and the last few issues edited by Kains Jackson are remarkable only for homosexual verses under a pseudonym from J. F. Bloxam, author of 'The Priest and the Acolyte' and editor of *The Chameleon*. Precisely as Kains Jackson administered cautious doses of Uranian material, so he avoided organizing any firm attitude towards 'decadence' and its embodiment, Wilde. To allow personal views and occasionally to attack Wilde and Gray gave them publicity and promoted circulation. But the failure of the magazine to adopt a distinct stance accords with its undistinguished format and vague attitude towards realism and naturalism in the visual arts. Kains Jackson's preference was for the ideal, but apart from gradual hardening towards the New English and more attention to Pre-Raphaelitism, it is barely visible. The paradox presented by the *Artist* is of a London provincialism, randomly permeated at an early date by

French Decadent theory and practice, dissolving Decadence from new-
ness into news.

THE DIAL (1889–97)

The Dial produced five highly sporadic issues spaced over five years,
printing two hundred copies at a price of 7s. 6d.; in its style and in-
frequency it foreshadows like periodicals by Gordon Craig and
James Guthrie. The circle which produced it gathered round the
enménagement of Charles Ricketts, painter, book-designer, stage-
designer and collector, and Charles Shannon, painter and illustrator, at
the Vale and later at Beaufort Street, Chelsea. Here, said Wilde, one
could hear the least boring conversation in London; the productive
circle included John Gray, Sturge Moore, Reginald Savage and Lucien
Pissarro—all young, virtually unknown, and interested in contemporary French culture and uniting the arts. The magazine had the largest
format of any of the period's little magazines; its cover, showing a
sun dial, was of thick biscuit-brown paper, owing something perhaps
to Whistler's famous brown paper for walls. It prolonged the Art and
Craft traditions of the *Hobby Horse* in its elegant use of type measure,
though it went well beyond the woodcut and wood-engraving idiom
of its predecessor. Its first issue was less achieved than subsequent issues,
and an article on Puvis de Chavannes, devoid of its continuation, indicates that the second issue was shortly to follow. In the event, it did not
appear for three years. Like *The Hobby Horse*, there are Pre-Raphaelite
affinities, though also a taste for Japanese art (Utamaro mainly, however, the Pre-Raphaelite of the Japanese). There is medievalizing,
though the note tends toward the playful and parodic. Contemporary
French literature (Verhaeren, Verlaine, Rimbaud) and art are more
accented, but the art pantheon resembles the earlier magazine: the
Pre-Raphaelites, Millet, Puvis. Gray remarks that the Pre-Raphaelite
movement seems to have 'died down', and that 'when it returns it will
be through France', coming back through Impressionist no less than
Symbolist art. There are sympathetic notes of the Exposition des
Vingts, Monet and the not too successful visit of Antoine's *Théâtre Libre*.
Ricketts's colour lithograph illustrating John Gray's 'The Great Worm'
reflects Puvis, as do Pissarro's woodcuts, Millet and Sturge Moore.
Calvert and Blake. Shannon's lithograph 'Atalanta' owes something to
Beardsley, though it also shows impressionist influence.

But only with the second issue is the purer impress of Ricketts's taste
clear. Now title page becomes identical with cover, and the tables of

contents are, in three issues, huddled at the back in a neat rectangle of type. Convention cedes to typographical rigour; page numbers are omitted. Decadent sensibility now shows in parodic and whimsical parable; Ricketts's story 'The Marred Face' is a version of the Salome theme; and decadent Catholicism appears in Gray's notice of Huysmans' *En Route*. The equivocal tone of decadence indeed seems evident in the title itself—a seeming promise of temporal determinism which the whimsical cycle of the periodical denies. Presumably Ricketts and friends brought out an issue when they had sufficient material: stability through eccentricity. *The Dial*, though perhaps less atomized than the magazines produced by single individuals, does extend the 'private effort' to its extreme. Cohesion is frankly a matter of personalities; there is no group or guild; the main programme is to exist as beautifully as possible.

THE YELLOW BOOK (1894–7)

In literary history, this is always *the* magazine of the 1890s. Yet it represents the point where the format and accent of earlier periodicals was taken up into commercial publishing. 'And it's not even yellow', Wilde reportedly remarked of its first number, displeased at being conspicuously overlooked in the battle order of eminences and notorieties announced as future contributors. And despite Beardsley's cover design, which must have startled eyes however habituated to jaundiced aesthetic tints, scrofulous French novels, railway yellow-backs, and the menace of the yellow east, Wilde was as usual perfectly correct. The publisher, shrewd son of a Devonshire farmer, turned book producer, viewed his periodical as speculation with slender risk and expectation of fat profit. What Lane intended to profit from was the need of the *avant garde* to advance from the safe world of the coterie to the dangerous open world of the 'new', and the complementary need of the popular press—the 'new' journalism—to find (or if necessary engineer) controversy. The position of the 'advanced' and the 'new' could be vulgarized and polarized: 'Has Marriage a Future?', 'The Question of Zola', or the problem of the New Hedonism. Such questions had to be incarnated in figures; but personality could barely be exploited by the press without some connivance. The models were Whistler and Wilde; Beardsley was a more desperate neophyte, though as insolent and witty. The 'new' was to hypostatize movements and type individuals. The 'new' woman was as old of course as Mary

Wollstonecraft, who stimulated, if that is the just word, her counterpart, the homosexual Dandy. There was the New English Art Club, which had tried to be French and had hardly been new at any time; the New Journalism, certainly new, largely American and intensely nasty, even nastier when yoked to Imperialism; the New Humour, though no one has yet been able to determine whether it was in the least new or particularly humorous. These words, as we can see from the newspaper reaction to the *Yellow Book* and other nineties magazines, were involved with others—'decadent', 'realist', 'impressionist', all deployed with a useful looseness.

The book itself was to be parodically sacred, that is, unparaphrasable: with the majesty of quarterly publication, asymmetrical cover design and highly elaborate illustrations profiting from the new photo mechanical processes so that any medium could be translated with clarity (though black and white travelled best). Lane's strategy—though Henry Harland, tepid literary editor, Ella D'Arcy, clever assistant editor, and the rogue Beardsley were the tacticians—was to spice the *Yellow Book* with some alarming names: Hubert Crackanthorpe for slices of refined misery; 'patchouli' Symons; 'George Egerton'; and Beerbohm, who soon attracted as much fear and contempt as Wilde or Beardsley himself. If Max didn't keep bad company, he certainly kept bad vocabulary, bad tone and worse subject matter: 'A Defence of Cosmetics' indeed; a eulogy of George the Fourth. Shyly to submit he was joking made Max's offence twice mortal, and J. A. Spender in the *Westminster Gazette* (probably stunting, as in his campaign against the 'New Fiction') apoplectically affirmed that nothing would meet the case of Beardsley but 'a short act of Parliament to make this kind of thing illegal'. Both press and 'decadents' knew this was good clean fun; Beardsley joined in by contributing drawings to the *Yellow Book* under an assumed name, to be praised by the same critics who had damned his acknowledged work. Beardsley also baited his publisher. Poor Lane dizzied himself, turning every drawing round and round to ensure that no saucy phallus poked occultly from some corner.

But the audience had to be reassured as well as moderately shocked. The letterpress included the 'safe' William Watson; though he had fired a pistol at an empty Royal carriage to draw attention to his own genius, and spent much time travelling about England carrying a carpet bag filled with constantly replenished French letters, he was, in poetry, agreeably tame. Then there was the Superintendent of the British Museum Reading Room; there was George Saintsbury; there was the esoterically respectable Henry James. Beardsley polemically separated the 'picture' side of things (no subservience to print), though the arrangement lasted for only two issues. Equally elegant but more mischievous juxtapositions: Beardsley plus seedy images from Sickert with Sir Frederic Leighton, President of the Royal Academy. Beardsley's own sinister, enigmatic 'Night Piece', an unaccompanied lady with mountainous coiffure, sharp whiteness of neck and bosom, composes her sexuality against a backdrop of houses and the East end of a Wrenish church. The drawing ushers in Symons's 'night piece' *Stella Maris*, a blasphemously cheery record of 'The chance romances of the streets, / The Juliet of a night', and on the other flank of the poem the innocuously entitled 'A Study' by the Chevalier Bayard of the Royal Academy: two Maenads dancing to a flutter of transpicuous draperies, the younger devotee cocking a leg in front of her taller partner. The classical distance, that sort of thing is excusable in the Greeks, becomes disturbing by context. At all events, the other paletted knights of the Academy were disturbed: Leighton contributed no more.

If the relationship of Lane to the contributors was not necessarily direct, it was not coincidental that so many came from his own list. (The *Yellow Book* was in a sense a house journal, the first of several: the *Chapbook* (1896–7); *Bodley Head Bulletin* (1900), *Methuen's Gazette and Literary Notes*, *Unwin's Chapbook* (1899–1900) with a Beardsley cover design.) The list of advertisements was large, indexed, and bound in at the back. Beardsley's cover design listed the contents on the back cover, a familiar witty device as we have seen with Ricketts, who enjoyed turning books inside out, disguising the title page, confusing the abstractly visual with the discursive. But the table of letterpress and pictures was also printed at the front: more unparaphrasable balancing. The proprietor was, it has often been observed, particularly hospitable to women writers and there was an increasing sect of educated and questioning women to write for and read the new venture.

Press reaction was all that might have been wished. The *Yellow Book* was widely and emphatically noticed. The *Academy*, for which Watson, Lionel Johnson, John Davidson, J. T. Nettleship and a number of Lane's other contributors reviewed, received the first number with a resigned acidity. The reviewer was Frederick Wedmore, writer of 'mood' short stories, art critic, who had failed to get onto the short list of those who were billed to appear in Lane's periodical, though Lane was Wedmore's publisher. Wedmore found Beardsley's cover 'cheerfully eccentric', while 'Education Sentimentale', that disturbing piece, was disturbingly, cleverly reduced to a 'comic puzzle, not without a certain attractiveness of line'; but, like most of Beardsley, too Japanesy, just as Laurence Housman's illustrations were too much 'the sexless Pre-Raphaelite'. James's 'Death of the Lion' was read as a satire on the 'larger latitude' or 'the licence to talk about ugly things inartistically'. As for poor Max and his lapidary joke, both were dismissed as a 'somebody' who had contributed 'a worthless silly article on an insignificant theme'. Arthur Waugh's article on 'Reticence in Literature' in the second number, carefully counterbalancing Crackanthorpe's which had preferred the larger latitude, in the first, was 'sane and manly', and Watson's inevitable sonnet had 'distinction and real dignity'. The anonymous *Academy* reviewer of the second issue (probably Wedmore again) was indeed more kind, but not very kind: was it not too bulky to be convenient, and far too full of 'short' stories which were too diffuse to be really short? While the pictorial side had improved, the literature remained for the most part merely 'letterpress'. And, as for Lane's young ladies, they were shrill amateurs with pet-names like the actresses at the Gaiety and far too displayed: so much for 'George Egerton' and 'Graham Tomson' and 'John Oliver Hobbes'. Yet a year later, Wedmore was mollified enough to write for the *Savoy*, a genuinely advanced periodical.

The general content of the *Yellow Book* reflected the 'mood' forms fashionable at the time: no full-length novels, no serials; but one-act plays; short poems as fillers; whimsically trivial essays. The achievement of the letterpress, indeed, is pretty well limited to its short stories, light on plot, heavy on mood, with not much visible climax. Indeed George Saintsbury grumbled that much fiction in this form had no ending at all, it simply guttered out. The central figure of most of these stories is the artist, a new passive hero, condemned to misunderstanding and muted disaster. Here, at least, the *Yellow Book* was genuinely decadent in suggesting an aesthetic of failure: in Sartrian terms, that existence and essence can never, after the moment of contingency, be reunited; that essence is by definition evanescent. This will cover Yeats's lyrics of *The Wind Among the Reeds* phase or Dowson's notion of the 'good moment', gone almost as soon as evidenced.

The exclusion of Wilde did not, by a strident irony, save Lane's enterprise from being engulfed in the *débâcle* of 1895. The sacred book was entirely paraphrasable: it was more than just dirty entertainment, it was like Wilde's paradoxes, for real. The 'new' journalism with its coarse deadlines was unable and unwilling to distinguish delicately.

For Wilde, for Beardsley, for Lane himself, the reckoning had come. The *Yellow Book* survived for two more years, until it ceased to pay dividends, but it had, as a contemporary said, 'turned grey overnight'. The later issues were more solid, introduced new talent—Arnold Bennett, John Buchan, Harold Frederic—but the attempted leap-frogging to Edwardianism merely resulted in a loss of identity. Certainly another contemporary who remarked that it 'died of acute preciosity' was very wrong. Still, it aimed to be 'modern', and in spite of compromises and contradictions, survives as the central magazine of the decade, for it reached beyond the coteries, the closed world of pornography, the invisible world of the esoteric. Which of its rivals has attracted a full-length book, reprints of its thirteen volumes and four selections from its offerings? Yet if it had not entered the public world so provokingly, it would not have failed so publicly, and narrowed the choices for its successors. Any coterie magazine was now liable to guilt by exclusiveness; yet any minority periodical which entered the public world was forced by the state of cultural politics to disavow 'decadence', which involved disavowing 'modernity'. The improved technical facilities in illustration and printing compelled more direct confrontation between artist and public. Mechanical punching, composition and linotype, all available by the 1880s, coincided with the first generations benefiting from the Education Acts of the 1870s and the Franchise Act of 1888. The readership of the daily press increased and the 'numbers' had been given a voice by the possible influence of emancipated and widely disseminated art and literature on a partially educated readership in search of entertainment rather than information or moral discrimination. The new mass media as has been suggested tempted artist and writer to publicize themselves: their activities had become the more exposed to a new glare and alerted civil authority.

THE SAVOY (1895-6)

The evasions and lack of success of the *Savoy* have to be understood in this context, and the context of Wilde's trial and of Beardsley's dismissal from the *Yellow Book* (his defiant mood indicated by the earlier version of the *Savoy*'s cover which shows a chubby Cupid micturating on a copy of Lane's magazine). It was an essentially Anglo-French enterprise, planned in Dieppe; for, in the later summer of 1895, England was no place to organize an 'advanced' periodical. The cast was

Arthur Symons, Beardsley, Charles Conder and that solicitor turned 'learned erotomaniac' and publisher of 'decadent' verse, Leonard Smithers. W. B. Yeats had been involved in discussions at Symons's flat in Fountain Court, the Temple—near to the Strand, where Smithers's office was located, and to that area of London vaguely surviving its former splendours known as the 'Savoy'. But the title suggested also a quarter studded with frail, informal gaities, ablaze with theatres and the 'iron lilies' of gas lamps. The context also explains Symons's defensive preface: the periodical would not be 'realist', 'naturalist' or 'decadent', it lamely judged that 'all art is good, which is good art', regardless of school. So, no originality for originality's sake; or audacity for the sake of advertisement; indeed there were no advertisements at all. Nonetheless, the *Savoy* still represented an attempt to conquer the 'open', the commercial world for 'advanced' art. Symons claimed, too, that he would not stud the *Savoy* with names. Pondrom justly remarks: 'instead of the magazine's reputation being enhanced by securing a major 'name' it was almost the other way around. Probably no other magazine has ever published so little bad material in proportion to the good.'[13] But it lasted for only a year, despite winning some reluctant press support. The decision both to be commercial, involving a crucial change after the second issue from quarterly to monthly, and to reject advertising, was too bold. And the publisher could not be altogether relied on to promote the periodical, since his main income came from pornographic publications. As Wilde remarked, Smithers tended out of habit to suppress *all* his publications. The decline of Beardsley's health also played its part. Although he profited from the innovations in reproduction, Beardsley was generally far from fusing text and illustration in the manner of those who sought to accomplish a union of the arts—an appeal to touch (quality of paper) as well as to the eye and the mind. Mostly he widened the gap between text and illustration, and had little interest in the total book. The calligraphy of the cover design of the individual volumes and the printing is inferior to the *Yellow Book*'s caslon, let alone to the *Hobby Horse* and the *Dial*. Yet, in its letterpress, there was no compromise: the fluent philistine was not allowed his say. The poetry of the *Savoy* is marked by 'decadent' features: Yeats's love poems, with their tremors of alienation and longing for apocalypse in falling rhythms; Johnson's sonnets celebrating religious heretics—Ann Lee, the Anabaptists of Munster and R. S. Hawker, expressing 'decadent'

[13] C. N. Pondrom, *English Literary Periodicals 1885–1918* (1966), p. 148.

warmth to the losers of history though Paterianly described as embodying 'altar fire astray'.

The *Savoy* is notable also for its frank and informed welcome to contemporary French literature. If the decadent element is somewhat muted, there can be no doubt about the *Savoy*'s importance in the history of international symbolism. Symons's notions of decadence had, of course, changed since his review of Verlaine's *Bonheur* (*Academy*, 18 April, 1891). The master is praised for destroying a language of classical perfection, transposing it into exquisitely tormented rhythms, assonances, arbitrary position of accents; but Decadence remains a matter of *personal* style, and Verlaine's innovations are only betrayed by 'the noisy little school of *Décadents*, the brain-sick little school of *Symbolistes*' who push Verlaine *à outrance*. This dismissal of any Decadent Movement, however, disappears in the article of that name which Symons contributed to *Harpers' magazine* of 1893—where he associates decadence with symbolism and impressionism as examples of 'modern' suprapersonal currents of creation, in a piece deriving largely from French sources. But, by 1895, when his close friendship with W. B. Yeats began, Symons revised his attitude to symbolism. It now struck him as a synthesis of decadent pessimism and submission to the *Zeitgeist* and impressionist cult of the moment; between a demonic nature and one subject to supersensuous illumination.

In the *Savoy* we encounter Symbolism if in theoretical more than creative form. A movement in France by 1884, a cliche by 1890 (though new symbolist magazines such as *La Plume* and *L'Ermitage* were established in that year), Symbolism became in the 1890s an international movement, extending to all the arts. But in Britain its practitioners were confined to the Celtic fringe. Indeed the Celt might well have appeared to embody the decadent turned symbolist: myth, magic, political listlessness (in the decade after the fall of Parnell the political messiah); everywhere a race, nowhere a nation. Its international quality proclaims the *Savoy* as representative of the decade (though internationalism means French, not Russian, German or Italian). There are translations from Verlaine, Moreas and Verhaeren. If decadence, symbolism and impressionism are diffused, a certain reserve towards naturalism appears in Ellis's comments on Zola, whose future fame is somewhat discounted and whose main value is seen as a crusader for the artist's freedom: enlarging subject matter and restoring vigorous, simple language, no longer muffled by periphrasis. Ellis, indeed, is the polemicist of the *Savoy*, conducting a sustained if discreet attack on the *cant Brittanique*: by his presentation of Nietzsche as a sane and brilliant critic, in the philosopher's middle phase, of the nineteenth century; by his quiet apology for Casanova, and by the brilliant tactic of 'A Mad Saint'. Here Nordau is undercut by the application of notions of degeneration and insanity to religious genius, and by treating the topic without histrionics. New uses are found for the primitive in Crackanthorpe's 'Courtship of Anthony Garstin', and Symbolism is evident in the supernatural peasant tales of Yeats and 'Fiona Macleod'; George Moore contributes the translation of a prose poem by Mallarmé and was to have contributed also his symbolist novel *Evelyn Innes* (documented naturalistically, however, from Yeats's Golden Dawn and Dolmetsch's *musica antica*) and the doctrine of symbolism appears unequivocally only in Yeats's three articles on Blake as illustrator. Here, French notions of total art as healing divisions of race, class and creed reinforce the occultism of Yeats's commentary on Blake's 'Symbolic System' in the edition he had accomplished with Edwin Ellis in 1893. Yeats develops a canon of Symbolist painting based on Blake's distinction between Symbol and Allegory, whose characteristics are to include reliance on Blake's wiry, bounding line rather than on Pre-Raphaelite 'subject', while the nervous rhythms of Symbolist line find their counterpoint in a phrase from Osman Edward's article on Verhaeren's free verse in the issue of November 1896: 'more supple, more free to catch and render the actual rhythms of life', the aim no less of Symons's impressionist travel pieces. However, the prescription barely fits the artists that Yeats admires in common with Image and Ricketts: Puvis de Chavannes and Gustave Moreau. Besides giving antithetical definitions of Symbolism and Naturalism, in his distinguished article Edwards isolates Verhaeren's attempt to confront industrialism and the city: to conquer them from naturalism.

It was one of the illustrations Yeats chose for the article on Blake that brought about the confrontation with Philistia which had broken the *Yellow Book*. Messrs W. H. Smith were shocked; orders had doubtless come from that mysterious Mr White, Smith's censor deputatus (or from his successor, since White retired in 1895) of whose activities we learn from James M. Glover's autobiography. According to Yeats, however, the hard morality could be melted if 'contrary to our expectations the Savoy should have a large sale'. The *Savoy* did not. From one number Beardsley's health had perfectly removed him. He returned to supply all the illustrations, as Symons supplied all the letterpress, for the final issue of December 1896: a gesture of economy, perhaps also of defiance.

SUCCESSORS

After the *Savoy*'s collapse, the most distinguished offering, the *Pageant* (1896–7), reverted to the extreme of an annual. A continuation of the *Dial*, its format was that of the gift book, Ricketts designing the cover, Lucien Pissarro the end papers. All the possible technical resources are once more amassed, and Edmund Evans, brilliantly connected with so many 'aesthetic' children's books of the eighties, oversaw the colour printing. French literature; impressionist and symbolist painting; post-pre-Raphaelitism are prominent in the letterpress. The canon is familiar, and the names too, both of writers and illustrators; their incidence still more remarkable since a number published both under pseudonyms and their own names. The situation is becoming imminent where contributors are beginning simply to address one another. The high price of the *Pageant* (6/–) foreshadows that of *The Anglo-Saxon Review* (1899–1900) which at four guineas a year clearly envisaged an audience of Liberal Imperialist clubs and country houses. Its covers were all based (in thick cloth masquerading as leather) on famous designs of the past and it welcomed 'names': established writers and the aristocracy. The *Evergreen* ran to five issues, four of which represented the seasons—a pre-determined limit to publication. Though promoting *art nouveau* and the Scots Celtic Revival, it remained programmatically hostile to decadence and the letterpress is mediocre.

The year 1897 witnesses the extinction of the *Yellow Book* and the *Pageant* and the inception of the *Dome*, as though the death of one minority periodical must generate another. The *Dome* announced itself as 'a quarterly containing examples of all the arts', but in its second series from October 1898, when it became a monthly, the ambitious sub-title was accurately omitted. The *Dome*'s survival stemmed precisely from its compromises with the bleaker climate of the later 1890s. Its editor, Ernest J. Oldmeadow (1867–1949), an ex-Methodist minister, was to find his vocation as one of the finest palates of his generation; strikingly handsome, it was not altogether coincidental that Gleeson White had encouraged him to found the *Dome* and that Sir Hugh Lane later found his arms 'picturesque'. Much of the actual financing was by his father-in-law, another Methodist minister, who needed cautious handling. The *Dome* opens with a ritual though good-humoured blast against decadence, naturalism, realism, and was never to be experimental. The Celtic *symbolistes* were safely idealist and Yeats contributed some of his most important early essays; 'Fiona Macleod' was prominent and Arthur Symons also supplied *symboliste* apologia. Oldmeadow had been converted to Roman Catholicism about 1896 and the Yeats circle was supplemented by Alice Meynell's drawing room and the professional lady writers of the Lyceum Club, particularly Miss G. Hudson ('Israfel') who wrote flippantly florid impressionist travel pieces. Of the *avant garde* of the earlier 1890s, a few survived in the *Dome*: Laurence Housman, Sturge Moore, Stephen Phillips, Rothenstein. But there is no Max, no Beardsley, no Ricketts. In spite of work by Gordon Craig, W. T. Horton, William Nicholson and William Strang, the art content is disappointing. But Oldmeadow's own musical interests ensured the impressive and frequent presence of Vernon Blackman and J. F. Runciman. Their contributions coincided with the beginnings of a healthier phase in British composing, and Elgar and Coleridge-Taylor are noticed; but the only foreign composers are the safely dead. The same British (or perhaps West British) exclusiveness is evident in the *symboliste* area; the *Dome*, unlike the *Savoy*, is introverted rather than international; and the appearance of several names later to become prominent Georgians confirms its role as preparing the arid immediately pre-modernist moment. The sub-title 'containing examples of all the arts' justly reflects the atomized and eclectic quality of content: a museum rather than a cathedral. Oldmeadow himself, with low-toned versatility, contributed under at least five pseudonyms. Confrontation having disastrously failed, genial compromise was deployed, and with some success, until the Boer War stopped all such frivolities.

In the little magazine of the period from 1850 to 1900 we witness not merely new sensibilities, forms and groupings at the beginning of their convergence, but watch the earliest crystallization of an *avant garde* dissociating itself from the high Victorian synthesis. The deconstruction of time, experience refining itself into critical 'moments' and the consequent instability of identity, the present becoming unpredictable, dangerous, open, is reflected in the 'mood' short stories, evanescent poems and impressionist travel pieces, to which such magazines were so hospitable. The deconstruction of space is evident both in the aspiration towards a total paradigmatic art and in the shift from the paradigms of antiquity and the national tradition to inter-

Bibliographical Note

Aestheticism and Decadence. A Selected Annotated Bibliography (1977) by Linda C. Dowling is indispensable; virtually the only offering on the topic. It contains an acute introductory essay on the historiography of the period 1880–1920. The *New Cambridge Bibliography of English Literature* 3 (1969), ed. G. Watson, is notably weak in this area and absurdly omits a number of the authors who appeared in the superior *Cambridge Bibliography of English Literature*, ed. F. W. Bateson (1940).

Aesthetes and Decadents of the 1890s: An Anthology of British Poetry and Prose, ed. Karl Beckson (1966), has a useful introduction and an enterprising selection R. K. R. Thornton's *Poetry of the Nineties* (1970) is a good alternative, with a sound prefatory essay.

Earlier books on the period which can still be read with profit include Holbrook Jackson's *Eighteen Nineties* (1913) which remains a classic account of the decade's energy and diversity. *The Beardsley Period* by Osbert Burdett (1925) has useful critical and biographical comment. A. J. Farmer's *Le mouvement esthétique et décadent en Angleterre 1873–1900* (1932) is a general history which retains some value while the erotic sensibility, or pathography perhaps, of the nineteenth century is covered in Mario Praz's brilliant *The Romantic Agony* (latest edition, 1951 with additional notes). A. J. Busst in 'The Image of the Androgyne in the Nineteenth Century' which appeared in *Romantic Mythologies*, ed. I. Fletcher (1967), traces the shift in this image from an earlier optimism to the pessimism of the *fin de siècle*. See also B. Dijkstra, 'The Androgyne in Nineteenth Century Art and Literature', *Comparative Literature*, 26, 1974. The image of Salome has been frequently discussed. Mandatory reading: Hugo Daffner's *Salome. Ihre Gestalt in Geschichte und Kunst* (1912); Reimarus Junior in *Stoffgeschichte der Salome-Dichtungen* (1913) and for the French treatments, Hertha Bren's *Die Gestalt der Salome in der Französischen Literatur* (1950). Helen G. Zagona's *The Legend of Salome and the Principle of Art for Art's Sake* (1960) is critically somewhat thin; rather more rewarding are an anonymous critic in the *Edinburgh Review* (1912); R. L. Peters's 'The Salome of Arthur Symons and Aubrey Beardsley', *Criticism* (1960), and the brilliant discussion by Nicolas Joost and Franklin E. Court, *Papers on Language and Literature* (1972). There is no commanding work on Narcissism and the *doppelgänger* in the period. The homosexual theme is discussed in Brian Reade's introduction to the anthology *Sexual Heretics: Male Homosexuality in English Literature from 1850–1900* (1971). Armand Bitoun in 'Aubrey Beardsley et l'esthéticisme homosexuel' in *Les Lettres Nouvelles* (1967) argues that hermaphroditism is the grand theme of nineteenth-century literature and art; a desire to experience a wider range of erotic experience. There are also useful comments on the role of burlesque in the English decadence. Rupert Croft-Cooke's *Feasting with Panthers: A New Consideration of Some Late Victorian Writers* (1967) is primarily a biographical account of Solomon, Symonds, Pater, Wilde, Gray, Johnson and others. It captures in a somewhat vulgar light something of the 'queer' half world. Susan Sontag's 'Notes on Camp' in *Partisan Review* (1964) have proved influential. Swinburne and Beardsley have a chapter in *The Aesthetics of Pornography* by Peter Michelsen (1971).

Of later general books, both J. H. Buckley's *The Victorian Temper* (1951) and Graham Hough's *The Last Romantics* (1949) tend to treat the 1890s as romanticism in decay, though Buckley's *The Triumph of Time* (1966) suggests connections between Pater and modernism. That work, though, appeared after F. Kermode's pioneering *Romantic Image* (1957) which decisively changed the prevailing view of the *fin de siècle* through discussion of the Romantic-Symbolist 'epiphany' in the work of Pater, Symons and Yeats. Kermode records the influence of dancers, both 'free' and symbolist, on literature and art in 'Poet and Dancer before Diaghilev', *Puzzles and Epiphanies* (1962), and suggests continuities between the 1890s and twentieth-century literature in terms of crisis and historical licence for the 'New' in 'Modernisms', an essay contained in his *Continuities* (1968). Ellen Moers, however, in *The Dandy: Brummell to Beerbohm* (1960) suggests that both Yeats's and Holbrook Jackson's images of the 1890s, as 'Tragic Generation', and as energetically diverse, respectively, appear less plausible from a distance; rather it is commercialism which is central to the decade, strongly connected with the new media. Barbara Charlesworth's *Dark Passages* (1965) reiterates with some subtlety the older view of the 1890s as diluting the insights of Rossetti and Pater. John A. Lester in *Journey through Despair* (1968) refreshingly concentrates on themes and this approach is elaborated in J. E. Chamberlin's *Ripe was the Drowsy Hour* (1977). Tom Gibbons explores the crucial evolutionary metaphors of the period in the mystical, elitist and anti-naturalist theories of art and literature adumbrated by Symons, Havelock Ellis and A. E. Orage in *Rooms in the Darwin Hotel* (1973). Connections between the nineteenth-century Decadence and avant-gardism are sophisticatedly made in R. Poggioli's *The Theory of the Avant Garde* (1968) and between Decadence and Barbarism in 'Qualis Artifex Pereo! or Barbarism and Decadence', *Huntington Library Bulletin* (1959).

Two books which attempt to set the period in the larger context of the other arts are Morse Peckham's *Beyond the Tragic Vision: The Quest for Identity in the Nineteenth Century* (1962) and Wylie Sypher's *Rococo to Cubism in Art and Literature* (1960).

As a consequence of Kermode's book, the historiography of the 'decadence' and the usefulness of the term itself has come under considerable scrutiny. H. E. Gerber's 'The Nineties: Beginning, End or Transition?' in *Edwardians and Late Victorians*, ed. R. Ellmann (1960), indicates areas for future scholarship and suggests that the term has only a limited usefulness. For attempted definition and demythologizing see: C. de L. Ryals, 'Towards a

Definition of "Decadent" in British Literature of the Nineteenth Century' in the *Journal of Aesthetics and Art Criticism* (1958). This was answered by R. L. Peters's trenchant 'Towards an Un-Definition of "Decadence" as applied to British Literature of the Nineteenth Century', *Journal of Aesthetics and Art Criticism* (1959–60), which also calls for more critical discrimination in the discussion of texts. Morse Peckham in 'Aestheticism to Modernism: Fulfillment or Revolution?' *Mundus Artium*, 1967, proposes the former. Several articles by Wendell Harris tend to argue for a sharp delimitation on the use of 'decadence' and 'symbolism' in the English context: 'English Short Fiction in the 19th Century', *Studies in Short Fiction* (1968); 'Identifying the Decadent Fiction of the Eighteen Nineties', *English Fiction in Transition* (1962); 'John Lane's Keynotes Series and the Fiction of the 1890s', *Publications of the Modern Language Association* (1968), and 'Innocent Decadence: The Poetry of the Savoy', *Publications of the Modern Language Association* (1962). Similar views are expressed in George J. Worth's 'The English "Maupassant" School of the 1890s: Some Reservations' in *Modern Language Notes* (1957). Two more elaborate essays in definition may be found in Ruth Z. Temple's 'Truth in Labelling: Pre-Raphaelitism, Aestheticism, Decadence, Fin de Siècle' in *English Literature in Transition* (1974) which suggests 'Aestheticism' might be dropped from the concert. 'Towards a Definition of the "Decadent" Novel' in *College English* (1961) by Richard A. Long and Iva G. Jones is useful if generalized. See also J. Lethère, 'Un Mot témoin de l'époque "fin de siècle"', *Esthète* (1964), and R. Gilmans, *Decadence: The History of a Word*, New York (1979).

M. L. Cazamian's *Le Roman et les idées en Angleterre: l'anti-intellectualisme et l'esthétisme 1880–1900* (1935) and her *Le Roman et les ideés en Angleterre: l'influence de la science 1860–1890* (1923) should not be overlooked. *The English Short Story in Transition 1880–1920*, ed. by H. E. Gerber (1967), is a useful anthology with a sound introduction which stresses the variousness of the period. The *1880s* are isolated as the focus of conflict between Victorian and Modern, involving romantic and realist notions of fiction, in Donald D. Stone's *Novelists in A Changing World: Meredith, James and the Transformation of English Fiction in the 1880s* (1972).

There is considerable literature on Anglo-French literary relationships in the late nineteenth century. Ruth Z. Temple's *The Critic's Alchemy: A Study of the Introduction of French Symbolism into England* (1953) provides the best introduction. It offers an early insistence on the relationship between decadence and modernism and on the importance of translations from the French. Christopher Campos's *The View of France from Arnold to Bloomsbury* (1965) has a slightly wider and more superficial sweep. A. E. Carter in *The Idea of Decadence in French Literature 1830–1900* (1958) discusses the decadent myth in its three phases: late Romantic, Naturalist and *fin-de-siècle*, and decadent style; but has one sentence only on Désiré Nisard. K. W. Swart's *The Sense of*

Decadence in Nineteenth-Century France (1969) is massively documented and deals passingly with the literary response. Philip Stephan's *Paul Verlaine and the Decadence 1882–1890* (1974) offers close chronological examination of 'decadent' poetry's emergence in periodicals, along with a detailed analysis of 'decadent' style. See also J. Lethère, *Le thème de la décadence dans les lettres françaises* (1942, 1963), and *Der rastlose Fluss Englische und Französ Geschichten des fin de siècle*. Herausgegeben von W. Pehnt (Stuttgart, 1967).

Fin de Siècle, Zu Literatur und Kunst der Jahrhundertwende, Herausgegeben von Roger Bauer, Eckhard, Heftrich ... (Frankfurt am Main, 1977), deals mainly with the German dimension and has enterprising illustrations. See also E. Koppen, *Dekadenter Wagnerismuss Studien zur europäischen Literatur des fin de siècle* (Berlin–New York, 1973). Also see Albert Cassagne, *La théorie de l'art pour l'art en France, chez les derniers romantiques et les premiers réalistes* (Paris, 1906: repr. 1959); Rose Egan, 'The Genesis of the Theory of "Art for Art's Sake" in Germany and England', *Smith College Studies in Modern Languages*, 2, 4 (July 1921), 5–61, and 5, 3 (April 1924), 1–33; Albert J. Farmer, *Le mouvement esthétique et 'décadent' en Angleterre, 1873–1900* (Paris, 1931); and Louise Rosenblatt, *L'idée de l'art pour l'art dans la littérature anglaise pendant la période victorienne* (Paris, 1931).

For Yeats's elaboration of the myth of the *fin-de-siècle* 'tragic generation' see *Autobiographies* (1922); 'Modern Poetry: A Broadcast' in *Essays and Introductions* (1961); the Introduction to *The Oxford Book of Modern Verse 1892–1935* (1936) and 'The Rhymers' Club' in *Letters from the New Island*, ed. Horace Reynolds (1934), an earlier and less ambitious account. *The Poetry of Ezra Pound: Form and Renewal 1908–1920* (1969) by Hugh Witemeyer, and N. Christopher de Nagy's *The Poetry of Ezra Pound: The Pre-Imagist Stage* (1960), discuss Pound's relation to the Decadence. Probably the best critical account of Johnson and Dowson can be found in Harold Bloom's brilliant and provocative *Yeats* (1970).

Index

Index

Academy 24, 173, 194, 195

accidie 104

actresses 152–4

The Adventures of Sir Henry Loveall 91

Aesthetic Movement 9, 11, 90, 102, 105–6, 174, 179–80, 189

algolagnia 90–106

Allen, George 180

Althusser, L. 123, 127–8

Amiel 19

The Anglo-Saxon Review 200

Antoine, André 191

Aquinas, St Thomas 127

Arnold, Matthew 28, 42, 56, 63, 78, 110, 118, 182

Art and Craft movement 179, 180, 188, 191

Art Nouveau 36, 53, 179, 181

Art Workers Guild 180

Artist and Journal of Home Culture 182, 183, 184, 188–91

L'Artiste 175

Artistic Japan 189

Ashbee, H. S. (Pisanus Fraxi) 90–3; *Catena Librorum Tacendorum* 91; *The Curiosities of Flagellation* 91; *Index Librorum Prohibitorum* 91

The Athenaeum 61

Augustus, Emperor 9

The Author 116

autobiography 33–5, 37–40, 50, 57

avant-garde 110

Baird, Julian 72

Baju, Anatole 18

Barrie, James 34

Bastien-Lepage, Jules 140, 141

Bataille, Georges 80; *Death and Sensuality* 68

Bate, Francis 182

Baudelaire, Charles 10–11, 15, 20, 110, 126, 129, 153, 170, 189; *Les Fleurs du Mal* 18, 103, 105, 106; *Franciscae Meae Laudes* 185; 'Le Mauvais Vitrier' 104; *Le Peintre de la Vie Moderne* 102–104

Bayard, Chevalier, 'A Study' 194

Beardsley, Aubrey 12, 16–17, 28, 51, 57, 189, 190, 191, 192–7, 199–200; *Morte D'Arthur* 181; 'Night Piece' 194; 'The Rape of the Lock' 53

Beerbohm, Max 51, 64, 158, 193, 195; 'A Defence of Cosmetics' 22, 193; '1880' 21

Benjamin, Walter 110, 11, 127, 129

Bennett, Arnold 127, 196; *A Man from the North* 145

Bergson 37

Bernhardt, Sarah 153, 154

Bernini, Gianlorenzo 7

Bertz, Edward 120

Besant, Annie 117

Besant, Walter 117, 120, 121; 'The Maintenance of Literary Property' 119

Bildungsroman 40, 42, 48, 52

Bion, *Lament for Adonis* 184

Blackman, Vernon 201

Blake, William 144, 191, 199; *Book of Los* 182; 'Gates of Paradise' 64–6; *Marriage of Heaven and Hell* 182

Blanchot, Maurice 96

Block, Lilian 183

Bloxam, J. F. 190

Bodley Head Bulletin 194

Bookman 25

Bourget, Paul, *Essais de psychologie contemporaine* 19–20; *Nouveaux essais de psychologie contemporaine* 19–20

Bradley 127

Brecht, Bertolt 127, 129

Breuer, Josef *Studies of Hysteria* 48

Bridges, Robert 25

Brown 180

Buchan, John 196

Buchanan, Robert, 'The Fleshly School in Poetry' 61

Burne-Jones, Sir Edward 190

Busst, A. J. L. 82
Butler, A. J., 'Mr Hardy as Decadent'
    123
Byron, Lord, 92, 120; *The Corsair* 129

Caillois, Roger, *L'Homme et le Sacré* 68
Callimachus 7
Calvert, Edward 191
Carlyle, Thomas 126
Carolus Duran, Emile Auguste 140, 141
Carter, A. E., *The Idea of Decadence in
    French Literature* 18
Casanova, Giovanni Jacopo 199
Catholicism 192, 201
Celtic Revival 28, 198, 200, 201
Century Guild 42, 179–83, 186, 188
The Century Guild Hobby Horse 20, 23,
    174, 179–88; *see also Hobby Horse*
Chaikin 141
Chambers, E. K. 24
Chapbook 194
Chekhov, Anton Pavlovich 166
Chiswick Press 180
Chorier, Nicholas, *Satyra Sotadica* 91,
    93
Church and Stage Guild 180
Church Reformer 179
Clausen 141
Cleland, John, *Fanny Hill* 92–3, 94
Clifford 139
Clough, Arthur Hugh 139
Coleridge, Samuel Taylor 41, 113–15,
    121
Coleridge-Taylor, Samuel 201
Colet, Louise 119–20
Collins, Churton 187
Collins, Wilkie 116; 'Thou shalt not
    steal' 118
Collinson, James, 'Child Jesus' 176
Conder, Charles 197
Conrad, Joseph 4; *Heart of Darkness*
    146–7
Cook, David A. 79
Copeland and Day 187
copyright 116–20
Corvo, Baron, *see* Rolfe, Frederick
The Court and Society 12
Cozens, Alexander 179

Crackanthorpe, Hubert 27, 111, 113,
    121, 193, 195; 'Courtship of Anthony
    Garstin' 199
Craig, Edward Gordon 154, 191, 201
Crosland, T. W. H. 173
Curll 91
Custance, Olive, 'The White Statue' 29

Dada 129
Daily Chronicle 23
Daily Telegraph 16
Damien 93
Dandyism 102–4, 153, 158, 174, 193
D'Annunzio, Gabriele 154, 164, 166,
    170; *La Città Morta* 163; *Il Fuoco*
    163; *La Gioconda* 163; *Il Piacere* 163
Dante 9
D'Arcy, Ella 193
Darwin, Charles 11
Darwinism 139, 155
Davidson, John 25, 125, 194
Le décadent 18
Le décadisme 18
Degas, Edgar 111
Deleuze 98
Les déliquescences 18
Derrida, Jacques 86
The Dial 189, 191–2, 197, 200
Dickens, Charles 120, 134; *Our Mutual
    Friend* 36
Dobson, Henry Austin 25, 28
Dolmetsch, Arnold 199; 'Consorts of
    Viols, the Viola d'Amore, the Lyra
    Viol and the Viola da Gamba', 187–
    188
The Dome 174, 200–1
Donne, John 190; *Songs and Sonnets*
    190
Douglas, Lord Alfred 55, 185
Dowling, Linda 8
Dowson, Ernest 8, 36, 52, 56, 179, 188,
    195; 'A Case of Conscience' 186;
    'Non sum qualis eram bonae sub
    regno Cynarae' 20, 27–8, 186
Doyle, Sir Arthur Conan 49
Dramatis Personae 24
Dryden, John 8
Du Bellay, Joachim 19

Dumas, Alexandre, *fils* 19; *La Dame aux Camélias* 156, 159, 162, 163
Du Maurier, George, *Trilby* 121–2
Duse, Eleonora 154–66, 168–71

Eagleton, T. 110, 111
Edwards, Osman 199
'Egerton, George' 193, 195
Elgar, Edward 201
Eliot, George 138–9; *Middlemarch* 36
Eliot, T. S. 7, 20, 21, 78, 126, 127, 167–8; *The Waste Land* 57
Ellis, Edwin 199
Ellis, Havelock 27, 112, 198–9; *Affirmations* 26; 'A Note on Paul Bourget' 19–20
ennui 104
epigrams 51–2
Equinox 174
L'Ermitage 198
eroticism 68–9; *see also* pornography
Evans, Edmund 200
Evening News 16
Evergreen 200

Fabian Society 38
The Favourite of Venus 91
Femme Fatale 90, 96–8, 99, 100–2, 153, 163–4
Field, Michael 21; *Sight and Song* 178
Fischer, Ernst 145
flagellation 90–5, 100
Flaubert, Gustave 19, 129; *Madame Bovary* 119–20
Forbes, Stanhope 140–1
Forster, E. M., *Howards End* 147–8
Foucault, Michel 114
Foxon, David 91, 93
Frederic, Harold 196
Freud, Sigmund 75, 93, 97; *The Interpretation of Dreams* 48; *Mourning and Melancholia* 48; *Project for a Scientific Psychology* 48; *Studies of Hysteria* 48
Fry, Roger 179
Frye, Northrop 8; 'The Drunken Boat' 32
Fryer, Peter 93

Futurists 129

Galton, A. H. 182, 183, 184, 186
Garnett, Edward 156
Gautier, Théophile 10–11, 15, 18, 187; *Mlle de Maupin*, 105
gender-role 89–90, 99–100, 105–6
The Germ 175–8, 180, 183, 188
Gilbert, W. S. 51
Giorgione, 'Fête Champêtre' 178
Girard, René, *Dionysos et la genèse violente du sacré* 68
Gissing, George 48, 120, 131, 134–5, 136–8, 144, 145; *Demos* 135, 137; 'Hope of Pessimism' 137; *New Grub Street* 133–4, 137–8; *The Odd Women* 137–8
Glover, James M. 199
Gluck, Christoph Willibald von, *Orfeo ed Euridice* 186
Goethe, Johann Wolfgang von, *Das Propyläen* 175
Goldmann, Lucien 85
Goncourt brothers 19, 24
Gosse, Edmund 25, 28
Gothic 96
Gourmont, Remy de, *Le Latin Mystique* 185–6
Grahame, Kenneth 34
Gramsci, A. 111, 127
Gray, John 12, 52, 125, 183–4, 189–192; *The Barber* 115; 'The Great Worm' 191; *Silverpoints* 28; *Spiritual Poems* 28
Gueunier, Nicole, 'La Production Littéraire' 129
Guild of Saint George 180
Guild of Saint Matthew 180
Guthrie, James 191

Haeckel 127
Hale White, William, *Mark Rutherford's Deliverance* 136; *Revolution in Tanner's Lane* 132–3
Hardy, Thomas 112, 120, 121; *Jude the Obscure* 56, 121, 122–5, 129, 152; *The Return of the Native* 36
Harland, Henry 193

Harper's Magazine 186, 198
Harper's New Monthly 124
Hawker, R. S. 197
Headlam, Stewart 179, 180
Hedonism 89–90, 93
Hegel, Georg Wilhelm Friedrich 80
Heidegger, Martin 52
Hello, Ernst 124
Henley, W. E. 15–16, 24, 25, 28, 112, 125
hermaphrodites 82–3
Heroism 103
Herzen, Alexander 110
Hiatt, C. J. 190
'Hobbes, John Oliver' 195
Hobby Horse 187–8, 189, 191, 197; *see also The Century Guild Hobby Horse*
Hofmannsthal, Hugo von 161, 166
Hollingshead, John 118
Homer 9
homosexuality 11, 53, 82, 184–5, 188–189, 190, 193
Hooper, W. H. 181
Hopkins, Gerard Manley 178
Horne, Herbert Percy 179–88; *Sandro Botticelli* 179
Horton, W. T. 201
House, Humphrey 175–6
House Beautiful 174, 188
Housman, A. E. *A Shropshire Lad* 7
Housman, Laurence 175, 195, 201
Hudson, Miss G. 201
Hugo, Victor 9, 10; *Les Misérables* 74
Hunt, William Holman 175
Hunt, Mrs M., *Thorneycroft's Model* 12
Huxley, T. H. 139, 141, 142–3
Huysmans, J. K. 12, 24, 26, 102, 115, 187; *A Rebours* 18, 22, 58, 96–7, 151; *En Route* 192
Hyder, Clyde K. 61

Ibsen, Henrik 111, 152, 154, 166; *A Doll's House* 141–2, 161–3; *Hedda Gabler* 161
Image, Selwyn 179, 181–4, 186, 199; 'In the Days of the Philistine' 183
Imagism 8
Impressionism 8, 151, 169–70, 191, 198

incest 82
Ingres, Jean Auguste Dominique, 'Angelica rescued by Ruggiero from the Sea Monster' 178

Jackson, Holbrook 9
Jackson, Moses 7
Jacobs, John 138–9
James, Henry 194; 'Death of the Lion' 195
Jay, Rev. A. Osborne 145–6; *Life in Darkest London* 146
John, Augustus 179
John-A-Dreams 188
Johnson, Lionel 12, 22–3, 25, 28, 52, 112, 178, 179, 182, 187, 194, 197; *In Honorem BVM de Winton Martyrumque Wicamicorum* 185; 'In Praise of Love' 184–5; 'A Note upon the Practice and Theory of Verse at the Present Time Obtaining in France' 20, 186; *Post Liminum* 123, 124
Jonson, Ben, *The New Inn* 27
The Journal of Philosophy 11
Joyce, James 55, 127; *Portrait of the Artist as a Young Man* 56
Juvenal 9

Kains Jackson, Charles 11, 188–90; 'The New Chivalry' 188
Keating, Peter 145–6
Keats, John 31, 34, 97, 182; 'To Autumn' 33
Kelmscott Press 180
Kermode, Frank 152, 168
Khnopf, Fernand 189
Kierkegaard, Sören 80
Kingsley, Charles 11
The Knight Errant 188
Künstlerroman 42
Kyrle Society 11

Laforgue, Jules 126
Lafourcade, Georges 63
Laing, R. D., *The Divided Self* 56–7
Lane, Sir Hugh 200
Lane, John 174, 187, 188, 192–6
Lang 25, 28

Lange, Antoni 20
Law Journal 119
Lawrence, D. H. 127
Leavis, Q. D. 116
Leconte de Lisle, Charles Marie 19
Lee, Ann 197
Lee, Vernon, Miss Brown 12
Lee-Hamilton, Eugene 190
Le Fanu, Joseph Sheridan, Uncle Silas
    96
Le Gallienne, Richard 25, 112, 187;
    'Considerations, suggested by Mr
    Churton Collins's "Illustrations of
    Tennyson" '22–3; 'The Decadent
    to his Soul' 27; English Poems 23–4;
    The Religion of a Literary Man 23
Lehmann, A. G. 10
Leighton, Sir Frederick 194
Leonardo da Vinci 41; 'Joconda' 156;
    Mona Lisa 155
Lesbia Brandon 52
Lewis 96
Little, James Stanley 190
little magazines 173–202
London 136–7, 145–7
The London Review 61
The Lotus 188
Louis XIV, King of France 9
Louis XV, King of France 93
Louis Philippe, King of France 10
Loüys, Pierre 189, 190
Lukacs, Georg 49
The Lustful Turk 93
Lyceum Club 201

Macdonald, George 34
Macherey 127–8
Mackmurdo, Arthur Heygate 179–81,
    183, 186, 188; 'The Guild's Flag Un-
    furling' 181; Wren's City Churches
    179
'Macleod, Fiona' 49, 199, 201
Maeterlinck, Maurice 24, 126
magazines 173–202
Mallarmé, Stéphane 11, 12, 17, 18, 24,
    46, 126, 190, 199
Malthus, Thomas 11
Marcus, Steven 93

Marholm, Laura, Modern Women 161–
    163
Marlowe, Christopher 93
Martial 9
Marx, Karl 115, 118, 128; Theories
    of Surplus Value 129
Marxism 110
masochism 92, 97–102
Massine 167
Mathews, Elkin 187, 188
Maturin, Charles, Melmoth the Wan-
    derer 56, 96, 97
Medici family 9
Meibomius, De La Flagellation Vener-
    ienne 91
Memoirs of a Maid 52
Mendès, Catulle 189, 190
Meredith, George 77, 112, 116
Merleau-Ponty 85
Methuen's Gazette and Literary Notes 194
Meynell, Alice 201
Mill, John Stuart 34
Millais, Sir John Everett 175
Miller, J. Hillis 63, 87
Miller, Jean François 191
Milton, John 83; Paradise Lost 129
mirror images 31–2, 51, 52, 53, 152
Mlle 188
modernism 109, 110
Monet, Claude 191
Moods 188
Moore, George 12, 36, 48, 57, 131,
    134–5, 145, 190; Evelyn Innes 50,
    199; Impressions and Opinions 141;
    A Mere Accident 185; Mike Fletcher
    12; A Modern Lover 140; A Mum-
    mer's Wife 134; 'Our Academicians'
    140–1
Moore, Thomas Sturge 179, 191, 201
Moreas, Jean 198
Moreau, Gustave 102, 199; Salome 96–
    97
Morley, John 61
Morris, William 34, 37, 38, 39, 51, 144,
    178, 179, 180; 'The Influence of
    Building Materials upon Architec-
    ture' 186
Morris, Faulkner and Co. 180

Morrison, Arthur, *A Child of the Jago* 145–6

National Observer 15–16
naturalism 9, 131–48, 166, 168–9, 199
Nerval, Gérard de 126
Nettleship, J. T. 194
New English Art Club 11, 182, 193
New Unionism 117
New York 188
Newman, John Henry 33, 53–4
Nicholson, John Gambril 187, 189
Nicholson, William 201
Nietzsche, Friedrich Wilhelm 86, 152, 199
Nisard, Desiré, *Etudes de mœurs et de critiques sur les poètes latins de la décadence* 9, 10, 18
Nordau, Max 45, 187, 199; *Degeneration* 152

Oldmeadow, Ernest J. 200–1
Organicism 168–9
Osborn, Percy L., 'Echelle D' Eros' 185
O'Sullivan, Vincent 15
Otway, Thomas, *Venice Preserved* 93
Oxford and Cambridge Magazine 178
Oxford Book of Modern Verse 25

Pagan Review 174, 189
Pageant 200
Parnassianism 8
Parnell, Charles Stewart 198
parody 51
Pater, Walter 11, 24, 26, 36, 48–9, 54–5, 112–16, 129, 141, 151, 155, 165, 170, 184, 187, 189–90; *Emerald Uthwart* 127; *Imaginary Portraits* 42–43, 44, 46–7, 56, 176; *Marius the Epicurean* 22, 34, 41, 44–5, 47, 55, 123, 163–4; 'On Style' 40; *The Renaissance* 19, 20, 40–4, 46, 123, 142
Patmore, Coventry 176
The Pearl 52
Perceau, L., *Bibliographie du Roman Erotique au 19e Siècle* 91–2
Pericles 9
Persecuted Virgin 90, 96, 97–8, 99

Persius 9
pessimism 132, 137–8, 146–7
Petronius 7
Phillips, Stephen 201
Piggot, Mostyn 51
Pinero, Sir Arthur Wing, *The Second Mrs Tanqueray* 156
Pioneer 19
Pirandello, Luigi 166
'Pisanus Fraxi', *see* Ashbee, H. S.
Pissarro, Lucien 191, 200
Plarr, Victor 179
Platonism 106
La Plume 198
Poe, Edgar Allan 170
Poggioli, Renato 7, 110, 111, 116
Pondron, C. N. 197
pornography 52–3, 89–100, 105–6
Pound, Ezra 7
Praz, Mario, *The Romantic Agony* 90, 95–7, 99–100, 102
Pre-Raphaelites 9, 12, 175–8, 180, 181–2, 190, 191
Prévost, L'Abbé 97
Punch 21–2
Puvis de Chavannes, Pierre 191, 199

Queensberry, Marquess of 15–16

Rachilde 189
Raffalovich 28
Reade, Charles 116
Realism 8, 167, 189–90
Redon, Odilon, 'Cyclops' 47
Renan, Ernest 19, 121
Revue des Deux Mondes 173
Rhymers' Club 179, 187, 189
Rhys, Ernest 187
Ricketts, Charles 175, 191–2, 199, 200; 'The Marred Face' 192
Rimbaud, Arthur 126, 191
Ristori 161
Rodin, Auguste 165
Rolfe, Frederick (Baron Corvo) 50, 189; *Hadrian VII* 56
Romanticism 31
Rose Croix school 189
Rossetti, Christina 182

Rossetti, Dante Gabriel 175, 180, 182, 184; 'From the Cliffs: Noon' 177; 'Hand and Soul' 176–7; 'Mrs Holmes Gray' 176

Rossetti, William Michael 66, 175; 'Fancies at Leisure' 176

Rothenstein, William 201

Royal Academy 175, 182

Royal Society 182

Runciman, J. F. 201

Ruskin, John 11, 37, 38, 39, 179, 180, 182

Sacher-Masoch, Leopold von 94; *Venus in Furs* 102

Sade, Marquis de 10, 91, 92, 93, 94, 96; *Juliette* 97, 99; *Justine* 93, 95, 97, 98; *120 Days of Sodom* 98–9

sadism 93, 97–100

Sainte-Beuve, Charles Augustin 92, 96

Saintsbury, George 193, 195

Saltus, Edgar 189

Sargent, John Singer 190

Sartre, Jean-Paul, *What is Literature* 109–10, 111

The Saturday Review 61, 122

Savage, Reginald 191

Savoy 17, 174, 195, 196–200, 201

Sayle, Charles 189; 'New Poet' 187

Scapin 18

Schopenhauer, Arthur 186, 189

Scott, W. B. 182

Scott, Sir Walter 120

Scottish National Portrait Gallery 184

Seaman, Owen 51

Selwyn, George Augustus 93

Shadwell, Thomas, *Virtuoso* 93

Shakespeare, William 9, 115

Shannon, Charles 182, 191; 'Atalanta' 191

Sharp, William 49, 174

Shaw, George Bernard 154, 158–60

Shelley, Percy Bysshe 31, 78, 144; *The Cenci* 95, 97

Sickert, Walter Richard 194

Smetham, James 182

Smith, George 119

Smith, Messrs W. H. 199

Smithers, Leonard 28, 197

Socialism 152

Socialist League 144

Society of Authors 116–19

Solomon, Simeon 82, 102

Spasmodics 11

Spender, J. A. 193

The Spirit Lamp 185

Sprigge, S. Squire, *The Methods of Publishing* 116, 117–18

Stanislavsky, C. 166

Statius 7, 9

Stendhal 19

Stephens, F. G. 175, 176–7

Stevens, Wallace 78–9

Stevenson, Rober Louis *Dr Jekyll and Mr Hyde* 49

Stoker, Bram, *Dracula* 48

The Story of O 99

Strang, William 201

Sudermann, Hermann, *Magda* 158–60, 163

Swedenborg, Emanuel 127

Swinburne, Algernon Charles 61–87, 105, 113; 'Anactoria' 71, 73, 79–80; *Atalanta in Calydon* 71, 80, 81, 84; 'A Ballad of Burdens' 76, 84; 'Dolores' 69–70, 73, 77, 81, 84, 100–1, 106; 'Faustine' 66; 'The Garden of Proserpine' 85; 'Hermaphrodites' 82–4; 'Hertha' 66–7, 74–5, 81; 'Hymn to Proserpine' 71–2, 76, 80; 'Laus Veneris' 70–1, 73, 76, 77, 81, 84; 'The Leper' 69, 73; 'The Masque of Queen Bersabe' 70; *Poems and Ballads* 61–4, 69–87; *Songs before Sunrise* 63; *Victor Marie Hugo* 74; *The Whippingham Papers* 100, 101; *William Blake* 64–7, 70, 86

Swinnerton, Frank 134–5

Symbolism 8, 17, 29, 125–6, 131, 139, 146–8, 151–4, 163, 165–70, 191, 198–9

Symonds, J. A. 182–3, 184, 187, 188

Symons, Arthur 12, 15–18, 26–8, 131, 139–40, 153–8, 160, 165–71, 186, 193, 197–201; *Amoris Victima* 25, 29; 'At the Cavour' 151; 'The Decadent

Symons, Arthur—*continued*
Movement in Literature' 20–1, 24, 113, 124, 125, 151; 'Idealism' 29; 'Impression: to M.C.' 28–9; *London: a Book of Aspects* 136; *London Nights* 16; 'Maquillage' 157; 'Nora on the Pavement' 29; 'Pastel' 157; *Silhouettes* 16; *Stella Maris* 194; *The Symbolist Movement in Literature* 17, 112, 125–6, 142, 152, 170

Taine, Hippolyte 19
Tatlin, Vladimir 129
Temple, Ruth Z. 25–6
Tennyson, Alfred, Lord 116, 187; 'The Lady of Shalott' 31–3, 45, 57, 58
theatre 152–71
Théâtre Libre 191
Thompson, Francis 25
Thomson, James 136
Ticknor, Lisa 181
'Tomson, Graham' 195
Trilling, Lytton 35
Trotsky, Leon 129
Tupper, John 176
Turgenev, Ivan Sergeevich 19, 141
Tyndall, W. 141, 142–3

Unwin's Chapbook 194
Utamaro, Kitagawa 191

Vallance, Aylmer 180
Verhaeren, Emile 191, 198, 199
Verlaine, Paul 11, 18, 24, 28, 126, 188–91; *Bonheur* 198
Villiers de l'Isle Adam, Auguste 24, 126
Vorticism 8, 47

Wagner, Richard 186
Walker, Emery 180
Watson, William 25, 193, 194, 195
Watteau, Jean Antoine 45

Watts, G. F., 'A Roman Lady in the Decadence of the Empire' 185
Waugh, Arthur 113, 122; 'Reticence in Literature' 195
Wedmore, Frederick 194–5
Wells, H. G. 48
Westminster Gazette 193
Westminster Review 9
Whistler, James Abbott McNeil 11, 187, 191, 192
White, Gleeson 188–9, 200
White, Mr 199
Wilde, Oscar 11–12, 15–17, 21, 27, 34, 36, 52, 111, 152, 174, 179, 182, 190–2, 195–6; 'The Critic as Artist' 39; *De Profundis* 53–8; *The Picture of Dorian Gray* 12, 22, 34, 37–8, 39–40, 47, 51; *Salome* 153
Winckelmann, Johann Joachim 41
Wollstonecraft, Mary 192–3
Woolf, Virginia 7
Woolner, Thomas, 'My Beautiful Lady' 176
Wordsworth, William 34
Wratislaw 189; *Caprices* 190

Yeats, W. B. 7–8, 29, 34–7, 41, 47, 125, 127, 131, 139–45, 167–8, 197–9, 201; *Autobiographies* 27, 38, 57, 109, 142–3; 'The Autumn of the Body' 111, 126; *The Body of Father Christian Rosencrux* 143; *Ideas of Good and Evil* 143; 'Leda and the Swan' 178; 'Mr Arthur Symons's New Book' 25; *Poems* 17; 'Secret Rose' 28; 'The Statues' 29; 'Trembling of the Veil' 144; *A Vision* 35, 44, 143; *The Wind Among the Reeds* 195
Yellow Book 17, 21, 22, 173, 174, 188 189, 192–6, 197, 199, 200
Yonge 116

Zola, Emile 9, 12, 18, 111, 140, 141, 184, 189, 198; *Thérèse Raquin* 131–2